CW01213416

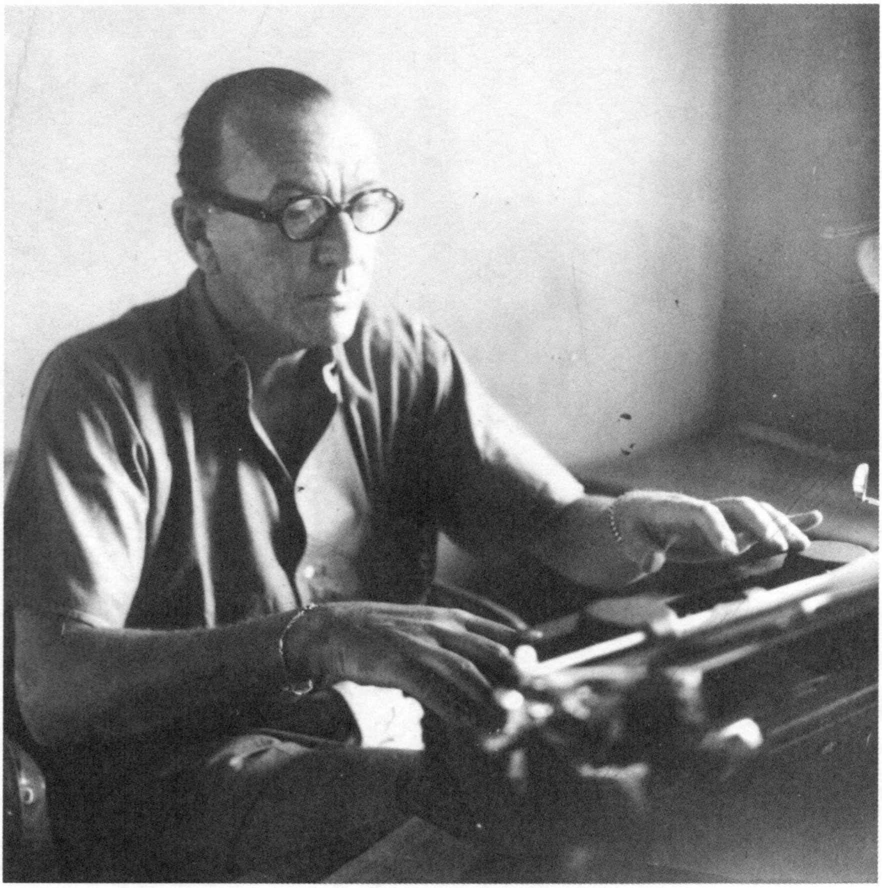

The Complete Verse of
Noël Coward

*For Jeremy —
In affectionate admiration
Barry

March 30th.
2012*

ALSO BY NOËL COWARD

COLLECTED PLAYS: ONE
(Hay Fever, The Vortex, Fallen Angels, Easy Virtue)

COLLECTED PLAYS: TWO
(Private Lives, Bitter-Sweet, The Marquise, Post-Mortem)

COLLECTED PLAYS: THREE
(Design for Living, Cavalcade, Conversation Piece,
and from Tonight at 8:30: Hands Across the Sea,
Still Life, Fumed Oak)

COLLECTED PLAYS: FOUR
(Blithe Spirit, Present Laughter, This Happy Breed,
and from Tonight at 8:30: Ways and Means,
The Astonished Heart, 'Red Peppers')

COLLECTED PLAYS: FIVE
(Relative Values, Look After Lulu!,
Waiting in the Wings, Suite in Three Keys)

COLLECTED PLAYS: SIX
(Semi-Monde, Point Valaine, South Sea Bubble, Nude with Violin)

COLLECTED PLAYS: SEVEN
(Quadrille, 'Peace in Our Time',
and from Tonight at 8:30: We Were Dancing,
Shadow Play, Family Album, Star Chamber)

COLLECTED PLAYS: EIGHT
(I'll Leave It to You, The Young Idea, This Was a Man)

TONIGHT AT 8:30
(We Were Dancing, The Astonished Heart,
'Red Peppers', Hands Across the Sea, Fumed Oak,
Shadow Play, Ways and Means, Still Life, Family
Album, Star Chamber)

COLLECTED REVUE SKETCHES AND PARODIES

THE COMPLETE LYRICS OF NOËL COWARD

COLLECTED SHORT STORIES

THE ESSENTIAL NOËL COWARD COMPENDIUM

THE LETTERS OF NOËL COWARD

POMP AND CIRCUMSTANCE
A Novel

PRESENT INDICATIVE

FUTURE INDEFINITE

The Complete Verse of Noël Coward

EDITED AND WITH A COMMENTARY
BY
BARRY DAY

Methuen Drama

METHUEN DRAMA

Methuen Drama, an imprint of Bloomsbury Publishing Plc

1 3 5 7 9 10 8 6 4 2

Methuen Drama
Bloomsbury Publishing Plc
49–51 Bedford Square
London WC1B 3DP
www.methuendrama.com

Verse and other material by Noël Coward copyright © by NC Aventales, as successor in title to the Estate of Noël Coward.

Introduction and commentary copyright © Barry Day 2011

The authors have asserted their rights under the Copyright, Designs and Patents Act 1988 to be identified as the authors of this work.

ISBN 978 1 408 13174 9

Available in the USA from Bloomsbury Academic & Professional, 175 Fifth Avenue/3rd Floor, New York, NY 10010.
www.BloomsburyAcademicUSA.com

A CIP catalogue record for this book is available from the British Library

Typeset by SX Composing DTP, Rayleigh, Essex
Printed in Great Britain by Martins the Printers, Berwick-upon-Tweed

Caution

All rights reserved. No part of this publication may be reproduced in any form or by any means – graphic, electronic or mechanical, including photocopying, recording, taping or information storage and retrieval systems – without the written permission of Bloomsbury Publishing Plc.

This book is produced using paper that is made from wood grown in managed, sustainable forests. It is natural, renewable and recyclable. The logging and manufacturing processes conform to the environmental regulations of the country of origin.

CONTENTS

Introduction   1

1. THE YOUNG IDEA (1907–?1922)
   '*Vegetable Verse*'   11
      Love Ditty to a Turnip   11
      'I had a little onion'   12

   The Animal Kingdom   13
      The Canary   13
      Sonnet to a Hermit Crab   14
      Any Part of Piggy   14
      The Great Awakening   15

   Romantic/Gothic   16
      Goblins   17
      The Blackness of Her Hair . . .   18
      Beyond   18
      Raratonga   19
      The Conversion of a Cynic   19
      If Wishes Were Horses   20
      Pierrot and Pierrette   21
      Columbine and Harlequin   22

   Nonsense Verse/Limerick   24
      The Island of Bosh   24
      Rhapsody   24
      'There was an old Marquis of Puno'   25

   Scenes of Suburbia   26
      Personal Reminiscence   26
      James and Belinda   28
      Elizabeth May   31

Suppositions and Expectations   33
Rubaiyat of a Man About Town   34
Tooting Bec   37
A Sad, Sad Story   38
Till I Return   39
Souvenir of Infancy   40

'Those Were the Days'   41
Letter from the Seaside 1880   41
1901   44
Honeymoon 1905   46

2. 'COD PIECES'
'The Swiss Family Whittlebot' (Sketch – 1923)   51
Early Peruvian Love Song   52
Exultance   52
Passion   52
The Lower Classes   53

Early Whittlebot Poems   54
Daddy and Boo   54
Gob   54
Heigho for Hockey   55

Poems by Hernia Whittlebot   59
'My Bedroom'   59
'To My Favourite Hostess'   59
'Agamemnon and Sappho'   60
'Sonata for Harpsichord'   60
'Apple Blossoms'   61
'Poor Shakespeare'   62
'The Bride Cake'   62
'To Noël Coward'   62
'The Dancing Class'   63
'To an Old Woman in Huddersfield'   64
'Pied-à-Terre'   64
'Greasy Garbage'   65
'A May Morning'   65
'Yellow Nocturne'   65
'Romance'   66
'A Country Fair'   67

Contents

Chelsea Buns (1925)   70
   Neurotic Thoughts on the Renaissance   71
   To a Maidenhair Fern   72
   Nous n'avons plus de chichi   72
   Chelsea Buns   73
   Contours   73
   Guava Jelly   74
   Garibaldi   74
   Family Circle   75
   Silly Boy   76
   Candelabra   77
   Children's Tales   77
   Written from a Mansard Window in a Velvet Dress   79
   Victorian Rhapsody for Lesser Minds   80
   Spotted Lilies   80
   Mrs Gibbon's Decline and Fall   81
   Sunday Morning at Wiesbaden   81
   Misericordia   82
   To My Literary Parasites   82
   To Badrulbador Frampton   82
   Contemporary Thought   83
   Send Me My Hat   83
   Theme for Oboe in E Flat   84
   Oleograph   85
   Hic Haec Hoc   85
   I Will Protect My Sister   85
   Christmas Cheer   87
   Caprice de Noël   87

Spangled Unicorn (1932)   89
 Janet Urdler   89
   Reversion to the Formal   89
   How Does Your Garden Grow   89
   Hungry Land   90
   Necromancy   90
 Elihu Dunn   91
   Harlem   91
   Ma People   92
 E. A. I. Maunders   93
   Moss   93

        Curve In Curve Out   93
        Church of England   94
    Tao Lang Pee   94
        Sampan   94
        The Emperor's Daughter   95
        The Voice in the Bamboo Shoot   95
    Serge Lliavanov   96
        Every Day   96
        Theatre Party   97
        Harlot's Song   97
    Juana Mandragágita   98
        Picnic Near Toledo   98
        'Flamenco'   99
        Torero   99
    Crispin Pither   100
        'Deirdre'   100
        'The Whisht Paple'   100
        'Pastoral'   101
    Albrecht Drausler   101
        First Love   101
        Freundschaft   102
        'Youth'   102
    Jane Southerby Danks   103
        Legend   103
        Sicilian Study   103
        Richmond Boating Song   104
        Old Things Are Far the Best   104
    Ada Johnston   105
        The Nursemaid   105
        Sunburn   106
        To Rudyard Kipling   106
        Dawn   106

3. 'FAMILY . . . FRIENDS . . . AND OTHERS'
    'Family' . . .   111

    Violet Coward   111
        Telegram to My Mother on Her Eightieth Birthday   112
        To an Octogenarian   112

Contents

Lorn Loraine   113
    To Lorn   144
    Lornie Is a Silly-Billy   114
    'Here I lie sweetly in bed'   115
    Reflections by Master on Awakening   115
    A Tribute to Lorn from Master   115
    'When I visit Venice, Italy'   116
    'In the deep hush before the dawn'   117
    'Lornie Darling, how I loved your news'   117

Joyce Carey   118
    'To pretty winsome Joyce'   118
    Ode to Joyce
    'Go, Joycie, with your upper parts uncovered'   119
    Saturday, January the Sixth (1940)   120

Jack Wilson   122
    'Baybay's gone . . .'   123
    'We came to the Ivy . . .'   124
    Don'ts for Dab   124
    Notes on the Correct Entertainment of Royalty   125

Kay Thompson / Graham Payn   127
    Darling Kay and Little Lad   128

Cole Lesley   129
    Birthday Ode   129

Gladys Calthrop   129
    'Lock your cabin door my darling'   129

'Friends' . . .   131
    Jamaica   131
    House Guest   133
    Goldeneye Calypso   134
    Goldeneye Opus No. 2   135
    'Morning Glory'   136
    Don'ts for My Darlings   137
    Toast to Sir Hugh and Lady Foot and Blanche Blackwell   139

Edwina Mountbatten   140
    'I could really not be keener . . .'   140

Hope Williams   140
    The Birth of Hope   141

4. WORDS OF WAR
    Personal Note   145
    'Lornie, whose undying love'   147
    'Pretty, Pretty, Pretty Lorn'   147
    'Why did you fall, Winnie?'   148
    'Reply-Reply'   149
    A Fallen Postscript   150
    'Dearest Mrs Lorn Loraine'   151
    'Because of the vast political intrigues'   153
    'Lornie, dear Lornie . . .'   154
    'Master's back and all alone'   154
    'Dearest sympathetic lovely Lorn'   155
    With All Best Wishes for a Merry Christmas 1939   156
    Bill   157
    Peter   158
    Paul   159
    Major Leathes   160
    Notes on Liaison   161
    News Ballad   162
    Reply-Reply   162
    'Sir Campbell is coming'   163
    Olwen, Olwen   164
    Fécamp   165
    These Are Brave Men   166
    Lines to a Remote Garrison   167
    Notes on an Admiral's Hangover   168
    Lie in the Dark and Listen   169
    Note on Our New National Heroine   171
    Political Hostess   173
    Sing of the Shepherd's Night   175
    We Must Have a Speech from a Minister   176
    'Where are the bright silk plaids . . .'   177
    Tintagel   178
    Convalescence   179
    Lines to an American Officer   180
    Canton Island   183
    Postscript   185

Contents

Happy New Year   186
I've Just Come Out from England   187

Bread and Butter   190
    'Dear Admiral . . .'   190
    To Admiral Sir James Somerville   191
    Bread and Butter Letter to Lord and Lady Killearn   191
    Casa Medina   192
    Bread and Butter Letter to Jean and Bill Fleming   193
    Bread and Butter Letter to Mr and Mrs R. G. Casey   195
    To His Excellency Field Marshal Viscount Wavell   196
    To Admiral the Lord Louis Mountbatten   197
    Reflections   198
    'Oh Lady Clementi!'   199
    Reunion   200
    The Battle of Britain Dinner, New York, 1963   201
    Let the People Go   203
    Not Yet the Dodo   206

5. SHALL WE JOIN THE LADIES . . . ?
    Mrs Mallory   229
    Social Grace   231
    I've Got to Go Out and Be Social   233
    The Lady at the Party   234
    Morning Glory   235
    In Masculine Homage   236
    Open Letter to a Mayor   237
    Quiet Old Timers   239
    Verse from *The Scoundrel*   240
Mary Baker Eddy   241
    What a Saucy Girl   241
    Midst the Hustle and the Bustle . . .   241
Marie Stopes   242
    If Through a Mist   242
Ella Wheeler Wilcox   243
    Whoops! Ella Wheeler Wilcox   243
Beatrice Eden   244
    'Oh, Beatrice dear, what a superb weekend'   244
    Letter to Beatrice Eden   244

6. INDEFINITE THOUGHTS ON THE INFINITE
    A Miniature   250
    Death   250
    Lines to God   250
    Meditation on Death   251
    Do I Believe?   251
    A Prayer: Most Merciful God   253
    This Is the Moment   254
    If I Should Ever Wantonly Destroy   254
    Condolence   255
    Nothing Is Lost   255
    Father and Son   256
    Ignatius Hole   260
    Onward Christian Soldiers   260
    Lines to a Little God   261

7. THE THEATRE: 'A TEMPLE OF DREAMS'
    The Boy Actor   265
    Ode to Italia Conti   267
    Concert Types   269
      The Pianist   269
      The Tenor   269
      The Contralto   269
      The Humorist   270
      The Child Prodigy   270
      The Soprano   270
    When Babsie Got the Bird   271
    To Meg Titheradge   272
    To Mary MacArthur   273
    Irene Vanbrugh Memorial Matinée: The Epilogue   274
    Tribute to Ivor Novello   275
    'Dearest Binkie, dearest Bink'   277
    Thoughts on Beatrice Lillie   278
    'Darling Alfred, dainty Lynn'   280
    I Resent Your Attitude to Mary   281
    Tribute to Marlene Dietrich   283
    Epitaph for an Elderly Actress   285

  Critics   287
      Routine for a Critic (Dirge)   287

Contents

  To Mr James Agate 288
  Lines to a Film Censor (1940) 289
  Novel by Baroness Orczy 290
  The Garden of Allah 291

Words . . . 293
  Tarantella 293
  Boots 294
  A Question of Values 295
  After a Surfeit of Sir Philip Sidney 295

. . . *and Music* 296
  Opera Notes 296

. . . *and a Literary Footnote* 298
  The Ballad of Graham Greene 298
  'Dear Mr Graham Greene, I yearn' 299

8. 'I TRAVEL ALONE'
  On Leaving England for the First Time 303
  P&O 1930 305
  Pleasure Cruise 325
  Souvenir 326
  Lines to a Fellow Passenger 326
  The Little Men Who Travel Far 327
  Malta 328
  Go to Malta, Little Girl 329
  Thoughts on Corsica 329
   Descriptive 329
   Hotel Napoleon Bonaparte, Ile Rousse 330
   Advice from a Lady Who Has Visited the Island Before 330
   Calvi 331
   The Bandit 332
  Venice 332
  Oh Walter Dear 333
  Bali 333
  Bora Bora 334
  Martinique 335
  Oh Dear 336
  The Quinta Bates (Aunt Bates) 337
  From One Chap to Another: A Complaint 339
  Jeunesse Dorée 340

9. 'If Love Were All'
    This Is to Let You Know   345
    I Knew You without Enchantment   346
    I Am No Good at Love   348

10. 'The Party's Over Now'
    When I Have Fears   351
    I'm Here for a Short Visit Only   352

ILLUSTRATIONS

1. Frontispiece: NC at typewriter
2. NC and Esmé 16
3. 'Goblins' (ms) 17
4. Waldegrave Road 26
5. *Poems by Hernia Whittlebot* (title page) 56
6. Hernia by Lorn MacNaughtan 68
7. Hernia by Gladys Calthrop 69
8. *Chelsea Buns* (cover) 70
9. *Chelsea Buns* (title page) 70
10. *Spangled Unicorn* (cover) 88
11. *Spangled Unicorn* (title page) 88
12. Violet Coward 111
13. Violet Coward and son 112
14. Lorn Loraine 113
15. Jack Wilson 122
16. Coley, NC and 'Little Lad' 127
17. 'Darling Kay and Little Lad' (ms) 128
18. NC and Kay Thompson 128
19. Coley 129
20. NC and Gladys Calthrop 130
21. Goldeneye 133
22. Canasta at White Cliffs: NC, Ian Fleming, Ann Rothermere and Joyce Carey 138
23. 'Unity Unity' (ms) 172
24. Noël in Imphal 184
25. NC and Lord Mountbatten 197
26. A dodo 226
27. 'The Lady at the Party' (ms) 234
28. 'A Miniature'/'Death' (ms) 249
29. A young Noël as Page with Sir Charles Hawtrey, in *The Great Name* 268
30. NC with Madge Titheradge 272

31. Binkie Beaumont 277
32. Mary Martin and Graham Payn 280
33. Marlene Dietrich 282
34. 'On Leaving England' (ms) 304
35. 'When I Have Fears' (ms) 351
36. Endpiece: NC in Jamaica 353

Every effort has been made to contact the copyright holders of the illustrations included in this edition. The agent will be happy to agree an appropriate permissions fee if necessary from any such holder with whom contact may be made after publication.

CREDITS AND ACKNOWLEDGEMENTS

All images courtesy of the Noel Coward Estate (N. C. Aventales a.c.) with the exception of: Corbis Images, on behalf of *Condé Nast,* for photograph 1; the English Heritage Library for 4; Pollinger Limited, on behalf of the Estate of Clemence Dane, for 22; the daughter of Squadron Leader 'Crasher' Archer (who appears on the far right of the photograph) for image 24; Lynne Carey for 26; and photographer Amador Packer for 36.

I would like to thank my editorial assistant, Lisa Foster, for helping to pull these far-flung elements together.

FOR DANY
The song is ended,
But the melody lingers on . . .

La chanson c'est terminée
Mais la mélodie c'est sans cesse

Introduction

'There is no time I can remember when I was not fascinated by words "going together". Lewis Carroll, Edward Lear, Beatrix Potter, all fed my childish passion . . .'

Later he would discover the Victorian romantic poets and have a particular affection for Wordsworth and Matthew Arnold.

A 1956 TV interview on CBS – *Small World* with Ed Murrow – was one of the few times he discussed his love of the form: 'There's one poem I particularly adore, because for many years I had a house on the very edge of the sea – just under the White Cliffs of Dover.'

The house was called 'White Cliffs' and the poem was Arnold's 'Dover Beach'. Noël could and did quote it from memory.

> The sea is calm tonight
> The tide is full, the moon lies fair
> Upon the straits; on the French coast the light
> Gleams and is gone, the cliffs of England stand
> Glimmering and vast, out in the tranquil bay.

These were words at the command of a genuine poet and one feels they humbled and inspired him in equal measure in approaching his own work. He always insisted that what he wrote was not poetry but verse. ('Those dear fairies at my christening at St Albans Church, Teddington endowed me with many rich gifts but a true poetic sense was not one of them.')

I can only assume that the compulsion to make rhymes was born in me. It cannot have been hereditary, for neither my mother nor my father nor any of my forebears on either side of the family displayed, as far as I know, the faintest aptitude for writing poetry or verse.

Throughout most of the years of my life, since approximately nineteen hundred and eight, I have derived a considerable amount of private pleasure from writing verse . . . It is an inherent instinct in the English character.

I find it quite fascinating to write at random, sometimes in rhyme, sometimes not. I am trying to discipline myself away from too much discipline, by which I mean that my experience and training in lyric writing has made me inclined to stick too closely to a rigid form. It is strange that technical accuracy should occasionally banish magic, but it does. The carefully rhymed verses, which I find very difficult not to do, are, on the whole, less effective and certainly less moving than the free ones. This writing of free verse, which I am enjoying so very much, is wonderful exercise for my mind and for my vocabulary. Most of what I have already done I really feel is good and is opening up, for me, some new windows. My sense of words, a natural gift, is becoming more trained and selective . . .

This volume contains all of Noël's published verse – the satirical 'cod pieces', *Chelsea Buns* (1925) and *Spangled Unicorn* (1932) and the verse collected in *Not Yet the Dodo* (1967). But it also contains a great deal of previously unpublished work discovered in the notebooks in his archive.

Not Yet the Dodo contained twenty-six verses – by Noël's own admission 'less than a quarter of my total output'. *Collected Verse* (1984), edited by his life partner, Graham Payn, and Martin Tickner, added another fifty-four but deliberately omitted what the editors referred to as 'private correspondence' by which they meant his 'verse letters' to friends and 'family'. This, I believe, was a mistake. Noël himself wrote that 'I have automatically enjoyed verse as a means of communication with my intimates ever since I can remember. Lorn Loraine, my beloved secretary and English representative for forty-six years, is an expert at squeezing the maximum of business information and personal news into rhymed cables and telegrams which, together with my own rhymed replies, has afforded us a lot of amusement.'

As with his recently published letters, I believe these verses show a personal and private and occasionally subversive side of this complex man that is of interest to his admirers. They throw new light on what he was doing and how he felt while he was doing it. By adding a linking commentary I have tried to set them in context.

I've also chosen to group the material by theme or subject matter rather than chronologically. It seems to me more revealing to see how – in the case of certain subjects such as the Theatre or Love – Noël's feelings evolved as he expressed them in verse.

When Noël had dated a verse I have included that information but for the most part they are undated and he would often return to a favourite subject throughout his life.

The Young Idea

The opening part ('The Young Idea') happens to be an exception to that rule of thumb. It's important with any writer to see where he came from and to identify the seeds of ideas and attitudes that would flourish and flower in the mature work.

The young Noël was inspired – perhaps 'egged on' would be more accurate – by his fellow actor, Esmé Wynne. Esmé, he recalled, wrote 'reams and reams' of overly romantic verse. Noël, ever competitive, felt impelled to prove he could do just as well. In addition to their individual efforts at verse, they collaborated on plays, the unfinished libretto for an opera and some 'excruciating' sketches in those early years.

Here we see Noël's early efforts at the Romantic – and occasionally Gothic – verse that was so popular in the literary salons of the day when people read verse aloud and the very idea of radio, television and the internet would have seemed a Gothic conceit in itself.

Words, written words, were the coinage to be played with, and clever writers like Lewis Carroll and Edward Lear made up wonderful mind games with them in the form of Nonsense Verse and the Limerick. Noël was only too happy to join in their games.

But there was an area where he felt most at home from the very beginning and that was in the observation of the lower middle class into which he had been born. Suburbia beckoned with its aspirations and affectations. Although he was to travel far and socially wide, emotionally he would never quite leave Suburbia and he would return to it in plays such as *Cavalcade*, *Fumed Oak* and *This Happy Breed*, as well as in countless song lyrics.

Having assembled the true juvenilia, we then see the mature writer looking back in nostalgia at these formative years that – in memory, at least – seemed to have so many 'English' qualities that were, like the Empire, subsequently lost.

'Cod Pieces'

Coming after the horror of a 'war to end all wars' – which it clearly *didn't* – the 1920s decided they couldn't abide anything that wasn't thoroughly *Modern*. Modern Art. Modern Verse. Noël for one found it difficult to impossible to take some of the 'Modern' manifestations seriously and in the second part we see his reactions to the reactionary.

In his 1923 revue *London Calling!* he has a sketch called 'The Swiss Family Whittlebot' in which a shrill poetess, Hernia, and her two brothers declaim surrealistically and at length until they are hustled offstage by the Stage Manager. The characters were clearly based on the real-life Sitwells – a fact that took Noël some forty years to resolve, and to achieve friendly relations with Dame Edith.

Nonetheless, he found great personal amusement in the literary doings of Hernia Whittlebot and proceeded to 'discover' more of her *oeuvre*, some examples of which he eventually published in the 1925 collection, *Chelsea Buns*.

The subject continued to amuse him as slim volume after slim volume of tortured verse appeared by and among the so-called *literati*. To Noël so much of what he read was literary snobbery. To be accepted as a True Poet one had to be a Russian *émigré*

(Chekhov was contemporary *primus inter pares* – or its Russian equivalent), Chinese, Latin, German – all in translation, of course. At a pinch you might get away with being a Scot, or a North Country spinster, as long as the accent was impenetrable enough.

In the 1932 *Spangled Unicorn* Noël parodies these and other literary idols . . . before literally closing the book on them.

The poets might be gone but Noël's urge to parody remained undimmed. Only the context changed.

In the 1945 revue *Sigh No More* and the 1960 novel *Pomp and Circumstance* he finds a place for the Pageant – traditionally a staged series of *tableaux*, invariably dealing at pompous and patriotic length with episodes of our glorious island race. Fortunately, it appears to be a form that has not survived the electronic age.

'Family . . . Friends . . . and Others'

'Family' was always important to Noël. Not merely the members of his biological family, of which there were all too few, but the 'family' he created around himself from his friends. Since the members chose each other, the bonds were tighter and chafed less than was often the case with the real thing.

His secretary, Lorn Loraine, his right-hand man, Cole Lesley, his life companions (early and late) Jack Wilson and Graham Payn, his designer Gladys Calthrop, actress Joyce Carey and writer/sculptress Clemence Dane . . . these were the core 'family' and Noël was in the habit of communicating in verse letters with all of them, when distance – or the excessive cost of phone call or cable – got in the way of a more direct narrative.

And then there were the friends . . .

Ian and Ann Fleming, whose long-distance London/Jamaica dalliance and eventual marriage were wryly recorded in Coward verse . . . the Mountbattens . . . Kay Thompson . . . and several others who stuck in his mind like burrs. None of them escaped being pinned down in Coward rhyme.

Words of War

World War II proved pivotal for Noël, as for so many people. He was at the height of his fame and – more important – at the height of his powers. Out of the war period would come songs such as 'London Pride', plays such as *Present Laughter* and *Blithe Spirit*, and films such as *In Which We Serve* and *Brief Encounter*.

His verse, too, tells of his personal odyssey, as he sees how war is conducted first hand: from the frustrating bureaucracy of running an Information Office in Paris, to the fact-finding trips for the Foreign Office as a part-time spy, to visiting our forces in every field of battle, to reporting on the Home Front and seeing the bravery of our boys in the air fighting the Battle of Britain, comparing it to the all too obvious detachment of far too many content to stay safely at home while others did their fighting for them.

And then – when war is finally over – his concern as to how we shall win the peace – or if, indeed, we shall – and the growing saddened conviction twenty years on that we hadn't and wouldn't.

Noël's War in Verse tells, in an accidental montage, as much as, if not more than, many a detailed and annotated history, and lets us see what all of us have lost and gained along the way.

Shall We Join the Ladies?

'Shall we join the ladies?' was the phrase used by the men at a dinner party when the port had been properly passed and it was time to return to the domestic ambience. As the years went by and Noël's celebrity grew, he seemed to meet everyone and everyone was certainly anxious to meet and claim acquaintance with that 'dear Mr Coward – *Noël*'. He was not always anxious to meet them but stellar *noblesse* must, of course, *oblige* . . .

The ones who fascinated – and frequently repelled – him were the ladies he met at parties.

There were the Social Gushers, the Social Crushers, the Social Climbers, the Social Predators, the Simple Bores and more. Noël saw them all, saw them whole and duly saw them off in verse.

Indefinite Thoughts on the Infinite

From his earliest years Noël was in two minds about the Great Beyond.

Did he believe in God? Well, in a sort of way, but, should there *be* a Hereafter, what kind of There would there be After? Perhaps because he was genuinely afraid to face the issue, he persisted in joking about it but – playing it safe – never entirely dismissing the possibility. What he was certain of was that if God really was in the details, he was getting a lot of the details wrong.

Perhaps his most honest – and certainly his most moving – observation comes in 'Nothing is Lost'. If all the words ever spoken and all the songs ever sung are still out there somewhere in the cosmos, then our own little living will have not have been in vain, because in some small way we shall all be part of Eternity. A thought worth hanging on to.

The Theatre: 'A Temple of Dreams'

A Life in the Theatre as seen through Noël's eyes:
'The Boy Actor' going through the agony of auditions, the joy of getting a part . . . the youthful professional's perspective on his fellow artistes and the challenges they all face each and every time they step on to a stage and bare their souls.

Then the seasoned actor reflecting on his contemporaries and their contributions to the craft they have in common . . . and a speculation on when and how to recognise the time to take that final bow.

Critics: Noël once said that he could take any amount of criticism as long as it was unqualified praise. It was a disarming way of dealing with something that never ceased to irritate him. 'I think it is so frightfully clever of them to go night after night to the theatre and know so little about it.' In his verse he became his own critic of critics.

He also became a critic himself. What was the point of endlessly debating who Will Shakespeare might or might not have been? Surely what mattered was that 'the Sonnets were written'.

As for opera: 'People are wrong when they say that opera isn't what it used to be. It *is* what it used to be – that's what's wrong with it.'

And if you want to settle a literary score with, say, a persistent critic like Graham Greene, perhaps a letter is taking things a trifle too formally. But a mocking verse or two . . .

'I Travel Alone'

As the lyric to one of his best known songs says, 'I travel alone. Sometimes I'm East / Sometimes I'm West . . .' He might have added North and South, because he was an inveterate traveller all his life.

He found travel romantic . . .

> A different sky,
> New worlds to gaze upon,
> The strange excitement of an unfamiliar shore . . .

It could be an escape . . .

> When the love-light is fading in your sweetheart's eye,
> Sail away – sail away.
> When you feel your song is orchestrated wrong,
> Why should you prolong your stay?

But, as the years went by, he was increasingly struck by the downside of travel – one's fellow travellers: 'Why must the wrong people travel?' In both lyrics and verse he would express his frustration.

But as a hopeful traveller himself, perhaps the *next* distant shore remained unspoiled?

'If Love Were All'

In a late TV interview Noël was asked to sum up his life in one word. Pausing uncharacteristically, he said, 'There *is* one word. *Love*. To know that you are among people you love and who love you. That has made all the successes so much more wonderful than they would have been anyway. And that's it really . . .'

But for Noël it was one of the few things in life he could never learn to control. 'If love were all / I should be lonely.' In later years he would become increasingly honest with himself:

> I am no good at love
> I betray it with little sins
> For I feel the misery of the end
> In the moment that it begins
> And the bitterness of the last good-bye
> Is the bitterness that wins.

But it didn't stop him trying.

'The Party's Over Now'

Strangely, when 'Time's wingèd chariot' started to 'goose' him, as he put it, Noël began to be fearful that when he was gone he would be forgotten.

In 'When I have fears . . .', his last verse, he begins to balance his emotional books. All in all, it wouldn't have been a bad run. Perhaps romantic love had let him down – or perhaps he had let it down – but there had been all those wonderful friends . . . 'and the jokes we had and the fun'.

'I'd like to think I was missed a bit.'

He needn't have worried.

BARRY DAY
2011

1.

THE YOUNG IDEA

(1907–?1922)

'Vegetable Verse'

In honest retrospection everything we write as a child is invariably derivative of what we've read. And since it's written too, to be read for the acclaim of proud parents, we're also determined to show how clever we are.

Noël was no exception: 'When I was rushing headlong towards puberty I wrote a series of short couplets under the general heading "Vegetable Verse" . . . I remember at the time of writing them I read them to my mother who was immediately struck by their brilliance . . . Even my own memory, which is retentive to an extraordinary degree, has refused to hold on to them. I can recall only two tantalising fragments:

> In a voice of Soft Staccato
> We Will Speak of the Tomato.

And

> The Sinful AspaRAGus
> To Iniquity will Drag Us.'

Notice the declarative capitals.

He had clearly forgotten the fact that when he was touring in *Charley's Aunt* in 1916 he wrote to Violet to break the good news that his Vegetable Muse had not deserted him: 'I have written two new nonsense rhymes (rhythms) which I enclose.'

Love Ditty to a Turnip

> Oh, Turnip Turn
> Those lovely eyes once more
> To me
> And let true love be ours
> Eternally
> Other I have loved before
> But none
> As much as thou, Thou art
> My Moon, my Sun,
>   My Star of Stars from out
> The Heavens above,

Come, Turnip mine
And let us yield . . . to love!

'I had a little onion'

I had a little onion
Its smell was rather strong
But it couldn't help its odour
'Twas its nature that was wrong.
It was Coarse and Avaricious,
Peculiarly Pernicious
And Disgustingly Suspicious
Pas Bon.

The Animal Kingdom

If vegetables were not safe from his versifying, neither were flora and fauna. The innocent domestic canary, for instance, was pinned down in the blankest of blank verse:

The Canary

The canary is a bird that sings.
It has yellow feathers as a rule, sometimes they are
Brown, if so, it is a linnet. Often they are purple,
Scarlet, or emerald green, then it is a delusion.
The canary is a singer, it is always singing,
Sometimes loudly, occasionally softly, often flat! But
It is always singing.
Some sewing-machines are called singers, but their
Song is quite different to the canary's, on the whole
More pleasant to the ear!
Occasionally a canary will lay eggs.
If it is a male, it won't.
When there are eggs, they are almost sure to be
Addled.
On these occasions the bird is addled, too.
I have a canary.
I have called it Ellen, because it is often terrified.
Canarys should be fed on seeds.
No intoxicants should be given to them to drink.
An aunt of mine fed her canary on caramels and whisky.
It was very hilarious for a time, then it died.
It would be unkind to leave a canary in tête-à-tête
With a cat!
Cats are so impulsive.
The worst way to talk to a canary is to purse up one's
    lips and make strange noises therefrom.
It is unwise to suddenly say 'Boo boo' to the bird.
If you do, it will probably expire from shock.
Some canarys are more sensitive than others.
I have said much worse to Ellen and she didn't mind
    a bit.

And some of his later speculations would have been unlikely to win any commendations from the RSPCA . . .

Sonnet to a Hermit Crab

These lines are written to a Hermit Crab.
O singular amphibian recluse!
Your predatoriness has this excuse,
That Nature fashioned you to smash and grab;
To be content with neither stone nor slab
But to appropriate for your own use
The homes of others. What perverse, obtuse,
Unkindly God designed a life so drab?
You have strong forward claws; a heart of steel,
But when your stolen shell becomes too tight
Out you must go, a larger one to find.
How sad to think that your Achilles heel
Lies in your mortifying, brownish-white,
Too vulnerable and too soft behind!

Any Part of Piggy

Any part of piggy
Is quite all right with me
Ham from Westphalia, ham from Parma
Ham as lean as the Dalai Lama
Ham from Virginia, ham from York,
Trotters, sausages, hot roast pork.
Crackling crisp for my teeth to grind on
Bacon with or without the rind on
Though humanitarian
I'm not a vegetarian.
I'm neither crank nor prude nor prig
And though it may sound infra dig
Any part of darling pig
Is perfectly fine with me.

The Great Awakening

As I awoke this morning
When all sweet things are born
A robin perched upon my sill
To signal the coming dawn.
The bird was fragile, young and gay
And sweetly did it sing
The thoughts of happiness and joy
Into my heart did bring.
I smiled softly at the cheery song
Then as it paused, a moment's lull,
I gently closed the window
And crushed its fucking skull.

Romantic/Gothic

In these days of gritty realism when – as Cole Porter puts it – 'anything goes', it's difficult to imagine the Edwardian context. No radio or television and if someone had mentioned an 'internet' it would presumably have been something to catch fish with.

Very few women worked and for the rest life was still within touching distance of the world of Jane Austen, where young ladies dabbled in watercolours, played the piano beautifully and read surreptitious romance stories in which no bodices were ripped and the hero went down on one knee to propose honourable marriage.

And while she was waiting for this to happen to her, the young lady might well turn her lilywhite hand to writing a little verse to express her romantic yearnings.

Noël and Esmé: youthful collaborators on 'excruciating sketches'. No literary form was safe from them

These flights of fancy would often take her – like Keats – to 'perilous seas in faery lands forlorn', full of Gothic fantasy and mythic happenings, all safely removed from dull modern reality.

Noël was introduced to this magic kingdom by a young Esmé Wynne.

As it happened, Esmé was a working girl – a part-time fellow actor and full-time Romantic. Noël recalled her as 'a podgy, brown-haired little girl with a bleating voice' but, despite that faint praise, she became a lifelong friend and his teenage Muse. 'She was determined to be a writer, an ambition that filled me with competitive fervour. She wrote poems. Reams and reams of them, love songs, sonnets and villanelles: alive with elves, mermaids, leafy gardens and Pan (a good deal of Pan).'

His own early efforts followed her fancy footsteps. These would seem to be in the great Esmé Romantic/Gothic tradition:

The Young Idea (1907–?1922)

Goblins

It's only just the Goblins,
Naughty little Goblins
Scampering through the trees.
Green ones, pink ones,
Little black-as-ink ones,
Down by the lake one sees them scurrying.
While the White Owl screeches in the tree-tops.
Come if you get the chance,
It's a wonderful sight
On a moonlight night
To watch the Goblins dance.

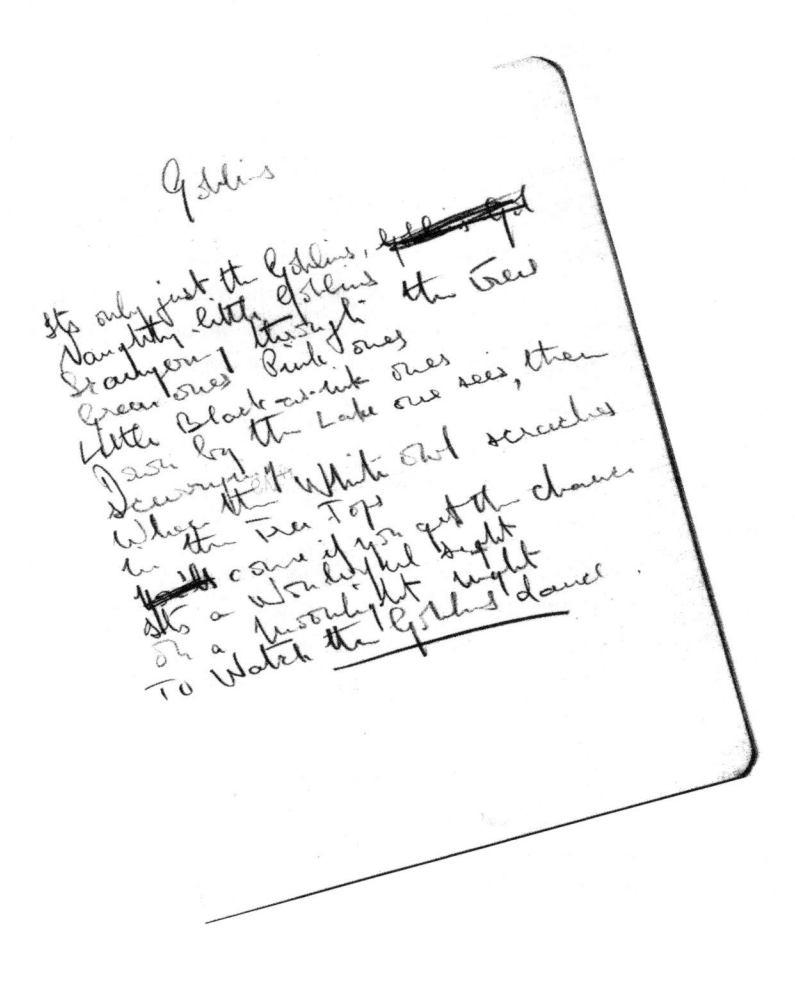

The Blackness of Her Hair . . .

The blackness of her hair outrivalled night,
Her skin was fairer than the morning light,
Her eye outshone the brightest star.
My young Yuntha, my young Yuntha.

Her soul was lofty as yon snowy height,
Her heart was true and strong with passion's might.
Her mind no worldly thought did mar.
My sweet Yuntha, my sweet Yuntha.

All that is left of Yuntha here,
A handful of dust beneath the snow.
Had that we ne'er met, 'twas better,
My love Yuntha, my love Yuntha.

The night was heavy with the scent of sleeping roses.
No breath nor sound disturbed the lifeless air,
The moon and stars in suspense seemed to stare,
As I confessed my love among the roses.

The scented dew fell gently o'er us from the roses,
The nightingale sang high among the trees,
A prayer of thanks came wafting o'er the breeze
As you gave me your lips among the roses.

Sparkling with the distant light of gold,
Full of heavy scent of many roses,
Alive with the music of the nightingale
And breathing forth a gladness yet untold.

Steeped in one long flow of golden wine
And all oblivious to the fleeting time,
With idols lying broken with his vows.
Omar Khayyam has weaved his poems fine.

Beyond

Beyond the purple covered hills,
Beyond the trembling sea

There is a land, a lover's land
'Twas made for you and me,
'Twas made for you and me.

No ship can ever take you there,
No aeroplane e'er flies
But only just the fleecy clouds
And birds know where it lies,
The birds know where it lies.

And love, dear heart, will take us far beyond.

Raratonga

You've heard of Honolulu and of Dixie Land,
Songs of old Kentucky sung on every hand.
But there's one place I love better than those.
It's a tropical island across the seas
Where the palm trees wave above my head,
While below the ocean gleams
And I'm dying to get there,
For someone I met there
Haunts my dreams!

There's a girl way down in Raratonga Town
And there she waits for me.

The Conversion of a Cynic

Love, the sowing of a seed divine
In a Cynic's barren wasted heart.
See in his eyes the tears of wonder shine,
Wonderment that tenderness so fine
Can make all sadness from his soul depart.

All his hard and bitter thoughts are flown
Like thistledown before some Zephyr's wings.
A love bird in his heart has built a throne
And taken all his being for its own.
A joyous, throbbing melody it sings.

And his version of the sixteenth-century nursery rhyme . . .

If Wishes Were Horses

If wishes were horses,
Then beggars would ride
Away from their sorrow and pain.
They'd leave the Grey City
Where happiness died
And never return there again.

One of Noël's first musical successes was his contribution to the 1923 revue, *London Calling!* – 'Parisian Pierrot'. Cecil Beaton considered it 'the signature tune of the late 1920s'. It was introduced by Gertrude Lawrence in her first appearance in a Coward show. 'The idea of it came to me in a nightclub in Berlin in 1922. A frowsy blonde wearing a sequin chest-protector and a divided skirt appeared in the course of the cabaret with a rag pierrot doll dressed in black velvet. She placed it on a cushion where it sprawled in pathetic abandon . . . Her performance was unimpressive but the doll fascinated me. The title "Parisian Pierrot" slipped into my mind and in the taxi on the way back to the hotel the song began.'

Noël's fascination with the character appears to have significantly pre-dated that encounter. Pierrot, Pierrette, Columbine and Harlequin were characters from traditional French or Italian pantomime.

Pierrot himself is always depicted as having a painted white face, white costume with a pointed hat and usually crying. Harlequin – a character from Italian *commedia dell'arte* – was usually dressed in multicoloured diamond-patterned tights and a black mask. Columbine was his lady love and the daughter of another character called Pantaloon, whose traditional dress included loose trousers and slippers. Noël uses him as a reference in 'Poor Little Rich Girl' (1925):

> You're weaving love into a mad jazz pattern,
> Ruled by Pantaloon.

In his 1915 notebooks he has two verses on the subject – 'Pierrot and Pierrette' and 'Columbine and Harlequin'.

Pierrot and Pierrette

Pierrot the gay – Pierrette the tender hearted
From fairyland once fled and so were parted.
The world, you see, is big and they are tiny.
So Pierrot, nearly sad, went back to find
His Pierrette but the Fates were unkind.
Pierrette's sweet eyes with tears were big and shiny
And she to find Pierrot as well soon started.

Columbine was in her garden playing
With her own pink roses, which were swaying.
In the breeze she danced for joy and youth
Pierrot found her and, as all his kind will do,
Quite forgot Pierrette and near Columbine he drew
And loved her golden hair and ruby mouth.

When Pierrot folk or Columbine's or Harlequin's do meet
A new love, they forget their old love was sweet.
But if they ever learn that their loves are untrue,
They die. (It is better than living to rue.)

Now Columbine stopped in her dance to admire
This Pierrot so brave in her scarlet attire
And Pierrot took care that the chance he'd not miss
And soon their lips met in a rapturous kiss.
A long day they lived midst sunshine and flowers
And on wingèd feet danced the wonderful hours.

But whenever Pierrot thought of Pierrette
And wondered what charm had e'er made him forget,
To Columbine turning he cried – 'I must go.
There's one I must find e'er the winter winds blow.'
She said – 'Pierrot, swear you will come back to me.'
He promised and said – 'There never will be
Anyone else in my life, dear, but you.'
He swore by the stars and sea of deep blue.

So Columbine kissed him and let him go.
She shed silent tears, for she loved him so.
Pierrette in her travels tripped lightly that way –
Passed Columbine weeping – no word did she say

But following the pathway that Pierrot had taken.
Columbine knew then that she was forsaken,
For Pierrot and Pierrette were of the same kind
And always they love if each other they find.
Columbine shed pearly tears – 'Ah,' she cried,
'He will forget' – then weary, she died.

Pierrette and Pierrot soon met and no more
Did he remember his love of before.
Gone from his mind was it all. It seemed
That all of his life before he had dreamed.
So together they danced and sang in delight,
Neither would go from the other one's sight,
Till sudden Pierrot spied Columbine there,
Lying quite dead – rose leaves in her hair.
But he remembered her not and said – 'See,
Harlequin's left her to die. Is not he
Heartless and cruel?' Pierrette answered not,
Though Pierrot said thoughtfully – 'Perhaps he forgot.'
But Pierrette she wept and o'er Columbine
She threw white rose petals with dew all ashine
And Pierrot flung over her several as well
But he was now under Pierrette's winning spell
And cried – 'Ah weep not, weep not, my Pierrette,
Come dance, laugh and sing, for we're living yet.'
Together they went to the land of their dreams
And lived always happy by clear silver streams.
But just 'fore they left her, Pierrette flung her fine
Gossamer veil over dead Columbine.

Columbine and Harlequin

Columbine sat on a window-sill
Watching the starlit sky,
While Harlequin in the road beneath
Tried hard to catch her eye.
But Columbine was haughty,
Columbine was naughty
And wouldn't hear his cry.

'Dear little Columbine, come, come away,
I've waited for you so long.
My heart's been throbbing the livelong day
With a passionate, joyous song.
Sometimes I'm sorrowful,
Sometimes I'm gay,
But always I long for you.
Dear little Columbine,
Pity this love of mine
And come along down here, do!'

Nonsense Verse/Limerick

Like all young writers, Noël experimented with all the currently fashionable literary genres. His fascination with verbal play naturally led him to the nonsense verse of Edward Lear (1812–88). Lear's *The Book of Nonsense* was published in 1846 and – like the verse of Lewis Carroll – soon became a classic.

Noël's teenage contribution:

The Island of Bosh

Have you ever been to the Island of Bosh?
It's the rummiest, scrummiest land
Where your thoughts are all wonderful, beautiful tosh
And golden birds feed from your hand.
There are palm trees that wave
And flowers that grow
And it's all very funny and quaint,
For the flowers and palm trees aren't real, you know,
For they're all made from cardboard and paint.
But everyone's happy when they've got the chance
And everything's right and just so
But if you are dull and don't care for Romance,
It's no use your trying to go.

Rhapsody

A Summer's Day,
A Golden Sun,
Sweet smelling hay –
A currant bun.

A garden fair
Of Dreams, thou art,
A jewel rare –
A treacle tart.

Although he didn't invent it – it probably derived from an early eighteenth-century form of nursery rhyme – Lear's adoption of the limerick certainly made it popular in the second half of the nineteenth century.

> The limerick, it would appear,
> Is a form we owe to Edward Lear.
> > Two long and two short
> > Lines rhymed, as was taught,
> And a fifth just to bring up the rear.

Just about everyone tried their hand at writing limericks, many of their efforts carrying a marked tinge of the scatological. In its evolution the form acquired a new rhyming end to its last line, instead of repeating the opening line. This 'punch' line, while sharpening the point of the verse, loses something of the charming nonsensicality that Lear brought to it.

> The limerick packs laughs anatomical
> In space that is quite economical,
> > But the good ones I've seen
> > So seldom are clean
> And the clean ones so seldom are comical.
> > > > (Anon.)

Typical of the modern limerick would be:

> There was a young lady of Wantage
> Of whom the Town Clerk took advantage.
> > Said the Borough Surveyor –
> > 'Indeed you must pay her.
> You've totally altered her frontage!'

Noël in later years liked to exchange limericks with his actress friend, Joyce Carey. Sadly, only one appears to have survived.

'There was an old Marquis of Puno'

> There was an old Marquis of Puno
> Who said, 'There is one thing I do know
> > A boy is all right
> > But for perfect delight
> A llama is *numero uno*.'

Scenes of Suburbia

5 Waldegrave Road (now No. 131), Teddington, Middlesex: Noël's birthplace

But it was when Noël began to write about his observations and the experiences of his own life that he started to find his true voice.

As a young man English Suburbia was his true *milieu* and in later years his memories of those early years were – if sometimes a little fragmentary – extremely vivid.

Personal Reminiscence

>I cannot remember
>I cannot remember
>The house where I was born
>But I know it was in Waldegrave Road
>Teddington, Middlesex
>Not far from the border of Surrey
>An unpretentious abode
>Which, I believe,
>Economy forced us to leave
>In rather a hurry.
>But I *can* remember my grandmother's Indian shawl

Which, although exotic to behold,
Felt cold.
Then there was a framed photograph in the hall
Of my father wearing a Norfolk jacket,
Holding a bicycle and a tennis racquet
And leaning against a wall
Looking tenacious and distinctly grim
As though he feared they'd be whisked away from him.
I can also remember with repulsive clarity
Appearing at a concert in aid of charity
At which I sang, not the 'Green Hill Far Away'
    that you know
But the one by Gounod.
I remember a paper-weight made of quartz
And a sombre Gustave Doré engraving
Illustrating the 'Book of Revelations'
Which, I am told, upset my vibrations.
I remember too a most peculiar craving
For 'Liquorice All-Sorts'.
Then there was a song, 'Oh, that we two were Maying'
And my uncle, who later took to the bottle, playing
And playing very well
An organ called the 'Mustel'.
I remember the smell of rotting leaves
In the Autumn quietness of suburban roads
And seeing the Winter river flooding
And swirling over the tow path by the lock.
I remember my cousin Doris in a party frock
With 'broderie anglaise' at the neck and sleeves
And being allowed to stir the Christmas pudding
On long ago, enchanted Christmas Eves.
All this took place in Teddington, Middlesex
Not far from the Surrey border
But none of these little episodes
None of these things I call to mind
None of the memories I find
Are in chronological order
Is in chronological order.

The young Noël began to find his own voice in verse when he dealt with events – and particularly people – he had observed in his own environment. English Suburbia was a context he instinctively understood. He remained fond of it and its idiosyncrasies throughout his career in songs, stories and plays such as *Cavalcade* and *This Happy Breed*.

If his early comic efforts were perhaps a little on the broad side, they rapidly became – rather like Norfolk – flatter and sharper.

James and Belinda

Belinda lived at Number 3
And James at Number 8.
She used to lure him in to tea
With sugar cake as bait.
He also saw her lots
When watering the pots
Of geraniums which flowered
Quite profusely by his gate.

Their friendship ripened day by day.
Their intimacy grew.
The Vicar's wife was heard to say
That what she knew, she knew!
Tho' far be it for her
To point out or infer
That James couldn't keep a rabbit
On the salary he drew!

One day Belinda disappeared –
Where no one seemed to know.
The Vicar's wife unkindly sneered
And murmured – 'Time will show.'
When James was also missed,
She positively hissed
With righteous satisfaction and
Exclaimed – 'I told you so!'

A year or more had fully passed
E'er home Belinda came
And tho' she looked a trifle fast

The Young Idea (1907–?1922)

Her nature seemed the same.
She'd been upon the stage,
Her singing was the rage
Of London and she said she found
Her parents rather tame!

When she'd been home a day or two
Her mother, quite in fun,
Inquired if it was Jimmy who
Had made her daughter run
Away from parents fond
Out to the world beyond
Where, so she'd heard, most murky deeds
Were very often done.

Belinda loudly blew her nose
And said – 'I cannot see
Why everybody should suppose
That James eloped with me.
Besides, I'm not the sort
To easily be caught
By such a poor and feeble-minded
Lunatic as he!

'As curiosity so low
Pervades your every tone,
I'd like you one and all to know
That I left home alone
And tho' he isn't bad,
He's not the sort of lad
That any bright, intelligent
Young girl would care to own!'

'Then what can have become of him?'
Belinda's mother cried.
'It would be sad if little Jim
Had been and gone and died.
We'll go and see his Ma,
Their villa isn't far,
Tho', as you know, that woman
Is the sort I can't abide.'

'Now, never mind your feelings low',
Belinda's tone was rude,
'I think that you should be above
Continuing your feud.
You've kept it up so long,
Besides to fight is wrong
Is what I say, tho' Heaven knows,
I ain't no blooming prude.'

So off went the determined pair
And knocked and rang the bell.
When James's mother saw them there,
She rudely murmured – 'Hell!'
But when she'd heard their tale,
She turned a trifle pale
And cried – 'I thought he was with you.
This is a rotten sell!'

Belinda with a thoughtful frown
Cried – 'Mother, wait a sec.
I think I'll just run up to town
And see a Private Tec,
Who rather lost his heart
To me, so I'll be smart
And wear my blue *crèpe de chine*
Or what about my check?'

'There isn't any time to waste,'
Her mother quickly said,
'I think it would be better taste
To wear your black and red –
It isn't quite so hot
As some others that you've got.
Besides, you mustn't look too
Bright, in case poor James is dead.'

At that his mother tore her hair,
Then called Belinda names
And cried – 'You neither of you care
What has become of James.
You heartless little cat,

Take that and that and that.
I hope that you will shrivel up
In purgatory's flames.'

And seeing she was so *distrait*,
In voices of alarm
They said they'd call another day
When she had grown more calm.
They went towards the door
And stood rooted to the floor,
For there was James himself
With wife and child upon his arm!

His mother kissed his horny hand,
Belinda hit his face.
Belinda's mother grasped the band
That kept his pants in place.
There followed after this
A scene of perfect bliss.
Of previous unpleasantness
There wasn't any trace.

To James's wife his mother may
Have been a trifle snappy,
But, taken in a general way,
Their after life was happy.

Elizabeth May

Elizabeth May
Lived down Kensington Way
And her manner was strangely reserved.
She'd a ladylike tone
And she'd never been known
From the Path of the Right to have swerved.
Her prettiness when
She met amorous men
Caused a largish amount of sensation.
They would fall on their knees
And say – 'Marry me, please!'

But she always resisted temptation
By saying to them –
'My name's Elizabeth May
And no one takes liberties with me.
I wasn't born yesterday and I
Know a thing or two, you see.'
When passionate gentlemen full of Romance
Cried – 'Darling, I love you, say I've got a chance!
If you'll marry me now,
I'll be faithful, I vow.'
'No one takes liberties with me!'

Elizabeth said
She would rather be dead
Than live with her mother at home.
She decided to go
In some West End show
At the Empire or Hippodrome,
So she tripped up to town
In a ravishing gown
To visit an agent called Vickers.
He said – 'You'll just do
For my latest Revue
But you'll have to wear
Transparent . . . stockings!!'

'My name's Elizabeth May
And no one takes liberties with me.
I wasn't born yesterday
And I know a thing or two, you see.'
The agent said – 'If you don't suffer from nerves,
You'll get off with your figure, it has
Such good curves.
But tell me, I beg,
Have you got a good leg?'
She said –
'No one takes liberties with me.'

Elizabeth danced and Elizabeth pranced
In the chorus for nearly three years
But she quickly got tired

Of being admired
By rather degenerate peers.
They wrote her sweet notes
Asked her to Brighton for weekends
But she'd always reply –
'You must think I'm a goose,
If I can't see beyond where my beak ends.

'My name's Elizabeth May
And no one takes liberties with me.
I wasn't born yesterday
And I know a thing or two, you see.'
They'd say – 'You're a topper and whopper, by gad!
I'd marry you straight, if it wasn't for Dad.
But don't fret about that,
Come and see my new flat.'
She'd say –
'Nobody takes liberties with me.'

(Alternative)
'Cos she never would take any charity
She'd say to them –
'I once went to one of those little Affairs
And a lovesick young man bit my neck on the stairs.
I left him in pain,
Having made it quite plain
That no one takes liberties with me!'

(Noël subsequently revised this verse and turned it into a song lyric.)

Suppositions and Expectations

Two young ladies once I knew,
Both had a passion grand
For an insignificant bank clerk who
Was living close at hand.
They hated each other with Deadly Hate
As to win his love they tried.
And when he took another girl to mate,
They banded together and cried.

I didn't suppose, you didn't suppose
That that was what he'd do.
And I didn't suppose that if others supposed
That what they supposed was true.
And now he's gone and married that hag
And will live with her until
She either does something really bad
Or nags at him 'til he's raving mad.
I don't suppose they'll come to blows,
But I jolly well hope they will.

Then two ladies full of pain
Went to a seaside town
To recuperate again
After their taking down.
They met a rich man who was not
Too robust in health.
For him they didn't care a jot
But simply loved his wealth.

I didn't suspect, they didn't suspect
That he suspected them
And as they were both so circumspect,
Nothing was proved *pro tem*.
The day he found their diary
And when he'd read his fill,
He went to his solicitor's
And altered a most important clause.
They hope to get money when he dies –
But I don't expect they will.

Rubaiyat of a Man About Town
(after Omar Khayyam)

I.
Awake, my valet soft in shirtsleeves white
Has pulled the blinds up, letting in the light.
The throbbing of my temples seems to say
I dined out wisely but too well last night.

The Young Idea (1907–?1922)

II.
And as in drowsy laziness I lay,
I heard a voice from out the bathroom say –
'You'd better hurry up and have your bath,
You've got to get your hair cut, sir, today.'

III.
E'en as I deftly wielded brush and comb,
A hated friend asked if I were at home.
With indescribable relief I heard
My valet say that I had gone to Rome!

IV.
The coolness of the morning after rain
Had eased from off my head the throbbing pain,
But since a modest luncheon at the Troc
It's unaccountably returned again!

V.
I wondered oft if life could be enjoyed
Were it entirely of the vine devoid
I think if alcohol were e'er debarred,
My father more than I would be annoyed.

VI.
Why is it when the barber us attacks
And with long scissors snips and pulls and hacks,
Should we emerge with smoothened shining poll
And horrid tickling hairs all down our backs?

VII.
Come, let us go like birds upon the wing
And leave this Music Hall in travelling.
We may forget the aged woman's voice
Which sounded as if forever it would sing.

VIII.
And often I, when watching a Revue,
Have sent round charming notes to one or two
To ask these pretty lissom little maids
To sup with me, if they've naught else to do.

IX.
Now, he who has Philosophy professed
Should not wake up at night angry, depressed
At hearing someone on the floor above
Return a trifle boisterously to rest.

X.
To those to whom in innocence we trust
Our favourite books, may they to Hell be thrust
When they return them not, and also let
Their souls be trodden quickly into dust.

XI.
Myself when young did once a week frequent
A cinema where threepence carefully spent
Enabled me to view with bated breath
The girl who cheerfully to the Devil went.

XII.
And oft between the hours of two and four
The mirth-provoking Charlie would arrive
And, as I watched his antics on the screen,
To hide my raucous laughter I would strive.

XIII.
For I remember halting by the way
To hear a barrel-organ's doleful lay.
The man with patches on his trouser's seat
Was grinding very flat 'A Perfect Day'.

XIV.
The servant problem's but a shadow show
Round which the frantic skivvys come and go
And some request a night out twice a week
To carry on with men in manners low.

XV.
Off to some Concert Hall our way we wend
To listen to the warbling of a friend
With voice discordant as the raven's croak,
Who sings, sans tune, sans feeling and sans end!

XVI.
Oh, my Beloved, fill the cup uncracked
With Billington's unequalled Beef Extract
To soothe the poignant agonies of one
Whose being is with indigestion wracked.

Tooting Bec

(with apologies to Mr Kipling)

In the 'Laburnum' Pub's Saloon Bar
In the High Street, Battersea
There's an apoplectic female
And I know she thinks of me.
I can guess her agitation
As to me she seems to beck
'Come you back, you dirty rotter,
Come you back to Tooting Bec!
Come you back to Tooting Bec,
If you don't, I'll ring your neck.'

On the road to Tooting Bec,
Where one can't get food 'on spec'
And the factory girls their Sunday
Hats with gaudy feathers deck.

I was sick of being honest and an upright working man
And my wife's eternal nagging drove me thinking of a plan.
So one day I broke the window of a jeweller's in the Strand
And when the Police arrested me,
I shook them by the hand.
They didn't understand
And they thought I was canned
When I went enthusiastically
And shook them by the hand.

On the Road to Tooting Bec, etc.

Take me to some restful prison cell
Where quiet I can find

And let me leave my irritating
Wife and kids behind.
I know that, if I'd stayed at home,
She'd soon have murdered me
And now she sits a-calling
In the 'Laburnum', Battersea.
'Come you back to Tooting Bec.
How I'd love to break your neck
And make your snubnosed countenance
A sanguinary wreck.'

On the road to Tooting Bec
Where you can't get food 'on spec'
And the factory girls their Sunday
Hats with gaudy feathers deck.

A Sad, Sad Story

Little Angelina stole into the pantry
Bent upon absconding with some tartlets from a plate.
Took them to the drawing-room, hid them 'neath the sofa cushion,
Meaning to devour them at some future date.
Now, father had a headache, having lunched unwisely,
Thought that he would lie down
As he felt inclined to snooze.
He flopped upon the sofa with a grunt of satisfaction
And Angelina, watching, saw the tarts begin to ooze.

Gee! But they oozed and oozed!

Half an hour later, mother entered quickly,
Intent on some domestic task she had to complete.
There she looked and saw an apparition horrible and sickly –
Her husband jammed all over from his eyebrows to his feet.
And as she gazed in horror, he gave out a gentle snore
And woke up asking sleepily for water.
With a shriek of outraged wifehood, she fell swooning
    to the floor.
Then his glaring eyes alighted on his daughter.

She was just busting her braces, laughing!

Poor child, she never laughed again.
The tale is sad to tell.
Her father's boot-jack found her brain.
Let's hope he'll be forgiven!

Shoplifting may seem to be an unlikely Coward topic but in *Present Indicative* he admits to a little light pilfering. Anxious to collect magazine episodes of the latest E. Nesbit book – she remained his favourite author – 'I stole a coral necklace from a visiting friend of Mother's, pawned it for five shillings, and bought the complete book at the Army and Navy Stores . . . in later years I told E. Nesbit of this little incident and I regret to say that she was delighted.'

Till I Return

When I am buying
Lean over me quietly, softly
Sneak, while the shop assistants
Speak
Anything that you spot,
So I may, when I return,
If there be a returning,
Slide me whatever you've nicked
Not a quarter or a half, but the lot.

But of course, all of these – however accurately observed – were imaginary people. Where his own youthful recollections were concerned, he was often somewhat less benevolently inclined . . .

The mature Noël was to find himself irritated on more than one occasion by the glamorous female stars who crossed his path. 'Great big glamorous stars can be very tiresome,' he once said and, 'God preserve me in future from female stars. I don't suppose He will.' And, fortunately for us, of course, He didn't. But it can be seen that Noël observed the warning signs early:

Souvenir of Infancy

Whatever became of those dear little girls
I used to dislike so much?
I can see them now as they came to tea,
Simpering slightly, aware of me,
Not as a friend, another child,
But as someone later to be beguiled
With roguish giggles and tossing of curls.
They were ready to squeal at a touch.
Whatever became of those dear little girls
I used to dislike so much?

'Those Were the Days'

Noël was born at the very end of the Victorian era and brought up as a typical Edwardian. Although he would travel far and see much in the years to come, the echoes of those more confident and leisurely days would remain with him.

Letter from the Seaside 1880

Dearest Mama
Here we all are
Safely arrived, with everything unpacked
Excepting the pilgrim basket and Laura's box
Which we are leaving until after tea
Because we want to go down to the sea
And look for seaweed and limpets on the rocks
And walk along the sands towards the caves
On the very edge of the waves.
We had, on the whole, a most agreeable journey
But for the fact
That poor Belinda
(Everything always happens to Belinda)
Got something in her eye, a piece of cinder.
You can imagine the relief
When Nanny cleverly managed to extract
The sharp invader with her handkerchief
The name of our landlady is Mrs Gurney.

Later. After tea.
Dearest Mama how glad, how proud you'll be
Arnold has paddled twice!
At first he was frightened and sat down and cried
On that hard kind of sand that's wrinkled by the tide
Until Nanny produced a piece of coconut-ice
Which we had bought in a shop on the Parade.

Soon his tears were dried, then suddenly, unafraid
Away he went, brave as a lion
Upheld on each side

By Belinda and Bryan
A tiny epitome of 'Hearts and Oak'
Kicking the little wavelets as they broke!

For tea we had shrimps and cake and bread and butter
And they were pink, the shrimps I mean, bright pink
Can you imagine what Aunt Knox would think?
Can you not hear the prophecies she'd utter?
Her disapproving tone, her fearful warning
That we should all be dead before the morning!

These lodgings are very comfortable
Though we haven't yet tried the beds
Belinda and Laura are in the front
With a lithograph of Cain and Abel
And 'The Light of the World' by Holman Hunt
Hanging above their heads.

Nanny's bedroom, which Arnold shares
Is across the landing, and down three stairs.
Bryan and I have two small rooms
On the very topmost floor.
His is in front and mine's at the back
And a picture faces my door
Which someone cut out of an almanac
A picture of dashing young Hussars
Galloping off to war.
On the chest of drawers by the looking-glass
There is – Imagine! – dried pampas-grass
Waving its fusty, dusty plumes
From a yellow Japanese vase.
But I can see over the sleeping town
To the curving line of the Sussex Down
And the sky and the moon and the stars.

Dearest Mama
Here we all are
Missing you so and wishing you could share
This pleasant gaslit room and the bracing air
And the prospect of to-morrow
For we are going on a picnic to a little bay

Beyond the lighthouse, several miles away.
Nanny has arranged with a Mr Wells
To drive us in his wagonette
(Unless, of course, it's very wet)
And Mrs Gurney says that we can borrow
A wicker basket that she has, with handles,
In which to put the shells
And coloured pebbles that we hope to find on the deserted shore
Because, it seems, this particular beach
Is out of reach
Of ordinary visitors and is therefore lonely.
Oh dearest Mama – if only – if only
You could be here with us. Now I must end
This untidy, rambling letter
For Nanny has come in with our bedroom candles.
We all of us pray Papa will soon be better
And that to-morrow's weather will be fine.
Your loving and devoted – Caroline.

Although he was far too young to remember the event itself, the passing of Queen Victoria imprinted itself on Noël's mind. In *Cavalcade* he has a scene in which the Marryott family watch the funeral *cortège* from their balcony.

Jane Marryott's young son, Joe, asks her: 'Why did Queen Victoria die, Mum?'

Jane Because she was a very old lady, and very tired . . . Now then, stand absolutely still – to attention, like father showed you.

The music swells as the band passes directly underneath them.

Jane Five kings riding behind her.

Joe Mum, she must have been a very *little* lady.

The lights fade.

1901

When Queen Victoria died
The whole of England mourned
Not for a so recently breathing woman
A wife and a mother and a widow,
Not for a staunch upholder of Christendom,
A stickler for etiquette
A vigilant of moral values
But for a symbol.
A symbol of security and prosperity
Of 'My Country Right or Wrong'
Of 'God is good and Bad is bad'
And 'What was good enough for your father
Ought to be good enough for you'
And 'If you don't eat your tapioca pudding
You will be locked in your bedroom
And given nothing but bread and water
Over and over again until you come to your senses
And are weak and pale and famished and say
Breathlessly, hopelessly and with hate in your heart
"Please Papa I would now like some tapioca pudding very much indeed".'
A symbol too of proper elegance
Not the flaunting, bejewelled kind
That became so popular
But a truly proper elegance,
An elegance of the spirit,
Of withdrawal from unpleasant subjects
Such as Sex and Poverty and Pit Ponies
And Little Children working in the Mines
And Rude Words and Divorce and Socialism
And numberless other inadmissible horrors.

When Queen Victoria died
They brought her little body from the Isle of Wight
Closed up in a black coffin, finished and done for,
With no longer any feelings and regrets and Memories of Albert
And no more blood pumping through the feeble veins
And no more heart beating away
As it had beaten for so many tiring years.

The Young Idea (1907–?1922)

The coffin was placed upon a gun-carriage
And drawn along sadly and slowly by English sailors.

But long before this the people had mourned
And walked about the streets and the Parks and Kensington Gardens
Silently, solemnly and dressed in black.
Now, with the news already a few days old
The immediate shock has faded.
The business of the funeral was less poignant than the first realisation of death,
This was a pageant, right and fitting, but adjustments were already
    beginning to be made.
This was something we were all used to,
This slow solemnity
This measured progress to the grave.
If it hadn't been for the gun-carriage
And the crowds and all the flags at half mast
And all the shops being closed
It might just as well have been Aunt Cordelia
Who died a few months earlier in Torquay
And had to be brought up to London by Great Western
In a rather large coffin
And driven slowly, oh so slowly
To the family burial ground at Esher
With all the relatives driving behind
Wearing black black black and peering furtively out of the carriage windows
To note for a moment that life was going on as usual.
For Aunt Cordelia was no symbol really
And her small death was of little account.
She was, after all, very old indeed
Although not quite so old as Queen Victoria.
But on the other hand she didn't have so much prestige
Except of course in her own personal mind
And that was snuffed out at the same moment as everything else.
Also, unlike Queen Victoria, she had few mourners
Just the family and Mrs Stokes who had been fond of her
And Miss Esme Banks who had looked after her in Torquay
And two remote cousins
Who couldn't rightly be classed as family
Because they were so very far removed
And only came to the cemetery because it was a sign of respect,

Respect, what is more, without hope
For there was little or no likelihood of their being mentioned in the will
But there they were all the same
Both tall and bent, in black toques with veils,
And both crying.

When Queen Victoria died
And was buried and the gun-carriage was dragged empty away again
The shops reopened and so did the theatres
Although business was none too good.
But still it improved after a while
And everyone began to make plans for the Coronation
And it looked as if nothing much had happened
And perhaps nothing much had really
Except that an era, an epoch, an attitude of mind, was ended.
There would be other eras and epochs and attitudes of mind.
But never quite the same.

For Noël – as for many others – the years that followed would never be quite the same.

Honeymoon 1905

'They were married
And lived happily ever after.'
They drove to Paddington Station
Where, acutely embarrassed, harassed
And harried;
Bruised by excessive jubilation
And suffering from strain
They got into a train
And, having settled themselves into a reserved carriage,
Sought relief, with jokes and nervous laughter,
From the sudden, frightening awareness of their marriage.

Caught in the web their fate had spun
They watched the suburbs sliding by,
Rows of small houses, neatly matched,
Safe, respectable, semi-detached;

Lines of gardens like pale green stripes,
Men in shirtsleeves smoking pipes
Making the most of a watery sun
In a watery English sky.

Then pollard willows and the river curving
Between high trees and under low grey bridges
Flowing through busy locks, looping and swerving
Past formal gardens bright with daffodils.
Further away the unpretentious hills
Rising in gentle, misty ridges,
Quiet, insular and proud
Under their canopies of cloud.

Presently the silence between them broke,
Edward, tremulous in his new tweed suit
And Lavinia, pale beneath her violet toque,
Opened the picnic-basket, lovingly packed
By loving hands only this morning – No!
Those sardine sandwiches neatly stacked
Lost centuries ago.
The pale, cold chicken, hard-boiled eggs and fruit
The cheese and biscuits and Madeira cake
Were all assembled in another life
Before 'I now pronounce you man and wife'
Had torn two sleepers suddenly awake
From all that hitherto had been a dream
And cruelly hurled
Both of them, shivering, into this sweeping stream
This alien, mutual unfamiliar world.

A little later, fortified by champagne
They sat, relaxed but disinclined to talk
Feeling the changing rhythms of the train
Bearing them onward through West Country towns
Outside in the half light, serene and still,
They saw the fading Somersetshire Downs
And, gleaming on the side of a smooth, long hill
A white horse carved in chalk.

Later still, in a flurry of rain
They arrived at their destination
And with panic gripping their hearts again
They drove from the noisy station
To a bright, impersonal double room
In the best hotel in Ilfracombe.

They opened the window and stared outside
At the outline of a curving bay,
At dark cliffs crouching in the spray
And wet sand bared by the falling tide.
The scudding clouds and the rain-furrowed sea
Mocked at their desperate chastity.
Inside the room the gas globes shed,
Contemptuous of their bridal night,
A hard, implacable yellow light
On a hard, implacable double bed.

The fluted mahogany looking-glass
Reflecting their prison of blazing brass,
Crude, unendurable, unkind
And then, quite suddenly, with a blind
Instinctive gesture of loving grace,
She lifted her hand and touched his face.

2.
'COD PIECES'

Noël was always suspicious of 'modern'. 'Modern art', 'modern poetry'; he distrusted both as certainly affected and probably bogus.

As far as 'the Abstract boys' in art were concerned, 'quite a lot of it is completely unintelligible'. He goes on to quote critic Wilenski – 'He talks a great deal of "emotive force" and "lyrical colour" and "constant functional forms", etc., and after he has described a picture in approximately these terms you turn to a coloured plate and look at a square lady with three breasts and a guitar up her crotch.'

He was to get his decisive revenge in *Nude with a Violin* in 1956.

'I don't think anyone knows about painting any more. Art, like human nature, has got out of hand.'

Sebastien in *Nude with a Violin*

As far as poetry was concerned, he'd made his views clear as early as 1923 in the revue *London Calling!* with a sketch called 'The Swiss Family Whittlebot'. The heroine was Hernia Whittlebot. Her brothers were called Gob and Sago.

> **Miss Hernia Whittlebot** *should be effectively and charmingly dressed in undraped dyed sacking, a cross between blue and green, with a necklet of uncut amber beads in unconventional shapes. She must wear a gold band rather high up on her forehead from which hangs a little clump of Bacchanalian fruit below each ear. Her face is white and weary, with a long chin and nose, and bags under the eyes. Her brothers* **Gob** *and* **Sago Whittlebot** *are dressed with self-conscious nonchalance in unusual clothes.* **Gob** *wears cycling breeches and a bottle-green velvet coat with a big floppy bow, cloth-topped boots and a tweed shooting hat.* **Sago** *is faultlessly dressed in a slightly Victorian morning suit. His shirt and boots are not quite right and his silk hat is upside down by his side. Their musical instruments are rather queer in shape.*

The sketch contained several pastiches:

Hernia   It is difficult for me to explain to you all in words which I have to say regarding Life and Art and Rhythm. Words are inadequate at the best of times. To me Life is essentially a curve and Art an oblong within that curve. Rhythm is fundamental in everything.

My brothers and I have been brought up on Rhythm as other children are brought up on Glaxo. Always we have tried to create Sound and Reality and Colour. My brothers on their various instruments (and they have many), and myself with all the strength and courage I can summon up, will endeavour to prove to you the inevitable Truth in Rhythmic Colour Poetry.

People have jeered at us – often when walking in the street. They have thrown fruit and vegetables at us – but it is all colour and humour. We see humour in everything – specially the Primitive.

But first is an early Peruvian love song . . .

Early Peruvian Love Song

Beloved, it is Dawn, I rise
    To smell the roses sweet,
Emphatic are my hips and thighs,
    Phlegmatic are my feet.
Ten thousand roses have I got
    Within a garden small,
God give me strength to sniff the lot,
    Oh, let me sniff them all.

Beloved, it is Dawn, I rise
    To smell the roses sweet,
Emphatic are my hips and thighs,
    Phlegmatic are my feet.

Hernia   The next poem strikes an exultantly gay note – the colours are vivid and ruthless because they are Life.

Exultance

Rain, rain, pebbles and pain,
    Trickle and truckle, and do it again;
Houp-la, houp-la, dickery dee,
    Fol-de-rol, fol-de-rol, fancy me!
    (*musical interlude*)
    Fancy me!

Passion

Passion's dregs are the salt of life
    Spirits trodden beneath the feet of Ingratitude.

'Cod Pieces'

>> Drains and sewers support the quest
> Of eternal indulgence.
>>> Thank God for the Coldstream Guards.

Hernia I will now give you a very long and intensely primitive poem entitled 'The Lower Classes'. I have endeavoured to portray the bottomless hostility of the Labour Party towards themselves and everybody else – I wrote most of the first part in a Lighthouse.

At this moment sounds become audible from the prompt corner. The **Stage Manager** *is making signs to them that their time is up.*

The Lower Classes

> War and life and the Albert Bridge
> Fade into the mists of salacious obscurity
> Street hawkers cry apathetically
> Mothers and children rolling and slapping
> Wet on the grass – I wonder why.
> Guts and dahlias and billiard balls
> Swirling along with spurious velocity
> Ending what and where and when
> In the hearts of little birds
> But never Tom Tits.
> Freedom from all this shrieking vortex
> Chimneys and tramcars and the blackened branches
> Of superfluous antagonism
> Oxford and Cambridge count for naught
> Life is ephemeral before the majesty
> Of Local Apophlegmatism
> Melody semi-spheroidal
> In all its innate rotundity
> Rhubarb for purposes unknown, etc., etc.

The **Stage Manager** *having despaired of making her hear, has signed to the Orchestra to strike up the next number. Unmoved by this* **Miss Whittlebot** *produces a megaphone – at last in desperation the* **Stage Manager** *begins to set the next scene and the* **Whittlebot Family** *are eventually pushed off the stage still playing and reciting.*

It just so happened that Dame Edith Sitwell (1887–1964) was – among other things – a 'modern poet' and she had two brothers, Osbert (1892–1969) and Sacheverell (1897–1988). When it became clear that Noël was satirising them and their 'art' with lines such as 'Life is essentially a curve and Art an oblong within that curve. My brothers and I have been brought up on Rhythm as other children are brought up on Glaxo', they were most definitely not amused. A *froideur* ensued that lasted for forty years but fortunately it ended happily. Noël and the Dame became close in the last years of her life and she would sign her letters 'Your ancient friend, Edith'.

Noël reflected – 'How strange that a forty-year feud should finish so gracefully and so suddenly.' But it didn't change his view that 'I really think that three quarters of it is gibberish. However, I must crush down these thoughts otherwise the dove of peace will shit on me.'

Early Whittlebot Poems

When Hernia was in full flow, Noël managed to disinter some of her 'Early Poems':

Daddy and Boo

> Goo Goo
> Daddy and boo
> Goo Goo Boo.

Gob

> Why is Gob so ugly?
> Perhaps in the Dawn
> God will tell me
> Why Gob is so ugly.
> Charlie and Phyllis are pretty
> And Mary is sweet.
> Why is my Gobby so ugly?
> Dear God in the Dawn,
> Tell me why Gob is so ugly.

Heigho for Hockey

Hockey, hockey – strike the ball,
Girls all bang together.
Hockey, hockey – cheerio
In nasty rainy weather.
Heigho for Hockey.

His notes from this period also include what would have been a complete 'slim volume' of *Early Poems by Hernia Whittlebot* – with an appreciation by Noël Coward. The book was typeset but never published – until now.

Here – and later in *Chelsea Buns* – I have retained Noël's 'cod' introductions, since they incidentally parody the way contemporary critics were able to swallow literary pretension as if it were caviar.

Errata

In 'My Bedroom', for 'Chimneys' read 'Communication Cord'.
In 'Sonata for Harpsichord', read 'Frab' for 'Dwad'.
In 'A May Morning', read 'Colwyn Bay' for 'Plymouth Sound'.

Other Works by Hernia Whittlebot

PEEPS AT MICE
HO! THERE POMPEII
GILDED SLUTS
AGATE-FACE AND BLUEBELLS
HAGGIS RE-VISITED

In Preparation

TWELVE RECIPES FOR MINCE PIES

POEMS

by

HERNIA WHITTLEBOT

With
AN APPRECIATION
by
NOËL COWARD

Hernia Whittlebot

An Appreciation
by
Noël Coward

I am proud of my task but the magnitude of it appals me. In the first place, may I say that even to mention the name Hernia Whittlebot is a far greater privilege than falls to the lot of most men, whoever they may be. And, secondly, that to attempt to analyse or so much as comment upon the supreme beauty of her fragrant work, is a prospect before which the boldest heart may well quail and the sternest hand falter.

In what magic hour was this juggernautic mite of inspiration – destined to meet in the course of life's story, such transcendent beauty and such woeful disillusionment – born into – Alack! Alas! A drear and sometime un-appreciative universe? That wonderful hour, the sustained fruits of whose mysteries spread today as a golden cloud, turning the mundane objects of this sordid world to facets of purest glory. That hour is sacred to her of whom I dare tremulously to write. (And to her mother.)

Must not the fairies from their elfin grots and darkling pools have pressed forward with dew drenched feet and ardent hands to waft the kiss of invisible bestowal upon the tiny puckered brow? Fated to become more puckered still as fortune's relentless grasp crushed the happy-hearted illusions of youth into what has become, at moments, a bitter pulp of ironic despair.

Love – Passion – Life – Hate!!! All, all have left their dreadful mark, and ultimately to what refuge has she turned in her bewildered frenzy? Creation! On second thoughts Creation is almost too small a word with which to endow the ineffable service which she has rendered to Poetic Thought in the British Isles; nay, wherever English is spoken, and possibly for future ages, wherever the stars may glimmer, and the sun shine.

It was one of my privileges to meet Hernia Whittlebot at Horsham, some years later at Sevenoaks, where she was taking tea with some friends, and one Easter at Sydenham – but to my task.

A slim volume in green snakeskin embossed vaguely, but unmistakably with the magic words 'Peeps at Mice', was the beginning. Words which within a few weeks became a clarion call to all that were born with the gem-encrusted spoon of Poesy in their mouth.

In 'Peeps at Mice', the freshness of girlhood is paramount, as evidenced by the ephemeral joy of the first poem beginning –

> Ah! Heaven, the sparrows seem so blue,
>   The cows go laughing tip-a-toe –

And finishing:

> Tramp, tramp, look at the lamp,
>   Daddy's asleep and my shoes are damp.

To even the most casual reader, the rhythm and above all, the rotation of these lines must convey an acute sense of the writer's extraordinary promise. Promise which was to be more than fulfilled in her next book, 'Ho! There Pompeii', with, lightly engraved on the fly-leaf, a reproduction of a frieze of the period, which caused an even more violent upheaval among the Epicurean few who were sufficiently *au courant* with her methods to understand a word of it.

As one turns the leaves, one shudders at the stark realism, allied to sensual splendour, with which every verse is saturated. Take at random, the opening lines of 'L'Après midi d'un Cocu':

> Said Cardinal Wolsey, rolling about,
>   Come in, come in, get out, get out.
> History says, and history's true,
>   Life's a game of See-Saw.

Or, again, an extract from her latest book, 'Gilded Sluts',

> 'Impromptu',
> Herrings shouting –
>   Pushing, pouting,
>   Snouts and snarls – !

These glittering lines with their fleet enchantment, conjure up such a haunting picture as shall never fade, of the vasty gloom and tender austerity of Canterbury Cathedral, where poor Thomas-à-Becket met such an untimely and exasperating end.

Hernia Whittlebot, I can do and say no more, but lay my tributes at your feet for all time.

NOËL COWARD

Poems by Hernia Whittlebot

'My Bedroom'

Dreary coal in a dirty grate,
And the crash of falling soot;
Out of the windows far away,
Where the smoke and clouds with the chimneys play,
I stare for hours and feel so gay,
With a corn on either foot.
Crawling flies on a murky pane
And the flies are nearly dead;
Along the floor where the draughts blow
Dust diaphanous to and fro;
There on an evening my thoughts will go,
As I sit and scratch my head.
Indescribably – adrift in space unutterable –
My thoughts like little cushion covers
In a Southsea boarding-house.
(Tender cushion covers these)
Like weary mothers who have been denied
The first fine principles of temperate existence,
And, therefore, by a hair's breadth
Have missed the ferry.
Perambulators, perambulators, not one of them mine!
So when my bedroom folds me round
In atmosphere grotesque,
I drop my orange and close my eyes,
And out of fistulating skies
The morning comes like a big surprise,
And I close my writing desk.

'To My Favourite Hostess'

Mary, with your vapid smile,
    Why not rest awhile?
Dispensing tea in tawdry room contemptible.

The dying sun
Shining alike on cake and bun,
    Turning the tarnished ornaments to beaten silver,
But leaving wistful and raddled the vulgar faces of the Dowagers
    Why not rest awhile?
The ugly teacups with their tasteless brew,
    Stinking to God of vast respectability
Madeleines with sodden ends in saucers,
    Sandwiches with butter oozing through,
Decorating Heaven's golden wheat
    With false pretentiousness.
Empty and vacant are your wandering eyes,
    Searching in vain for dissimilitude.
Clackerty clack your tongue wags on,
    Mouthing and spitting filth unutterable,
For filth to me is life, and life is filth,
    When it is strung on leaden threads, not gold.
Mary, you are my friend, and yet your breath is vile,
    Why not rest awhile?

'Agamemnon and Sappho'

Pull! Pull with a will, pull!
    Pool, pool with a whirlpool;
Rustle and scratch, and heave and snatch,
Open the window, the walls aglaze,
Nothing matters – ecstasy
The great God Pan is Lord of all.

'Sonata for Harpsichord'

Cock!
    Cock!
A-doodle-doo!
    Blankets and Ribston pippins
Unproduberous animal grab.
    Round as a Boh and square as a dwad,
Ann with her brush and a pail and a weary wail,

> Writing her Indian mail.
Prevail
Snail
The Holy Grail
> A-doodle-doo!
> > Cock!
> > Cock!

'Apple Blossoms'

When Arthur said Boo to the parlour maid,
> She felt afraid,
And her fingers played
> A rude tattoo
> > On the chimney flue.
For when he said Boo
> She always knew
> > What he meant to do
To the Irish stew.
> So she felt afraid
> > Poor parlour maid.
Said Bridget the cook
> With a nasty look
> > It's time he took
> A button hook.
For men like these
> Are thick as peas,
> > No Cheddar cheese
> > > This morning please.
But Master Art
> Would play a part,
> > And made a start
> With a raspberry tart.
Oh, Arthur, fie?
> Oh, Arthur, shame!
Even to think of such a game;
> For parlour maids are dainty folk
> And simply loathe a doubtful joke.

'Poor Shakespeare'

Blow, blow thou winter wind,
    Rough and rude like a goat's behind;
Helen of Troy and Lesbia fair,
    Catch a cloud in their matted hair.
Eagerly seeking
    Raddled and reeking,
Speaking
    In
        Gasps
With tongues like Asps
    Fresh from the Convent of Sacré Coeur,
And Queen Elizabeth's virginity.

'The Bride Cake'

Cups
    Pups,
Finding their mecca,
Drums and Madarines
    Minos was not so
Hard as any goat-footed Agapè
    Call to God
        For succour.
Winds
    Without
        Buds,
            Roads dust of June,
Tendrils of flame
    And where – ?

'To Noël Coward'

Pale faced rat!
    Wallowing in the pit of middle-class degeneracy.
Juggling clumsily with the immortal souls

'Cod Pieces'

    Of your superiors.
Illogically defying the very canons of beauty.
    Defiling with your touch the plangency of Art,
Restlessly groping with inadequate comprehension
    Among the tinsel stars and tawdry imaginings
Of a squalid mentality.
    Pitifully mean, your very appearance an offence.
Slimy as the ooze of a sluggish river.
    Rough to the insensate touch,
Rough to the insensate fingers.
    Pig-brained, pig-eyed and stupid,
Vulgar, blatant and self-confident,
    Early beginning of a nauseating manhood,
If such term can be applied to you.
    Hob-Goblin habits in an ass's skin,
Picking your mental food from garbage heaps
    Rotting in the sun.
Drab – Putrefying – Soul-sickening!
    And anyhow you smell awful.

'The Dancing Class'

The dim brown bush is waving
In the Sirocco
The far-off splash of the golden pool.
Love, if you could see me now,
Discordant as a gramophone,
Yet full-toned as a parrot's cry.
Tinsel and glamour and jagged edges,
Rough here, smooth there.
Pussy runs in her playful way.
In the Sirocco, and I laugh.
Such are the fruits of domesticity,
Privacy and aloneness.
The lupins drip.
My heart is flamboyant as the roses of China.
Whistle and I shall hear,
Whistle loud, whistle long –

Ah – h – h – h – h – h – h –
And so to breakfast.

'To an Old Woman in Huddersfield'

JADE, Agate,
    And the ivory degeneracy
Of down-at-heel profligacy,
    Sing us your song.

In the mine's
    Confines
Lines endless tortuous.

Bubble and whoop,
    As children with croup,
With stitches of pain,
    Again and again.

And again
    And again,
Again . . .

'Pied-à-Terre'

Oh! To be a small brown Nubian boy,
Muffled in strong bright tweed,
To lay my dark, flat ear
Upon the paving stones of immortality;
To twine my thick red hands
In the chypre-scented curls of
Orpheus;
To splook and namp in the mighty
River –
Men call satiety.
Mute your every trumpet hosts of
Impeccability;
The morass of evolution is a-quiver
To engulf the yearning shoots of my
Desire!

'Greasy Garbage'

In the perfumed air are butterflies
Singing to heaven of iridescent love;
Rapture and kisses and the dusk-scented dreams
Of poppy leaves.
Your mouth is my mouth,
And their mouth is Bournemouth.
Mauve splashes and scarlet berries,
And ninety-two columbines dancing to the echoes
Of fragrant melodies.
Oh God. How beautiful is ratafia flavouring,
Specially in gooseberry pudding.
Pay at the desk, please.

'A May Morning'

Berries red, berries white,
    Very round.
Spasms of gold darting,
    Naughty laughter
In the grass,
Scurry, scurry – happy
    It is me.

It is I,
I feel it, I know it – eternal movement
    Whirling for ever
And further still
To the utter vastness of my entity
    And Plymouth Sound is blue—

'Yellow Nocturne'

The tapestry is like bread to-night
    And the gardener picks his teeth.
Hampstead Heath.
    My dainty sheath,

With maggots underneath.
My soul is oblong, Sunset's Twag
    Rains down like jewelled froob;
My thoughts are gambolling like sharks
    Or Oxford undergraduates.
Away, away,
To-morrow, to-day,
Soldiers play
In new mown hay;
Golden spray
A roundelay,
Sometimes clay
Will join the fray;
Asses bray
Diddledy fay,
Green decay,
A-lack-a-day.
Caraway,
Isabel Jay,
Evelyn Lay,
Henry de Bray,
Maisie Gay,
Akerman May,
Edith Day,
Edna May,
Gabrielle Ray,
Helen Hay,
Watch and Pray.

'Romance'

In C sharp minor

So, this is all that Love has left,
Good Lord, the hours are slow,
My mouth is like a Lion's den,
My breath is crackling like a stove,
Or the whip of the Ring-Master.
The night light gutters,

'Cod Pieces'

And so does he – My lover once.
Good Gracious!
Fool that I am, and always was,
Take my dreams in your strong brown hands,
Roll them under the bed;
Take my hair (it is over there)
And cram it in my wardrobe;
Take my soul between your knees
And bite it and tear it please!
What have I left to give your feet,
To leap upon and crush?
My heart's too heavy, your heart's too light,
To balance the twain together;
Take my body, each tingling pore,
And paint it red and blue,
And take, oh take my eyelids, do,
And fling them about the yard;
Maul and tear, and nuzzle and beat,
And shake me like a rat;
Spit and choke, and cough and laugh,
Clap both your hands and writhe;
Quaff a drink of Burgundy
And throw me at the dregs,
And when you have jumped and rolled your will
And left me shattered utterly,
Go out into the rollicking Sunlight,
And leave me to eat my egg.

'A Country Fair'

Chipperty, chap
    Croperty, bibberty,
Snib, Snobb,
    Mop in wooh,
Clinter, clanter,
    Shinter, shanter,
Oggledy, boggled, roops a hoo!
    Danderloy, Plockinsnitch,
Keedle-weedle, keedle bim

Rift,
    Toft,
        Keek,
            Snoop,
                Piddery,
                    Frickerty,
                        Ramperty toop
        Griberty grap,
            Voberty, Viberty,
        Drib. Drob,
            Yock in fooh,
        Younter, Yanter,
            Minter, Manter,
                Nutlety, puttlety, Oggsie, Booh!

In 1925 Miss Whittlebot *did* see the light of print.

Lorn Macnaughton's portrait of the lady has been replaced – while keeping it in the Coward 'family' – by Gladys Calthrop's Picassoesque rendering.

Hernia by Lorn MacNaughtan

Hernia by Gladys Calthrop

Chelsea Buns (1925)

Chelsea
Buns

BY
HERNIA WHITTLEBOT

EDITED BY
NOEL COWARD

CHELSEA BUNS

BY
HERNIA WHITTLEBOT

EDITED BY
NOEL COWARD

WITH AN INTRODUCTION BY
GASPARD PUSTONTIN

LONDON
HUTCHINSON & CO.
PATERNOSTER ROW

Foreword

There can be no two opinions about Miss Whittlebot's work. She has steadily climbed the precarious ladder of poetic Conquest, and from the height of her unassailable pinnacle she now bestows upon an eagerly expectant public this new proof of her iridescent genius.

There is something flamboyant in her gallantly coloured phraseology – she affects one like 'Jumbles' or a merry-go-round in a Turkish bath.

She scatters the tepid tea-leaves of Victorian Aspiration and Georgian achievement with the incisive *mesquinerie* of a literary Bonaparte.

Nothing is spared the flail of her titulative satire. The cacophonous charm of Harlequin and Columbine evaporates like withered potpourri before the oncoming hurricane of her merciless pen. Hostesses retired battered, to the sombre tranquillity of the de Goncourts, and the *baroque* naughtiness of Madame de Sévigné.

In the puerile deprecations of her poetic contemporaries one senses the lurking and resentful machinations of wheels within wheels. They rise to the elusive bait of her audacity as crayfish to a nocturnal lantern – only to discover that in the searching illumination of her mental causticism their very vices are twisted into mediocre virtues; and they sink back abashed to find solace and consolation in the healing balm of their own particular satellites. In France, Hernia Whittlebot has been hailed and extolled even more perhaps than in England. Within the obscure translucent gloom of the Bois members of the Whittlebot 'cult' may be observed wandering like contented spirits temporarily released from the narrow confines of ungarlanded graves, and in their shining eyes the knowledge that at last they have found the source of life's inspiration.

NOËL COWARD
1924

Neurotic Thoughts on the Renaissance

He's in the Lancers, sir, she said,
Sir, she said, she said.
He prances high on horses yellow:
Trundle, trundle, hearty fellow.
Sugar mice like billiard balls

Go skit-a-wit,
Mouthed to nothingness
With infantile paralysis.

Silly, painted shrieks
Snick through constipated air.

Her baize-green face
Glares treacle sweet
Down wounded hills,
With chuckling gorse a-murmur,
With the indiscreet avowals
Of sadic curates in their laity.

To a Maidenhair Fern

You pretty thing,
Each dainty frond unbending,
Supple unending,
    Like pearls on a string –
Your message in sending
    A promise of spring.

Nous n' avons plus de chichi

Chelsea streets are trim and grand,
Trams are fortresses of pride,
And the tortoiseshell cat of the violinist
Stalks mincingly through the ordure.
I string my beads of parrot sound,
And clap my soignées mental hands,
A-loop the loop – they swing and float,
Immeasurably sensible –
Gauds in the aquarium of some vast infinitude,
Globe-like breasts of tender Americans
Glimmer through the fragile night
'A party in this lovely house.
How darling heavenly!'

The Town Hall's still there,
Godstone green and Purtle red,
And all the poets spew their potted shrimps
And don the velvet boots of turpitude.

Chelsea Buns

Along the thundering pavement roars
    and screams
A mouse-inclining to 'The Good
    Intent'
For conversation's toasted cheese –
Salisbury plain and twopence coloured.
A country joke, ha-ha – ho-ho – ha-ha!
The Restoration plays were *far* the best.
Let us be humorous and so obscure,
Because our minds of rainbow-coloured
    clay
Insist on Marcel-wavèd friends
And blameless notoriety;
Our hair drips this and that way with
    the wind
Of shrill falsetto sycophantic laughs.
Ha! let's be bawdy with our Oxford
    wits,
And pornographic in a foreign tongue,
And flick away the genius of an age
With Nuttall's Etymology.
Pass the spotted dog,
Which looks like Aunt Maria's belly!

Contours

Round – oblong – like jam –
Terse as virulent hermaphrodites;
Calling across the sodden twisted ends
    of Time.

Edifices of importunity
Sway like Parmesan before the half-tones
Of Episcopalian Michaelmas;
Bodies are so impossible to see in retro-
　　spect —
And yet I know the well of truth
Is gutted like pratchful Unicorn.
Sog, sog, sog — why is my mind amphi-
　　bious?
That's what it is.

Guava Jelly

Anne Boleyn, you were not half so bold
As those who whispered of your sensi-
　　bility,
And trickling through the corner of a
　　biscuit tin,
The india-rubber leaves fly click-a-clack;
For Henry was a man of passing tender-
　　ness
With spheroid hands that groped away
　　your dreams
Fantastical, elliptical his slavering lips,
Like cherry tart.
Puritanical were the forest trees;
And, ah! The sharpness of the moon's
　　decay,
With oblong beams adrift in sensuality,
Came drifting through the purlieus of
　　your soul.

Garibaldi

　　Immaculately fine
　　　　Like Elderberry wine,
　　　　　　And old Tokay's decline;

Impassioned as a bog,
>   Cavorting like a dog
>   >   Or brindled gollywog;

Resembling the short
>   Thin lessons we were taught
>   >   Of lazy battles fought;

Grandiloquent we see,
>   In all simplicity,
>   >   The trousered bumble-bee.

And all the afternoon
>   Disgruntled colonels swoon
>   >   Like wafers of the moon;

And tea-cups, dancing, pass
>   Along the azure grass
>   >   To where the monkey was.

The stilted elfin talk
>   Like buttered tomahawk
>   >   Destroys the Deacon's stalk.

Unfathomable, deep,
>   The pornographic sheep
>   >   Like bus conductors creep.

Interminable, boring,
>   Like festooned launches snoring
>   >   From Maidenhead to Goring.

Family Circle

A table spread
With vegetarian naughtiness,
Lasciviously the Burgundy
Grunts to see.
The Petite Suisse
Is no less pale
Than botched poetic faces
Thick as cream

That's curdled in the telling.
The saucy butler hovers
With blue-veined legs
A-twitch with varicose ambiguity;
Spatulate hands nark
At the multicoloured gems
Of still-born conversation.
'We'll give a grand recital Tuesday
    week'
With marmalade fingers plaiting dreams
Of conquering blasts among beslaug-
    tered literature
Blind drunk with stale achievement,
Seeking more to rend with elephantine
    fingers
Some poor web of silly weed
Athwart a stagnant pool
Of excellent bred ability;
Scorbutic brains, a-grapple and a-swoon,
Mazed with good living and effusive
    friends,
They keek and preen among the scented
    woofs
Bewoven for their ultimate decline
Towards the sullen breast of mediocrity.

Silly Boy

Wait, I must wash my hands in rasp-
    berry beer.
The saucepan's azure face sheds Anda-
    lusian beams
According to the segregating tears
    Of wayside urchins on St Crispin's
      day.
Devotedly I hope that you are well –
    Your asthma better? Good.
And now your teeth –

Paradoxical is the pain of life,
Spatulate, transcendent,
Empujamos la mesa.

Candelabra

Things come into your mind
And are gone again
Like drops of silly, truculent rain.
Do I like butter?
Who am I to question Nature's sanctity?
Ah! Gorgeous, gorgeous is the sun,
Shining out loud with a rum-tum-tum;
I stretch my naked limbs and writhe
About the desiccated drive –
Which doesn't rhyme with writhe, but
    Still,
Without the 'a' saliva will.

Children's Tales

(1)
My mother said to me:
Beware of gipsies bold,
Who lure you with their cold
Tight fingers to where the wood
Is spatulate and thin,
Like eager casks of tawny port im-
    placable.

(2)
My mother said to me:
The brindled cow has taken up
A Kreisler theme in G;
The posturing moon
Is thrilling like a maiden for her lover's
    touch;
And, ah! See how

The brindled cow
Importunate
Prepares evasive legs to mark the rhyme.
A little dog, hysteria unchained,
With raucous grunts goes lolling o'er the
    downs.
The willow-pattern dish to Gretna Green
Must fly
And sigh
A threnody.
Leave out the spoon, it doesn't mean a
    thing.

(3)
My mother said to me:
Clinkerty clank clonk
Clinkerty clank clonk
Clonderloo.
Felinity, enstrangled in the treacly depths
Of turgidity,
Who with foreceful red hands
Has sealed with sharp masculinity
Her mousing conquests?
Little Tommy Thin.

(4)
My mother said to me –
A flaxen figure, glassy hair a-spin,
And broken as a doll;
The yielding green of darkling
    spears
Abandoned to her sad posterior
A bowl like cod's eyes,
Sharp and thin;
Chalcedony and agate waferous May
    blossom
Floating in and out,
Like country vicars' wives
Intent on deadly kindnesses
Obstetrically scientific

Like the motherhood of spinsters
Behind the cashmere veils,
Phantasmagoric, gluttonous.
With fervent tentacles agrasp,
Beside the custard hot and green,
On, on the wooden article aglaze,
The sunset's haze
Amaze;
The foxgloves bobbing on inadequate stalk:
I think I shall get out and walk.

(5)
My mother said to me –
The angular extremities
Of glaring thin tin mugs,
Apocryphal, dynamic,
In matricate dythiambics
Rock, choke, creak:
Wednesday week
Will be the birthday of the Infanta.

(6)
My mother said to me –
In harlequined fancy
Pantaloon,
With conventional red-hot poker
Prodding the hopes of Messalinian
   adolescence:
Rock-a-bye baby.

Written from a Mansard Window in a Velvet Dress

Tell me your moth is yellow,
    I will laugh –
Flinging high the loofah in the bath,
    Exacting measured honey from the
        sluice.
Ah well-a-day!

Victorian Rhapsody for Lesser Minds

They're so attractive, flowers under glass;
    The little waxen buds are *too* divine!
Those dear, delicious snowstorms are
    such fun –
    Amusing, don't you think?
I've got a beaded footstool – such a dear.
Intriguing bubbles on a chandelier
Give me *such* inspiration for my work –
    So subtle, darling,
I've only eaten syllabubs for years.
Daguerreotypes *are* jolly – one appears
    Ineffably bucolic.
    Oh, to be different!
Give me an antimacassar for my dress
And several chignons for my happiness.

Spotted Lilies

Hey, hey, let her go
With clicking heels and furbelow,

With welcome written on the mat
And little pebbles round and fat,

And all the dust of Purgatory,
And flatulent streams,

From the mustard depths
Of old man's beards.

Shallow fishes fly about my eyes,
Exacting toll like dragonflies.

Of all the thoughts the best insure
The almond-colour paramour.

Call back the cattle, Mary, dear,
Like aged festering potentates,

Their horns are posters on a hoarding,

Flaunting their tattered nonchalance;

The hermits in their caves of glass
(My breasts are round and square and
    green).

Clorinda's cracked the soup tureen.
Bring cigarettes and matches fat.

As ballet dancers' legs,
Golf-croquet is like daisies' eyes –

Whirling, twirling ecstasies,
Invertebrate – mausades – bodeuses –
    moqueuses

Where are my garters?

Mrs Gibbon's Decline and Fall

Sibilant apples glistering now
In your mauve hands,
Like priests that hold a tortoise to their
    mouth,
And Macabre days of tan and blue
Go hopping one, two, three.
Good God, it's time for tea!

Sunday Morning at Wiesbaden

I sometimes think that shrimps and
    sprats
Should wear enormous Homburg hats,
And swim about with cricket bats
    Suspended from their ears.

Importunate the rolling downs,
Like very rare provincial clowns,
In knitted Jaeger dressing-gowns
    Upon the end of piers.

Misericordia

My breasts have sprung to meet you like the
 moon,
The nodding kingcups set my head
 aswoon.
If it were not Whit-Monday afternoon
I'd take a corrugated tinsel spoon,
Coagulate as golden macaroon,
Best syncopated passion as a coon
Would write the honeyed phrase of Lorna
 Doone . . .
What matters it if Love be over soon?

To My Literary Parasites

I'll give you wooden phrases –
Words for horses –
Mechanical contrivances.
You give me adulation – emulation –
And dribble at my feet.
What's it to you?
You've had the Russian Ballet!

To Badrulbador Frampton

The Day of Judgment crackling down
The hills of time,
Like mother going to her bath –
One for sorrow, two for joy;
Like any little carking boy
Whose sex unfolding, calls to mind
The water-melon purity
Of Mrs Hodgson's chignon,
Nettled like a grape;
And gardener's corduroys
All mottled by the verisimilitude

Of passing horses.
I think a swan has leather kidneys!

Contemporary Thought

Stravinsky, let me clutch your hand,
    And nuzzle at your breast,
The golden road to Samarkand
    Has made me so depressed.
Picasso, with your painted soul,
    Inspire me with a glance –
A flaunting Gauguin carmagnole
    Has set my pen a-dance.
Hey-ho, hey-ho, hey-hominy-ho,
    With a which and a what
And a where shall we go?

Send Me My Hat

Sob your heart out, child of mine,
    And fling away your train;
The clock is striking half-past nine
    And I must go to Spain;
The speckled flowers incarnadine
    Will ease the body's pain.
    Grub
    Grub
    Grub
The tuck shop bell is ringing
    And
    Swinging
Ding-a-ding-a-dinging.

Athwart the fat bald head
Of Mr Ebenezer Satterthwaite,
With small lascivious tartlets
    On
    A
    Plate.

For all the world like withered Mr Keats
Tossing on high the multi-coloured
    sweets
Of villanelle's intoxicated muse
I will not hear a word against the Jews,
    As,
    After
    All,
    They've
    Done
    A lot
    Of
    Good.
What's the use of grumbling – we should
On all occasions, like some striped
    rocking-horse,
All pull our weight around the garish
    course
Of life's betattered race.
The King and Queen not there – how
    strange!
Without a bowler hat on Derby Day.

Theme for Oboe in E Flat

    Zebubbah, zebubbah,
    Zooboom tweet tweet
    Pidwiddy piddwiddy,
    Pidantipatiddy

    Dark – round –
    Suggestive beads of sound.

    Zebubbah zebubbah,
    Tweet Tweet.

Oleograph

A cottage in the westering sun
    (This is my real mind speaking now),
The curling smoke when day is done,
The happy-hearted children run
To help their father pull the plough.
    If only peace were not so sad,
And happiness of rose-white youth
Were stained to glory mouth to mouth,
    I'd feel my heart serenely glad,
Would only intellect allow
(This is my real mind speaking now).

And even then Hernia had not quite written herself out . . .

Hic Haec Hoc

(on a postcard)

    Cups
    Pups
    Finding their
    Feet and wandering
    Minos was not so
    Hard on my goat-footed Agapè
    Call to god for succour
    Winds without buds
    And road's dust of June
    Tendrils of flame
    And where —— ?

I Will Protect My Sister

    I will protect my sister
    From low scorbutic wits
    Who say her hair is nasty
    And often full of nits,

Who say her inspirations
Are epileptic fits.
They also say she's frowsy
And some have said she's crude
And Harold Peter Spoopin
Was very nearly rude.

I *will* protect my sister
With teeth and feet open
No more shall she be baited
By literary men.
She's anyhow a lady
And charming in the home,
Who does her hair twice weekly
And never breaks the comb.

I *will* protect my sister
In spite of what they say.
She isn't mean, she doesn't cheat,
She's honest as the day.
I think her teeth are pretty,
I rather like her ears.
She won't be half bad looking
When her complexion clears.

Strong is my manhood,
Strong is my new found strength
Strong!
Liars, slanderers, degenerates,
Leave me to my family affection
And the river when the birds are calling,
The barrows with their fresh plucked fruit
Are drab – compared with her.
Love
Brotherhood
Protection.

Hernia was to make one final appearance. Noël claims to have visited her when she was resting after a heavy lunch. The poetess was anxious to find the appropriate vibrations for the spirit of Christmas. After two helpings of Christmas pudding she was able to write:

Christmas Cheer

> Snow and Pudding
> Life and Death,
> Nothing,
> And yet Everything.
> For shame, Good
> King Wenceslas!

Then, after coffee, she was further inspired and produced a verse which – Noël believed – 'has all the elusive "something" of a genuine Whittlebot'.

Caprice de Noël

> Holly berries twinkle red;
> Oh! How red they are!
> Parlourmaids with cheeks aglow
> Scream beneath the mistletoe.
> Footmen, footmen, stuff your calves
> Wrapt in patriotic scarves;
> Portsmouth harbour, Portsmouth harbour,
> Dreams of Francis Drake.

And then, one assumes, Miss Whittlebot went to visit that Great Salon in the Sky. She was certainly never heard from again.

There was a sense – even at the time – that 'a joke's a joke' but that this one had probably gone far enough. One critic went so far as to say – 'One almost feels sorry for Miss Sitwell, even though she has been, in the vernacular, "asking for it for years".'

There was to be one rather muted encore, as far as the 'cod pieces' were concerned. In 1932 a now distinctly famous Noël Coward published *Spangled Unicorn*, supposedly an anthology of obscure poets, several of them in apparent translation. (Like James Thurber's subsequent 'Unicorn in the Garden', this was a literary 'mythical beast'.) By and large it was well received as 'a gorgeous display of literary fooling' but there was one unforeseen problem.

The 'poets' were depicted in a series of old photographs that Noël had acquired in a junk shop years before. What he failed to consider was that, although the subjects of the photos were safely departed, their relations were not. And, like the Sitwells, they were not amused to see their ancestors being mocked.

A certain amount of money had to change hands to keep the law at bay!
That particular joke was now most definitely over . . .

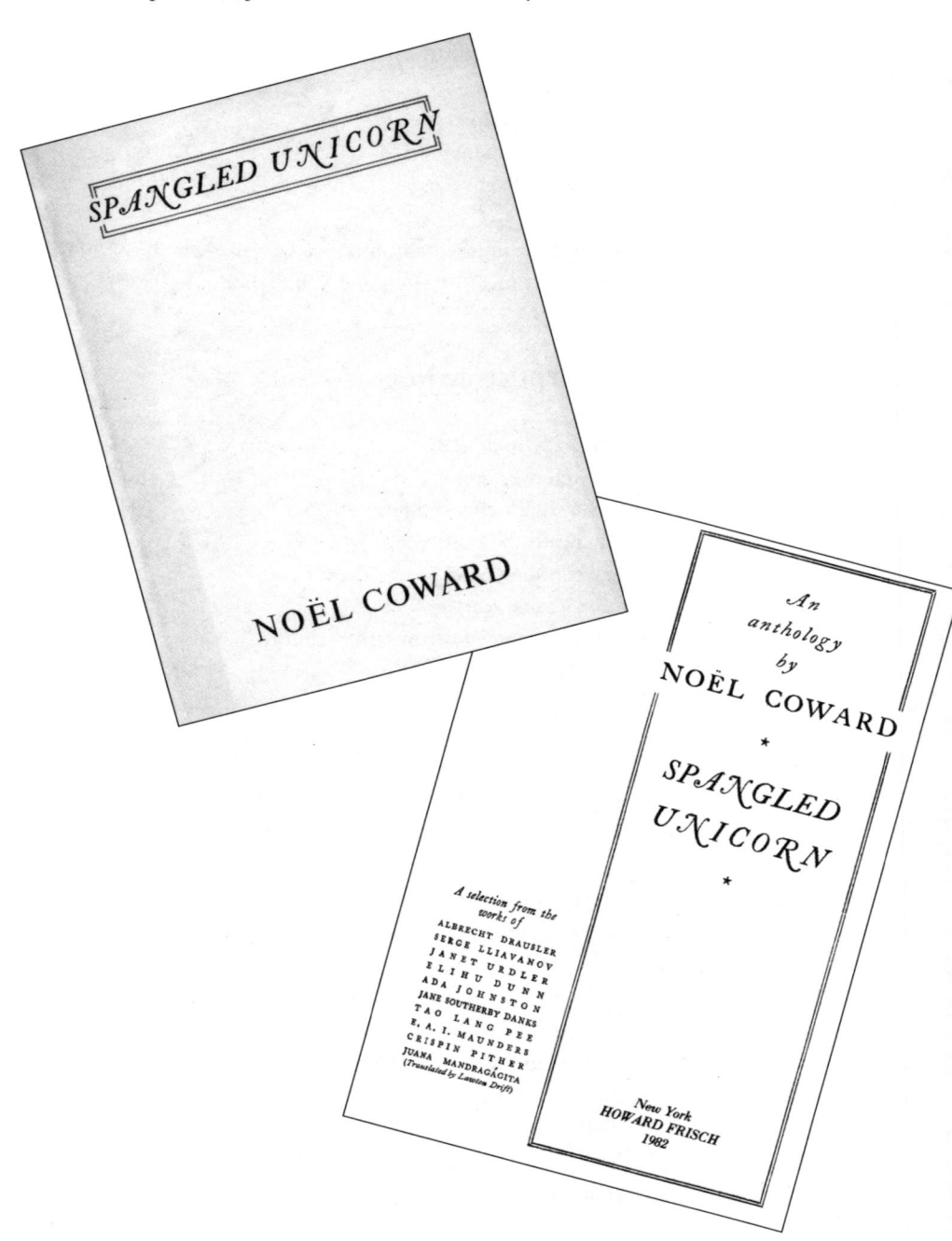

Spangled Unicorn (1932)

Janet Urdler

Reversion to the Formal

Emma housemaid sees the shepherdess shepherdess with crook lambs' tails up crying up tying gate hinges creak scream soul hinges scream creak no love no love Emma housemaid round red hands chimney smokes at sunset blue beads in thick sentimental air with children near women's children spherical butter skins and legs sausage swollen job the Ploughman big Job bug Job more children nuzzling and crying mother Emma mother Emma Emma no mother no love no love dairy-fed produce lush pasturage gate hinges scream creak happy scream love scream creak happy scream love scream women scream Job goes home laughing Job big laughing Job windows shut door shut hot body hot air Emma housemaid no love waiting no love lonely.

How Does Your Garden Grow

Silly lady with your trowel
Consecrating female energy
On small male plants
Outside your garden wall
Plains stretch limbless
To odd horizons
Inside there is peace
Sequestered foolish tranquillity
Shut away from vital urge
Stupid Arabis
Sanctimonious Hollyhocks
Bestial Lobelias
Concealing their obscenity in Prettiness
Like Vicars' daughters
In Organdie
What is there above but sky
What is there beneath but earth

Thick hot earth alive with jostling seedlings
And strange lewd bulbs
Silly lady with your trowel
How does your garden grow?

Hungry Land

Earth in chains and hunger
Tadpoles in Ponds
Cows retching
Drought
Famine
Milko
Oh No
Cattle come home
No home
Speed the Plough
No Plough
Hen bane
No Hen
Night Shade
No Shade
Only Night
Hungry Night

Necromancy

Ma skin is black
As an ole black crow
Ole black crow
Vo dodeo do
Ma Pap was white
As de wind blown snow
Wind blown snow
Vo dodeo do
Ma Mammy was brown
As chicken soup

'Cod Pieces'

Chicken soup
Boop oop a doop
She knocked my Pappy
For a loop
For a loop
Boo poop a doop
Ma sis is pale
As a piece of Gruyère
Piece of Gruyère
Halleluia
But ma skin's black
As an ole black crow
Ole black crow
Vo dodeo do.

Elihu Dunn (*to Robert Andrews*)

Harlem

Yellow brown black
Limbs writhing in rhythm
Rhythm writhing limbs
Hot Momma Hey Hey
Where is Death if this is life
Night Life Night Death
Crazy 'bout you honey
Hey honey ma baby
African drums beatin' our soul rhythm
African blood coursing thru
Dark streets
Hot dark breath
Shutters with light seepin' thru
Makin' black shadows
Black shadows of black loves
Saxophones moanin'
Groanin' groanin'
Where are de cotton fields

Where is dat blue grass
Where are dem ole oat cakes
No here Nigger
Hot Momma Hey Hey

Ma People

Ma People
Call back ober your shoulder
Way back to Jungle land
Come to Glory
Come with yo po hearts a-weary
Yo po souls a-stretchin' upwards to de light
Neber yo mind when de white folks
Stand in the dusty streets a-nid noddin'
Der fool white heads
And a-laughin' and a-jeerin'
De Lord lubs yo same as he lubs the King fisher
In de corn brakes
An de bees an de flowers in de Dixie fields
Ma People
Come on ma people
Lift up yo po hearts
Lift up yo po hands
Raise yo po eyes
The Lord knows yo po backs is a-bendin'
Under yo po burden
An dat yo po feet is a-aching
In yo po shoes
Come on, yo po people
Ma People.

E. A. I. Maunders

Moss

Sound is elliptical
Sorrow is sound
Sorrow is round
Curved like a ball
David and Saul
Knew about sorrow

Pain is a thing
Pieces of string
Tie them together
Wondering whether
Death is away

Thank you for nothing
Take it away
Over the hills
Back to beginning
Lying and sinning
Laughing and loving
Pushing and shoving

Curve In Curve Out

Catch time with a net
Nor yet embrace eternity
Like thin flute notes
Beads in ether – skipping down
Short stubby streets at evening
Without the vulnerable heel
Dr Juno's Anvils
Babying Gods with comforters
And small edged clouds to ride
And jelly in sand the sea had left
Causing mirth in the basement kitchen

And making foolish extra editions
Trackless dust leaves no tracks
But animals know
Beyond small imagery
The history of the crooked stars
And wildly breaking light.

Church of England

(to F. Tennyson Jesse)

Gertrude loves the Church of England
Font and Pew and Font
Hassock and Cassock and me
Pulpit pains are Gertrude
Gertrude is Ancient and Modern
And new and old.
Gertrude loves the Church of England
Choristers and boots and Adam's apples
Where through coloured saints sun dapples
Gertrude's cheek and hat bird
Gertrude's big umbrella
All the responses
Candles in sconces
Gertrude loves the Church of England.

Tao Lang Pee

Sampan

Waves lap lap
Fish fins clap clap
Brown sails flap flap
Chop sticks tap tap
Up and down the green long river
Ohè ohè lanterns quiver
Waves lap lap

Fish fins clap clap
Brown sails flap flap
Chop sticks tap tap

The Emperor's Daughter

There she sits
Wao Ping
With her gold nails
Scratching memories
Lacquer memories of other days
Other lovers
Chow Ho of the casual limbs
Oo Sang Po of the almond teeth and sweet
    breath
Plong How of the short legs and careful
    eyes
There she sits
Wao Ping
In her scarlet Pavilion
Watching the gold carp mouths
Opening tremulously
Dying of love
Because it is Spring in the Lotus Pool
And Spring's lute is cracked
Cracked and broken with too many tunes
Love songs long since sung.

The Voice in the Bamboo Shoot

The water is silver
Gliding softly by the Lotus pool
Softly softly softly softly softly
Little Princess Li Chung Ho
Daughter of a thousand stars
Imprisoned in an azure bowl
Where oh where is your lover

Your warrior lover
Lithe and tall helmeted for battle
Helmeted for honourable death
While you wait in your lacquer Pavilion
Tears dropping through the lattice
Tears like the jewels of Mei Tang Poo.

Serge Lliavanov

Every Day

Ivan is lost in the snow
The wolves are howling.
Each bough bends beneath its weary load
Maria Ivanovitch rocks
Rocks by the fire and weeps
Ivan is lost in the snow
In the Nevsky Prospect the snow has been
    cleared away
To allow the Droshkys to pass
Over towards Oomsk the sky is red
Ivan went out with a basket
And swiftly became lost in the snow
In the squares of the city
And in the taverns
There is warmth by the stoves
And good wine
And the thick stocky women of the people
With strong square breasts
And jolly red cheeks
Red as the sky in Oomsk
And sturdy legs,
But Maria Ivanovitch rocks
Rocks by the fire endlessly
Ivan went out with a basket
And was immediately lost in the snow.

Theatre Party

Here we are. Programme quickly
Sit yourselves down
The Play begins
See the funny man
How he pretends to be hurt
No No Life is not so easy
Chocolate Panskys for the asking
Delicious are they not
To while away the time
Before the funny man cometh again
To teach us to laugh at sorrow
Ha-ha-ha – ha-ha-ha –
Ho-ho-ho – ho-ho-ho.

Harlot's Song

Buy me. Buy me. Cheerio. Tip Top.
I will please you
With my happy laughter
And my gay Butterfly ways
Now bold now timid
How you will laugh to see me.
Run from you in mock fear
And then back again
Now sprite now woman
Which will you choose?
Buy me. Buy me.
Love is cheap to-day
Because fish must be bought at the market
Haddocks strong and fine
Small tender mussels for my mother
Buy me. Buy me.
I am young am I not
Young and gay. Cheerio. Tip Top.
I will please you.
You cannot buy my heart

That belongs elsewhere
In the trees and mountains and streams
In the deep valleys
My heart is not for sale
It belongs to Michael Michaelovitch
And he is dead
And never again will I see him
Because he is so dead.
But my heart is with him
Under the thick warm earth
You cannot buy my heart
Bid what you will
But I will sing for you
Sing and dance for you
A dance of old days
One two three so
One two three so
There does that not please you
Buy me. Buy me.
Cheerio. Tip Top.

Juana Mandragágita

(translated by Lawton Drift)

Picnic Near Toledo

Life is a moment
A moment of life
Is Life giving
Life loving
Life is love
Love loving
Love giving
Cathedrals rotting
In hot sunlight
Mellowing for Death

Death giving
Death loving
Death loving Life
Life loving Death
Why are we waiting
Why sigh
Why cry
Why cry
Why sigh
Why sigh cries
Why cry sighs
Death Death Death.

'Flamenco'

OHÈ Ohè
La – a – aňňa
Lacalacalacalaca – aňň – aňňa
Nyah Nyah
Carista Carista Caristagarcon
Baňero
Paňero
Carista Carista Caristagarcon.

Torero

Bull Blood
Blood Bull
Red Red
Hola Hola
Gallant Parade
Ladies and Laces
Voluptuous faces
Music is played
Bull Blood
Blood Bull
Red Red
Hola Hola

Crispin Pither

'Deirdre'

Deirdre the sorrowful smile of you
Deirdre the Spring sweet guile of you
Calls me back when the red sun's failin'
Calls me back like a sea-bird wailin'
Deirdre the hard hard heart of you
Maybe the Banshee's part of you
From County Kerry to County Clare
I smell the smell of your tangled hair.

'The Whisht Paple'

As I were lolloping down the lane
On Michael Mulligan's Mary Jane
I spied a whisht man all in green
Bedad says I, 'tis a Ragaleen.
I lolloped on wid a troubled mind
Shure the Davil himself was close behind
Now Father Snuffy I chanced to see
'Mother of Jaysus,' says I to he,
'The wee whisht paple are near at hand.'
So he drew a circle in the sand
And squatted down in his cassock green
To make a mock o' the Ragaleen.
'Begorrah,' says I, ''tis all in vain
The Davil himself is home again,
So climb the Tower and ring the bell
For all of the souls you've prayed to hell.'
Then Father Snufy on bended knee
Strangled himself wid his Rosary
And there where a minute ago had been
A Holy Priest, was a Ragaleen!

'Pastoral'

'Ah, where are ye goin' Macushla Macree?'
Wid a toss o' her curls she's replyin'
'Och, I'm climbin' the mountain to Bally Macbog
Wheer me grandmother Bridget is dyin'
Wid a maingadoo aday
And a maringadoo "adaddy o".'

'And whin you're returnin', Macushla Macree
Is it niver a present you're bringin'?'
'Och, I'll bring ye a part of me grandmother's heart
An' the part that I'm bringin' is singin'
Wid a maringadoo aday
And a maringadoo "adaddy o".'

'And what if you stay there, Macushla Macree
An' lave me this soide of the water?'
'Och, I'll lave you the pigs and jolly white legs
O'Father O'Flanningan's daughter.'
Wid a maringadoo aday
And a maringadoo "adaddy o".'

Albrecht Drausler

(*Gemütlichkeit*)

First Love

Lisa's eyes were full of trouble
When she looked at me last Sunday.
Girl's trouble
Her face was blotched and shiny
Where the tears had trickled.
She said she must go down to the Willows
Where we loved.
I do not understand the girl's trouble
Perhaps I do not understand love
But hot bread I understand

And Apfelstrudl and my mother's hot sweet belly
When she bends over in the Abendstunde
And says 'Curly head my Krochlein'
I asked her yesterday why Lisa had hanged herself
Down by the willows.
'Girl's trouble,' she said. 'Girl's trouble
Curly head my Krochlein.'
Perhaps I do not understand girl's trouble.

Freundschaft

I will wear your cap
If you will wear my cap
I will give you raspberries
If you will give me raspberries.
I will caress your body
If you will caress my body
I will give you a sabre cut
If you will give me a sabre cut
I cannot give you my boots
Because Fritz loves them so.
When I have a wife I will give her to you
And you will give me your heart
But not all of it. Just a slice of it
Because of memories and Heinrich
And Spring snows on Eisenthal.

'Youth'

Franzi is fair and Gretchen is dark
And Marlchen's hair is like the Farmer's boy at home
But all heads are alike against the dark Osiers
Karl's head caught the flame of the dying sun
When I kissed his mouth
But it was redder when he came out of the Professor's room
The Frau Professorin was red too
When she pulled Gretchen to her

Why does Herr Dornpfner look at me like that
When he talks of München
In the Geography lesson
Yesterday there was hay on his waistcoat
Why does everything remind me of the Farmer's boy?

Jane Southerby Danks

Legend

Slap the cat and count the spinach
Aunt Matilda's gone to Greenwich
Rolling in a barrel blue
Harnessed to a Kangaroo
Pock-marked Ulysses approaches
Driving scores of paper coaches
Eiderdowns and soda-water
What a shame that Mrs Porter
Lost her ticket for the play
(Aunt Matilda's come to stay)
Prod the melons, punch the grapes
See that nobody escapes.
Tea is ready, ting-a-ling
Satan's bells are echoing
Father's like a laughing Ox
Mimsying a paradox
Aunt Matilda's pet canary
Freda, Sheila, Bob and Mary
All combine to chase the bed
Now that Aunt Matilda's dead.

Sicilian Study

Dust
Lava
An old man

Two fish baskets
Tarentella Tarentella
Have you seen my blue umbrella?
Fanny left it on the beach
Out of reach, out of reach.
Careless Fanny, careless Fanny
Come to Granny, come to Granny.
Dust
Lava
Peppermint chimes
Dither through the valley
The Campanile totters
In yesterday's gentility.

Richmond Boating Song

Apples and cheese
Come hold my hand
Trip it, Miss Jenkins, to Kew
The Wooden Horse is panting – O!
But that's no argument
Look at Frank.
They brew good beer at the 'Saucy Sheep'
With a derry dun derry and soon may be
One for all and all for one.
Parrots are blue in old Madrid
And barking tigers screech the song
Rum Tiddy, rum Tiddy
Peculiar.

Old Things Are Far the Best

Old things are far the best
So measure compound interest
On all infirm relations
And let them wait at stations
And never catch the train of Life

Through being too immersed
In conning passion's Bradshaws with 'derrieres' reversed
Towards the World of Strife
So cherish Aunty Amy
And dear old Uncle Dick
And think of Mrs Roger-Twyford-Macnamara-Wick
Who bicycled to Southsea
When over eighty-two
And never left the handle-bars
To contemplate the view.
Though Grandmamma may dribble
Don't point at her and laugh
She gave you Auntie Sybil
A train and a giraffe –
Old things are far the best.

Ada Johnston

The Nursemaid

I wish to bathe my feet in the Turgid Stream of Life
And catch the cherry blossoms as they fall
One, two, one two.
The dreams that men have made
Live on in Tunnels underground
I think
A sword to the web of destiny
Would be a comfort in the winter months.
Parrot sound is angular
And wicked edges of the glass people
Crushed insensate
Have rattled like the tin of stones
Designs are futile
Why parody the inevitable
With mystic cherubim, afloat in treacle
By the Norfolk Broads.

Sunburn

Mabel, Mabel,
How blue you are and yet how tawny brown
Your aspidistra feet are soft
And firm as oft
They pound my consciousness
To plastic emptyness.
But I shall borrow matches from the moon
When it is Easter Day.

To Rudyard Kipling

Troll cried the wind
Troll cried the sea
Troll cried the Emperor
What price me.
Thrilling to the touch of your wet, wet hands
(Abaft, belay, adjust the boom)
A little wind goes trickling through
The sunset unfurls like Madeira cake
Inviolable the Sanctuary
With a dish and a dash and the scuppers full
Throw the cook overboard,
He won't play.

Dawn

A thousand Thanks my father said
Then flung his collar to the swine
That browse in Andalusia
It was raining that day
But beyond
The sun was carolling athwart the blue
And with a laugh we ran
And plucked the shimmering ropes of golden swings
It's wonderful the peace contentment brings

> And all the ewes are white again
> And stark with misty dew
> And angular as sheets of light
> Beneath the comet's cloudy vest
> Innumerable buttons shine
> Like pigs in amber.

Not that the urge to parody ever left him. The Kiplings, G. A. Hentys and other popular poets and storytellers of his youth still had their echoes somewhere at the back of his mind, ready to be summoned up.

In *Sigh No More* (1945) – his only post-war revue – he stages an historical pageant and in the light of England's recent victory, he has the actor playing Nelson declaim:

> Dear Friends of this fair sea-girt isle,
> This stronghold of an ancient race
> Where storm-wracked men may rest a while
> In some deep-loved and hallowed place.
> I, who have braved the foaming main
> With fifty gallant ships of sail
> And see the fleets of France and Spain
> Stand battle – close to fight – and fail,
> I tell you now, dear English kin
> If France's might or Alien threat
> One blade of English grass would win,
> We'll drum them down the channel yet.
> Cheer me no cheers, though I may be
> Lord Nelson, Admiral of the Blue
> And keeper of the inviolate sea,
> I spring from that same soil as you.
> We are, sweet friends, a brotherhood
> Who claim the pride of English birth
> And foursquare to the world have stood
> From Plymouth Hoe to Solway Firth,
> God speed those men who stand on guard
> In English ships of English oak
> From Afric's shore to Plymouth Hard
> To save us from the tyrant's yoke.
> Their unborn centuries yet shall see
> The flag of liberty flying high
> With England safe and Britannia free.

Even then, one senses, he was travelling hopefully.

He turned to the pageant in his novel, *Pomp and Circumstance* (1960). This time the Coward tongue was more firmly in the cheek.

The inhabitants of the island of Samolo, Britain's last remaining possession in the South Seas, are awaiting a state visit from Queen Elizabeth and Prince Philip.

Their *pièce de résistance* is to be a water pageant. The script has been entrusted to a local writer, Kerry Stirling. When he delivers it, it becomes apparent that he obviously had no more than a nodding acquaintance with the poetic muse. His verse, hovering uneasily between Scott, Macaulay and Ella Wheeler Wilcox, was at its best merely serviceable and at its worst almost excruciatingly banal. There was a great deal of heavy-handed allegory interspersed with flowery rhyming couplets such as:

> Long, long ago in time's primaeval dawn
> This island paradise, in fire, was born
> And fire and water, striving hand in hand
> Wrought, on this desolate, small coral strand
> Strange music where, as yet, no birds had sung
> And whilst the ancient universe, still young,
> Gazed down upon a sea of azure blue
> Amazed to see a miracle come true,
> Far out, beyond the breakers' thunderous boom,
> Other small islets born of Neptune's womb
> Rose up like jewels from the deeps below
> Thus to create our archipelago.

'Fancy Neptune having a womb!' whispered Sandra. 'I always saw him as rather a hearty type.'

3.

'FAMILY...
FRIENDS...
AND OTHERS'

'Family'...

Violet Coward

The only significant member of Noël's biological family was his mother Violet Veitch Coward. His father, Arthur, was a bent-and-soon-to-be-broken reed . . . his elder brother, Russell, died before Noël was born and his younger brother Eric (Erik) was sickly, in perpetual awe of him and died conveniently young.

Violet was the life force that propelled Noël forward – not that he needed much propelling – and came to live her own frustrated life through her son.

Fifty years of mutual love and irritation. He was a good son and was with her when she died at ninety-two. 'She will always be with me in my deepest heart,' he wrote.

He wrote to her every week when he was away from her in those years and, fortunately, she kept all of his letters and other memorabilia in 'Mum's Suitcase' that came to light in Chalet Coward after Noël's own death. The letters occasionally contain a verse but – with two exceptions that have come to light – the verses were not about her. Nonetheless, they tell a great deal about the kind of woman she was even in advanced age.

Telegram to My Mother on Her Eightieth Birthday

Eighty years ago to-day, as tho' she'd heard her cue,
Little Violet Agnes Veitch sprang firmly into view.
Later, being well equipped to organise her life,
She became a mother, having first become a wife.
Later still, while sleigh-bells rang and Christmas roses flowered,
She gave birth triumphantly to Master Noël Coward.
Thus, tho' often harassed by her family concerns,
We can hope she'll always have the happiest returns.

Violet Coward and son at the height
of their fame (New York, 1942)

To an Octogenarian
from her Middle-Aged Son, April 20th 1943
on Her 82nd Birthday

Should an octogenarian wear a gay hat
Or some lace on her silvery hair?
The answer to this will be given you at
No. 10 Eaton Mansions, Sloane Square.

Should an octogenarian always be borne
Here and there in an invalid chair?
The answer to this is a volley of scorn
From 10 Eaton Mansions, Sloane Square.

> Should an octogenarian wear a bright scarf
> Or devote herself bleakly to prayer?
> The answer to this is a hell of a laugh
> From 10 Eaton Mansions, Sloane Square.

Noël's real 'family' was the one he pieced together over the years from the people who became close to him: 'Lornie' (Lorn Loraine), his secretary from the mid 1920s until her death in 1967; 'Coley' (Cole Lesley), his assistant from the mid 1930s and successor to Noël's Estate with 'Little Lad' (Graham Payn), an actor/protégé who became his life companion; 'Blackie' (Gladys Calthrop), another friend from the twenties who became his designer for many years; 'Joycie' (Joyce Carey), an actress whose mother, Dame Lilian Braithwaite, had been Noël's leading lady in his breakthrough 1924 play *The Vortex*; 'Winnie' (Winifred Ashton aka Clemence Dane), writer, painter, sculptor and serial dropper of verbal bricks; and for many years 'Dab' (Jack Wilson), an American who became Noël's manager and sometime lover from the mid 1920s until alcohol displaced the Master in his affections. These were the people who knew at least part of Noël's 'secret heart'.

Lorn Loraine

Lorn Loraine (née MacNaughtan), Noël's secretary and right hand for over forty years

Prima inter pares – and keeper of the gates of his personal and professional life – was definitely Lornie.

To Lorn

There are certain ladies in our land,
Still living and still unafraid
Whose hearts have known a lot of pain,
Whose eyes have shed so many tears,
Who welcomed pity with disdain
And view the fast encroaching years
Humorously and undismayed.

There are certain ladies in our land,
Whose courage is too deeply bred
To merit unreflecting praise.
For them no easy, glib escape;
No mystic hopes confuse their days
They can identify the shape
Of what's to come, devoid of dread.

There are certain ladies in our land
Who bring to Life the gift of gay
Uncompromising sanity.
The past, for them, is safe and sure.
Perhaps their only vanity
Is that they know they can endure
The rigours of another day.

For the forty plus years they worked together, Noël and Lorn would indulge in an ongoing game of charades in which Noël was the omniscient but kindly 'Master' tolerating Lorn, the hapless servant. It was a typically English way of cloaking the deep affection that could never be adequately expressed.

Lornie Is a Silly-Billy

Lornie is a silly-billy,
O my *God*, is Lornie silly?
Lornie is sillier than Willy
Graham-Browne and he *is* silly.

Master, on the other hand, is witty,
Talented and *very* pretty,

Prettier than Dame May Whitty
And God knows, she's *really* pretty.

[William Graham-Browne (1870–1937), actor/director husband of Dame Marie Tempest. Dame May Whitty (1865–1948), English actress who emigrated to Hollywood.]

Noël might write about their invariable morning ritual, when Lorn would bring him the day's post:

'Here I lie sweetly in bed'

Here I lie sweetly in bed
And wait for Lornie's dancing tread.
Here in bed I sweetly lie
Anticipating Lornie's high
Well modulated senseless bray
Mouthing the topics of the day.

Or:

Reflections by Master on Awakening

A lovely lady dressed in blue
Has come to have a chat with you.
The answer to my deepest prayers
Is now advancing up the stairs.
A little grunt, a stretch, a yawn,
And then – heigh ho! For tea with Lorn!
That which supplies my carnal needs
Is Lorn when hung with coloured beads.

Rather more surprising is:

A Tribute to Lorn from Master

Through all these weary working days
Of toil and strife and strain
There's one who all fatigue allays
And makes me gay again.

Her dainty, happy little face
Is Youth personified
I really could not stand the pace
Without her by my side.

Her lissom grace enchants my eyes
When I am tired and worn
I cannot over-emphasise
My gratitude to Lorn.

. . . until one notices that the Tribute to Lorn is *by* Lorn.

Wherever in the world he might find himself, the teasing continued. From a trip in 1937 on HMS *Arethusa*:

'When I visit Venice, Italy'

When I visit Venice, Italy
Lorn's before me pouting prettily
Then again vast Yugo Slavia
Reeks of Lorn's divine behavia
Fishes in the Adriatic
Gasp for Lorn, become ecstatic,
Dive and swoop and dive again
Bubbling 'Viva, Lorn Loraine!'
In Albania every peasant
Makes a really most unpleasant
Rude grimace if I refuse
To tell them Lornie's latest news
Serbians and Slavs and Croats
Make strange noises in their throats
When they sight the *Arethusa*
Crying 'Lorn!! You mustn't lose her'
Everywhere, now here, now there
In the water, in the air,
On the mountain, on the plain
Comes again and yet again
That persistent fierce refrain –
'Viva, Viva, Lorn Loraine!'

During an intense theatrical tour in 1943 he was forced to recuperate in isolation at a hotel in Tintagel, Cornwall. From there he wrote to Lorn:

'In the deep hush before the dawn'

In the deep hush before the dawn
I hear the seagulls screaming 'Lorn'.
A baby hare cries on the leas
'Where is your secretary, please?'
A rain-drop on my window pane
Spells as it trickles – 'L. Loraine':
Small shell-fish moan on rocky shores
'How is that pretty friend of yours?'

Even in the midst of war, his mind was constantly flitting back to matters domestic, such as the Actors' Orphanage of which he was an active and involved President. He knew Loraine would sort things out.

'Lornie Darling, how I loved your news'

Lornie Darling, how I loved your news
Also all those lovely press reviews
Not to mention the delightful praise
That you lavished on my little plays.
I have read, unflagging, page by page
Yours and Winnie's stuff re Orphanage
And I am thrilled that that which was obscene
Has been purified by Mr Green
Certainly he sounds a pearl of pearls
Let us hope he doesn't grope the girls
Let us also hope his secret joys
Aren't concerned with pinching little boys!
Mrs Green sounds very very nice
Should she later prove to have a vice,
Let us pray with utter concentration
That it isn't based on sex frustration.
Something clear, straightforward and direct
Would, I feel, be so much more correct

Such as taking all the bathroom towels,
Smothering Miss Clarke and Mr Howells,
Cutting off the elder children's hands
And ultimately burning Silverlands.
Though that last line doesn't quite scan
You must please forgive it if you can.
What a shame about poor Joyce's dentures
And poor Winnie's terrible adventures.
I have now no more to say or write
So, my darling pretty Lorn, Good Night.

Joyce Carey

Noël was lucky to have literate ladies in his life, who could hand out as well as take his banter.

Noël teased Joycie about a production – one of the many in which she had appeared as a supporting actress – that had lived down to expectations:

'To pretty winsome Joyce'

To pretty winsome Joyce,
The Queen of old revivals,
Confronted by the awful choice
Of hunger or *The Rivals*,
Le Maître qui vous adore si bien
Hopes for the love of Mike it
Will amount so soon to *rien*
And poor old *As You Like It*.

In 1937 she appeared with Noël and Gertie in the Broadway production of *Tonight at 8:30*. Towards the end of the run Noël's health forced him to take a short break and he and Joyce went down to the Bahamas.

March 30th 1937
Nassau

Ode to Joyce

This is Joyce's natal day
Harass her with loving care
Tangle garlands in her hair
Do not let her get away
Give her oil and Lille lotion
Angry fishes from the ocean
Laugh, whatever she may say
Keep on asking how she's feeling,
Scratch her where her skin is peeling
This is Joyce's natal day.

This is Joyce's natal day
Burgeon her with kindliness
Tie her shoes, unhook her dress
Keep your conversation gay
Listen with apparent bliss
Should she wish to reminisce
Let her tell you of the play
That she hopes soon to complete
Stroke her bottom, kiss her feet
This is Joyce's natal day!

'Go, Joycie, with your upper parts uncovered'

Go, Joycie, with your upper parts uncovered
Bright Phoebus rides impatiently the sky
His horses cleave the early clouds asunder
Aching is he thy bosom to espy.

Go out, sweet girl, fear not Apollo's kisses
Unfold thy petals in the scented air
Let every wand'ring zephyr seek for shelter
The thicket of your slightly tangled hair.

Let slip, and slipping, soon unswathe thy wonder
For Neptune's wanton armies to invade
The pagan gods of sea and sky await thee
Go out, fond Joycie, nude and unafraid.

During the early months of the war, when he was stationed in Paris, the sudden interruption of his normal family routine disturbed him greatly. Never one to keep his feelings to himself, he made it clear to all concerned that if you couldn't be with your nearest and dearest, your nearest and dearest had damn well better be with *you* and writing regularly . . . To Joyce Carey:

Saturday, January the Sixth (1940)

Beastly, horrid, idle, vile Joyce Carey,
Throwback from some dank and ancient ghetto.
Why, by all tidings brought to Mary,
Do I get no wire, post-card nor letto?

I who once was loved but now forgot
Starting the New Year in pain and wonder
Realise the bleakness of my lot
Absence does NOT make the heart grow fonder!

Joyce could give as good as she got . . . From Joyce Carey, 8 January:

More numerous than all those loaves and fishes
Sent down by Dod to feed the girls and boyce
Are the devoted, half-semitic wishes
That reach you hourly from your loving Joyce.

Although your stern reproaches I deserve,
Think Christian thoughts and grant this tiny boon
Just blame my lack of news – not lack of lerve.
Herewith my heart: a letter follows soon.

By now we can see the first traces of a private language of baby talk creeping in. 'Dod' was God, 'Dood' was Good. Joyce became 'Doycie', Jack Wilson, for some reason, was christened 'Dab' or 'Baybay' and so on.

To Mr C. – from Joyce Carey:

Noellie's very witty
And Noellie's very sweet
He's inordinately pretty
And his intellect's a treat,
Though writing is his pigeon
And the theatre his domain

'Family . . . Friends . . . and Others'

He minds about religion,
Art, and Mr Chamberlain.
He can handle human cargo
Or a European war
He can argue in an argot
That he's never heard before,
He's been to Bali and Penang
To Egypt and Soho
There's abso-bloody-lutely *rien*
That Noellie doesn't know.

So, if he says the hole you're in
Is round and you are square,
Suggests that you'd look better thin
And if you dyed your hair,
If he proclaims that page by page
Your book gets worse and worse
Or says you ought to leave the stage
And be a district nurse –
If he counsels you to marry
Or to up and leave your wife
And go off to Tucumcari
And begin a brand new life –
It isn't wise to grumble
And it's a waste of time to fight
      You might just as well be humble
      Because Noellie's always right.

Jack Wilson

John C. (Jack) Wilson – aka 'Dab' or 'Baybay' – entered Noël's life when he came backstage in 1925 during the run of *The Vortex*. They met again when the production went to Broadway and shortly afterwards became business partners as well as lovers. Jack became Noël's US representative.

For Noël's sake Lorn tolerated but never really trusted Jack and even Noël came to share her unease. What saved Jack for the longest time was Noël's propensity to see in those close to him only the qualities that he wanted to see.

There was a hint in Lorn's . . .

> Just because your friend from Yale
> Climbs to heights you cannot scale,
> Don't forget your secretary
> Made her curtsey to Queen Mary.

as well as:

> It's quite a big expense to us

> Transporting Little Dab.
> He never travels in a bus
> And seldom in a cab.

On one occasion in 1930 Jack sailed to America while Noël stayed in England. Noël sent him a cable to the ship:

'Baybay's gone...'

> Baybay's gone, the moussies play
> Fifteen cheques went out today
> Richmond Park is grey with sorrow
> Thirty cheques go out tomorrow.
>
> Darling Baybay, darling Jack
> Just a kleptomaniac
> Pinching gifts from Poppa's house
> Like a predatory louse
>
> Taking slyly without stint
> Here a photo, there a print
> Still, although you snatch and grab
> Poppa loves his darling Dab.

And in that last line lies the answer to why a situation that seems clear in retrospect could not be dealt with. Noël didn't want to see it.

In this particular exchange Jack, now in New York, had the last word:

> Why is Pop in such a pox
> I only took a priceless box
> Shut down that reproachful lay
> And write a nice successful play
> The biggest hit on this here street
> Is Noël Coward's *Bitter Sweet*.

For the duration of their professional partnership this equivocal undertone continued. When in 1934 Noël parted company with the C. B. Cochran management that had been so successful for him and set up his own production company, Transatlantic Productions, with his old friends Alfred Lunt and Lynn Fontanne, Jack was made a full fourth partner and Lorn wrote:

> Great though the love we've always loved to give
> To Baybay Wilson, Big Executive

> An added veneration we must show
> To Baybay Wilson, Impresario.

Nor was it long before he began to act like one. On 25 September 1935, Noël, Lorn and Gladys Calthrop happened to be lunching at their favourite London restaurant, the Ivy. What they saw inspired a joint creation:

'We came to the Ivy . . .'

> We came to the Ivy and what do we see
> On this wet and horrible day?
> The Baybay is lunching with Vivien Leigh
> In order to irritate Ray.
> We really had not the remotest idea
> That Baybay was quite such a masher
> If this goes much further we all of us fear
> A cable must go to Natasha.

(Wilson was currently paying court to Natasha Paley.)

At one point Noël even went so far as to make Jack's 'social scorecard', and one is left with a distinct feeling of the surface banter covering a genuine uneasiness.

Don'ts for Dab

> Refrain from twitting Juliet Duff
> On her abnormal height
> You've criticised her quite enough
> And dine with her to-night.
>
> Refrain from telling Syrie Maugham
> She's stupid, old and dirty
> It's not considered decent form;
> Her lunch is at 1:30.
> Please realise it's impolite
> To pan Dorothe's relations.
> Her party is on Tuesday night:
> Dancing and decorations.
>
> Refrain from telling Pip Sassoon

(It's hardly courtly is it?)
His skin is yellow as the moon;
Did you enjoy your visit?

> Don't tell the merry Baron those
> Queer lips are too inflated.
> Quaglino's . . . then, I suppose
> Backgammon's indicated.

> Please do not steal a piece of jade
> From Brook House as a mascot,
> Nor murmur 'Jews' as you parade
> Edwina's box at Ascot.

> *Prends garde, cher Dab, lorsqu' à Paris*
> *Tu rencontres la lucinge*
> *Ne dit pas 'Princesse, je t'en prie*
> *Est-ce que tu es une dinde?'*

And again:

Notes on the Correct Entertainment of Royalty

Refrain from giving vent to gales
Of laughter at the Prince of Wales
Because, poor dear, he failed to guess
The dance was tails – not fancy dress.

Don't, if the Queen should come to tea,
Discuss exclusively George Gee;
Refrain as well from bawdy yarns
About Alf Zeitlin or Fred Barnes.

When dear Prince George arrives to dine,
Don't from excess of shyness
Snatch at the food and gulp at the wine
Before his Royal Highness.

When spending Christmas with the King
At your or someone else's house,
Please realise it's not the thing
To scare him with a clockwork mouse.

The hostess who has any brains
Particularly ascertains
Whether the Princess Royal cares,
Before she leaves, to go upstairs.

Although the Duke of Gloucester's tall
And has a nice complexion,
Do not upon his bosom fall
And slaver with affection.
P.S.
The Queen of Norway may not wish
To lunch *entirely* on fish.

When, after the war, he began to produce and direct on Broadway and even to put a tentative toe in the Hollywood water, Lorn wrote:

Long years ago when first we knew
Our dear John Chapman W.
His latest talents were confined
To efforts of a simple kind.
A homely wit, a merry sense
Of fun at your and my expense
A criticism here and there
Of Peggy Wood and Mary Clare;
A trifling bagatelle may be
Of error in accountancy,
Pictures and books – a brooch or so
Those were his limits long ago.
But as the years that speed apace
Have added girth to Baybay's face
They've stretched the fields of enterprise
On which he casts his penny eyes.
Where wicked murmurs once were heard
All Broadway trembles at his word
The acid jokes that used to be
Reserved for Blackheart [*Gladys*], you and me
Are now the *bons mots* of the day
In syndicated USA.
And – Oh, it only goes to show –
That oaks from little acorns grow . . .
It used to be enough for Dab

> To pinch, appropriate or grab
> Such trifles as he wished to use
> From Goldenhurst or Burton Mews.
>> But, as a child outgrows its nurse
>> So Baybay's pocket and his purse.
>> Now he finds investors just the thing
>> To suit light-fingered pilfering
>> And when he's had his fill from them . . .
>> OH, DO BE CAREFUL MGM!

In this instance there is no record of Jack's reply.

Matters did not improve – not helped by their almost total separation during the war and Jack's increasing mismanagement of Noël's financial affairs that led to a humiliating wartime government fine for him.

The post-war years were sad, with Jack drifting further and further into alcoholism. In October 1961 his wife Natasha found him dead in his bedroom.

Noël wrote in his *Diary*: 'What a hideous waste of life! . . . I am almost sure he was aware of inadequacy . . . Of course I am sad. But not nearly as much as I might have been. To me he died years ago.'

Kay Thompson/Graham Payn

'Coley' (Cole Lesley), Noël and 'Little Lad' (Graham Payn): the Three Musketeers

Even his nearest and dearest could never be quite sure when an admonitory verse might come hustling in their direction.

During the war Noël lost his Kent country home, Goldenhurst, to the Army. While he was waiting to take it back, he rented White Cliffs at St Margaret's Bay near Dover. Among the regular – and often noisy – weekend guests were Kay Thompson and Graham Payn ('Little Lad').

One evening Noël left them a little note in verse:

Darling Kay and Little Lad

Darling Kay and Little Lad,
  Do not think our manners bad
  But we had to hit the hay
  After an exhausting day.

Darling Little Lad and Kay,
  Pray forgive us if we say
  When you both have drunk and fed,
  Please go QUIETLY to bed.

Neither sing nor dance nor leap,
  Exercise some self control.
  Go to bed and go to sleep.
  Yours sincerely, Cole and Nole.

September 25th, 1954

Noël and Kay Thompson playing duets at Chalet Coward

Cole Lesley

Cole Lesley received the same teasing treatment:

Birthday Ode

(with love from Master, March 6th, 1963)

Coley now is fifty-four
Creaking on towards three score.
Blow the trumpets, bang the drums.
Aching joints – receding gums,
Upper plate and lower plate
Wretchedly inadequate.
Hacking cough and thinning hair,
Hernias almost everywhere.
Weathered like an ancient oak,
Pressing on toward a stroke.
Short of breath – all passion spent
Arteries hardening like cement.
Shout Hosanna – shout Hooray
Coley's fifty-four today.

Gladys Calthrop

Gladys also received the Master's concern:

On a transatlantic voyage years before she had met American actress Eva Le Gallienne and a brief, unsatisfactory affair had ensued. Anxious to avoid a repetition, when Gladys was making another trip in 1938 Noël sent her an admonitory cable:

'Lock your cabin door, my darling'

LOCK YOUR CABIN DOOR MY DARLING
LOCK YOUR CABIN DOOR
OTHER THINGS THAN WAR MY DARLING
THINGS WE ALL ABHOR MY DARLING

THREATEN YOU ONCE MORE MY DARLING
WHEN AWAY FROM SHORE MY DARLING
LOCK YOUR CABIN DOOR.

Noël and a reflective Gladys Calthrop

But perhaps his pithiest rhymed missive was in a cable to Gertie Lawrence on the occasion of her marriage to Richard Aldrich:

DEAR MRS A HOORAY HOORAY
AT LAST YOU ARE DEFLOWERED
ON THIS AS EVERY OTHER DAY
I LOVE YOU NOËL COWARD

'Friends...'

Then there were the *friends* . . .

Ian Fleming became a friend in later life. They had both been 'Little Bill's Boys' – part of the spy network set up by 'Little Bill' Stephenson, Churchill's 'Man Called Intrepid', who co-ordinated Anglo-American information services – but it was the post-war era that brought them together. And a shared interest in Jamaica.

Jamaica

Jamaica's an island surrounded by sea
(Like Corsica, Guam and Tasmania)
The tourist does not need to wear a topee
Or other macabre miscellanea.
Remember that this is a tropical place
Where violent hues are abundant
And bright coloured clothes with a bright yellow face
Look, frankly, a trifle redundant.
A simple ensemble of trousers and shirt
Becomes both the saint and the sinner
And if a head-waiter looks bitterly hurt
You can wear a jacket for dinner.

Jamaica's an island surrounded by sea
(It shares this distinction with Elba)
It's easy to order a goat *fricassée*
But madness to ask for Pêche Melba.
You'll find (to the best of this writer's belief)
That if you want rice you can get it
But visitors ordering mutton and beef
Will certainly live to regret it.
There's seldom a shortage of ackees and yams
Or lobsters. If anyone's caught them.
But if you've a passion for imported hams
You'd bloody well better import them.

Jamaica's an island surrounded by sea
(It has this in common with Cuba)

Its national tunes, to a certain degree,
Are founded on Boop-boop-a-dupa.
'Neath tropical palms under tropical skies
Where equally tropical stars are
The vocal Jamaicans betray no surprise
However off-key their guitars are.
The native Calypsos which seem to be based
On hot-air-conditioned reflexes
Conclusively prove that to people of taste
There's nothing so funny as sex is.

Jamaica's an island surrounded by sea
(Like Alderney, Guernsey and Sark are)
It's wise not to dive with exuberant glee
Where large barracuda and shark are.
The reefs are entrancing; the water is clear,
The colouring couldn't be dreamier
But one coral scratch and you may spend a year
In bed with acute septicaemia.
The leading hotels are extremely well run,
The service both cheerful and dextrous
But even the blisters you get from the sun
Are firmly included as extras.

Jamaica's an island surrounded by sea
(*Unlike* Ecuador or Guiana)
The tourist may not have a '*Fromage de Brie*'
But always can have a banana.
He also can have, if he has enough cash,
A pleasantly rum-sodden liver
And cure his rheumatic complaints in a flash
By shooting himself at Milk River.
In fact every tourist who visits these shores
Can thank his benevolent maker
For taking time off from the rest of His chores
To fashion the Isle of Jamaica.

In 1948 Noël bought land and built his first house there but before that he had rented Ian's house, Goldeneye, where he wrote most of the James Bond books.

At the end of his stay Noël wrote his traditional 'Thank You' letter:

'Family . . . Friends . . . and Others'

Goldeneye: Ian Fleming's Jamaican retreat that Noël once rented (to his cost!)

House Guest
(Noël Coward's Memorial Ode)

Alas! I cannot adequately praise
The dignity, the virtue and the grace
Of this most virile and imposing place
Wherein I passed so many airless days.

Alas! I cannot accurately find
Words to express the hardness of the seat
Which, when I cheerfully sat down to eat,
Seared with such cunning into my behind.

Alas! However much I raved and roared,
No rhetoric, no witty diatribe
Could ever, even partially, describe
The impact of the spare-room bed – and board.

Alas! Were I to write 'til crack of doom
No typewriter, no pencil, nib nor quill
Could ever recapitulate the chill
And arid vastness of the living-room.

Alas! I am not someone who exclaims
With rapture over ancient equine prints.

Ah no, dear Ian, I can only wince
At all those horses framed in all those frames.

Alas! My sensitivity rebels,
Not at loose shutters, not at a plague of ants
Nor other 'sub-let' bludgeoning of chance
But at those hordes of ageing, fading shells.

Alas! If only commonsense could teach
The stubborn heart to heed the cunning brain,
You would, before you let your house again
Remove the barracudas from the beach.

But still, my dear Commander, I admit,
No matter how I criticise and grouse
That I was strangely happy in your house –
In fact I'm very, very fond of it.

Goldeneye, Oracabessa, Jamaica

For ever after he christened it 'Goldeneye, Nose, Throat & Ear' and celebrated it in calypso:

Goldeneye Calypso

Mongoose dig about sunken garden
Mongoose murmur 'Oh my – Oh my!
No more frig about – beg your pardon
Things are changing at Goldeneye!'

Mongoose say to Annee
Mongoose say to Annee
Your man as shady as mango tree
Sweet as honey from bee.

Hey for the Alka-Seltzer
Ho for the Aspirin
Hey for the saltfish, ackee, ganja, Booby's eggs, Gordon's gin.

Mongoose listen to white folks wailin'
Mongoose giggle, say, 'Me no deaf.
No more waffle and Daily Mailin'
Annie Rothmere's Madam F.'

Mongoose say to Annee
Carlyle Mansions N.G.
Goldeneye a catastrophe
Whitecliffs too near the sea.

Hey for the blowfish, blowfish.
Ho for the wedding ring
Hey for the Dry Martinis, old goat *fricassée*, Old Man's Thing.

Mongoose love human sacrifice
Mongoose snigger at Human Race
Can't have wedding without the Bryces,
Both the Stephensons, Margaret Case.

Mongoose say to Annee
Now you get your decree
Once you lady of high degree
Now you common as me.

Hey for the piggly-wiggly
Ho for the wedding dress
Hey for the Earl of Dudley, Loelia Westminster, Kemsley Press.

Goldeneye Opus No. 2

Ah Goldeneye! Sedate, historic pile
Haven of peace for those in dire distress
Welcome oasis in a wilderness
Of dreadful rumour and most wild surmise
Dear sanctuary, screened from prying eyes
Sylvan retreat, impregnable and kind
Giver of solace to the weary mind
To you, to you we fly to rest awhile
Here to this gracious home, this grateful harbour
Wrought, not by Vanbrugh, but Scovell and Barber.

Here, in this paradise of palm and pine
(Perhaps not pine nut but anyhow sea-grape)
The hunted and the harassed may escape.

The troubled and tormented may relax

And lie about in ease in shorts and slacks
Wincing a bit perhaps when sunlight falls
On all those horses' arses around the walls
But soothed by architectural design
Wishing the wicked world could be as well built
As this old shack that Barber and Scovell built.

Ian was conducting a long-distance affair with Ann, Lady Rothermere – wife of the press baron Lord Rothermere, one of whose publications was the *Daily Mail*. On one occasion she prevailed upon Noël to put pen to paper on its behalf. She may have wished she hadn't . . .

'Morning Glory'

Epic in commemoration of the 50th anniversary of the Daily Mail

All Harmsworths, Northcliffes, Rothermeres
Deserve from us resounding cheers
While Camroses and Beaverbrooks
Have earned from us the blackest looks
And Kemsley to his lasting spleen
Is nothing but a might-have-been
And all because through hell and snow
The *Daily Mail* has charmed us so
In Peace and War and flood and fight
The *Daily Mirror* is *always* right
Through famine, pestilence and strike
The *Daily Mail* says what *we* like
To Tory truths and Labour lies
This *lovely* paper puts us wise
Although our bloody heads are bowed
This *darling* paper does us proud
In any crisis that occurs
This *angel* paper *never* errs
This classic home of journalese
Where ne'er a cliché fails to please
This epic of the printing press
We humbly and devoutly bless.

> O amiable, devoted, kind,
> Impeccable, serene, refined
> Most exquisite, most dignified,
> Dear emblem of our Nation's pride.
>
> In case some feeble mind should miss
> The point of this analysis
> I wrote it at the firm and clear
> Request of Lady Rothermere.

Ian and Ann eventually married but not before a good deal of what they believed to be clandestine assignations – a version of which Noël used in his 1960 novel *Pomp and Circumstance*.

To mark the great day he had a little advice to offer bride and groom:

Don'ts for My Darlings

> The quivering days of waiting
> Of wondering and suspense
> Without regret can at least be set
> In the Past Imperfect tense.
> The agonies and frustrations,
> The blowing now cold, now hot,
> Are put to rest, and there's no more doubt
> As to whether you will or not.
> We all of us knew so well
> Lo and behold can at last be told
> To the sound of a marriage bell.
> All the stories that could be written,
> The legends the world could spin
> Of those turbulent years you've lived, my dears,
> In excessively open sin.
> Permit me as one who adores you,
> An eminent *éminence grise*,
> To help you in finding some method of minding
> Your marital Qs and Ps.
> Don't, Ian, if Annie should cook you
> A dish that you haven't enjoyed,
> Use that as an excuse for a storm of abuse

Canasta at White Cliffs: Joyce Carey, Ann Rothermere, Noël and Ian Fleming
Painting by Clemence Dane

Of Ann or Lucien Freud.
Don't, Annie, when playing canasta
Produce a lipstick from your 'sac'
And drop your ace with a roguish grimace
While giving dear Delia the pack.
Don't, Ian, when guests are arriving
By aeroplane, motor, or train
Retire to bed with a cold in the head
And that ever redundant migraine.
Don't be too exultant, dear Annie,
Restrain all ebullient *bons mots*,
The one thing that vexes the old boy's old Ex's
Is knowing the status quo.
Don't either of you, I implore you,
Forget that one truth must be faced –
Although you may measure repentance at leisure –
You HAVEN'T been married in haste.

To balance the hedonism of the tropics, there were certain social obligations that were inevitable in any British Colonial context. Despite their Socialist leanings, Noël became fond of the Governor General and his wife – Sir Hugh and Sylvia Foot – and would occasionally dine with them at Government House.

On one occasion his old friend Blanche Blackwell was also present and this inspired a toast:

Toast to Sir Hugh and Lady Foot and Blanche Blackwell

I will now propose a toast
To the land we love the most,
Though the land we love the most may be kaput-put-put,
But to get a social jolt
We are lunching at 'The Bolt'
With the Governor and Lady Foot-Foot-Foot.

I should like to drink a Stein
For the sake of Auld Lang Syne,
Though the thought of Auld Lang Syne is far from sweet-sweet-sweet,
So to get a social thrill
We are trudging up the hill
To have luncheon with dear Blanchie and the Feet-Feet-Feet.

Edwina Mountbatten

The Mountbattens – Lord Louis and Lady Edwina (1901–60) – were friends from the early thirties. Edwina was something of a free spirit and was reputed to have had a number of affairs, including one with Indian Prime Minister Pandit Nehru. In 1937 she invited Noël to join her in an official visit to Canada. He wrote to Lorn:

'I could really not be keener...'

I could really not be keener ...
On a week-end with Edwina
From the moment that one rises
Life's a series of surprises.
On emerging from the lu-lu
One's confronted by a Zulu,
And one gives a sharp shrill cry on
Being pounced at by a lion;
So it's natural at dinner
One's appreciably thinner.
Still I just could not be keener
On a week-end with Edwina.

Hope Williams

He met Hope Williams (later Mrs Hope Read, 1897–1990) in the early 1920s. She enjoyed a 'brilliant but disappointingly brief stage career'. She also appeared with Noël in his one American film, *The Scoundrel*, in 1935.

In 1957 he was visiting her in Wyoming and wrote this to celebrate her sixtieth birthday:

The Birth of Hope

(Lines written to commemorate the sixtieth birthday of the eccentric Mrs Read. Deer Creek Ranch, Valley, Wyoming, August 11th, 1957)

Sixty years ago today
On a radiant August morn
Day of days and date of dates!
In these bright United States
Just imagine who was born
Sixty years ago today!

Sixty years ago today
Weary, flustered, harassed, hot,
Little did they know or heed
That the future Mrs Read
Lay there dribbling in her cot
Sixty years ago today.

Sixty years ago today
On Wyoming's mountain trails
Moose and bear and stag and steer
Hadn't got the least idea
Who, one day, would twist their tails
Sixty years ago today.

Sixty years ago today
(Blow the bugles. Beat the drums.)
Hopie entered upstage centre,
Upside down and bright magenta
Hanging from the doctor's thumbs
Sixty years ago today.

Sixty years ago today
In a stately shuttered room
Not too far from New Rochelle
Hopie with a piercing yell
Sprang from the maternal womb
Sixty years ago today.

4.

WORDS OF WAR

In our city darkened now, street and square and crescent,
We can feel our living past in our shadowed present . . .

> Grey city,
> Stubbornly implanted.
> Taken so for granted
> For a thousand years.
> Stay, city,
> Smokily enchanted,
> Cradle of our memories, our hopes and fears.
> Every Blitz
> Your resistance
> Toughening,
> From the Ritz
> To the Anchor and Crown,
> Nothing ever could override
> The pride of London town.
>
> 'London Pride' (1941)

Personal Note

> Creative impulse whether fine, austere
> Or light in texture; great in scope, or small,
> Owes to its owner, if it's true at all
> Some moments of release in this dark year.
>
> Feeling my spirit battered, bludgeoned, sore,
> All my ideas so pale, oppressed by doom.
> Like frightened children in a burning room
> Scurrying round and round to find the door.
>
> Feeling the world so shadowed, and the time,
> Essential to clear processes of thought,
> So much accelerated, I have sought
> Relief by those excursions into rhyme.
>
> I must confess I have no mind right now
> To write gay Operettes, Reviews or Plays
> Nor leisure, for these swiftly moving days
> Have set my hand to quite a different plough.

> And what a different plough! An office desk;
> Large trays marked 'In' and 'Out'; a daily load
> Of turgid memoranda, and a code
> That lends itself too glibly to burlesque.
>
> From this new language that I have to learn,
> From these dull documents, these dry reports,
> From this dank verbiage, from these cohorts
> Of qualifying adjectives, I turn –
>
> And for a while, perhaps a few brief hours,
> My mental muscles gratefully expand
> To form these unimportant verses and
> Like Ferdinand the Bull, I sniff the flowers.

Noël's war was his commitment to repay a debt.

In the first 'war to end all wars' he had been a reluctant late recruit who had served ignominiously. Even his mother gave his performance a poor review. This time he was determined things would be different.

His personal war began as far back as 1938 when he was recruited as an unofficial spy by Sir Robert Vansittart, a high-ranking member of the Foreign Office. Noël was to go around, as he normally would, being 'Noël Coward' but now taking care to sound out high-level opinion in the countries he visited and report back to his 'Control'.

This he did, but when it became clear in the summer of 1939 that hostilities were only weeks or even days away, he made his bid to do something significant. He visited Winston Churchill, then out of office but 'waiting in the wings' to be recalled, and asked for his advice. Couldn't he do something that would use his intelligence?

Churchill chose to hear Intelligence with a capital 'I'. 'No, no,' he said, 'you'd be no good in Intelligence – too well known.' Noël should go off and sing 'Mad Dogs' to perk up morale 'in the cannon's roar'.

Noël refrained from pointing out that if the cannons were roaring, it would mean that the crew were on deck and, in the unlikely event that anyone remained behind in the mess, they wouldn't hear a word he sang for the noise!

Returning to his London home he met Sir Campbell Stuart who – with Vansittart's approval – told him that it had been decided that when war was declared, Noël was to fly immediately to Paris to set up an office of propaganda. It was far from what he had hoped for but when it was pointed out that his French counterparts would be the eminent French writers André Maurois and André Malraux, he could scarcely argue the point.

A few days after 3 September he was on a military plane en route for the 'city of lights'.

There would be letters to the Coward 'family' and to Lornie in particular. In October he writes to her on British Embassy stationery:

'Lornie, whose undying love'

Lornie, whose undying love
Pursues me to this foreign clime
Please note from the address above
That Master is not wasting time
In pinching all that he can see
From his Britannic Majesty.

Master regrets he has no news
To gladden Lornie's loving heart
Hitler's still beastly to the Jews
And still the battle does not start.

Kindly inform my ageing Mum
That I am reasonably bright
Working for peace and joy to come
By giving dinners every night.
Give her my love and also Joyce.
Thus echoing your Master's voice.

And as for you, my little dear,
Please rest assured of my intense
And most devoted and sincere
And most distinguished compliments,
And if you do not care a bit
You know what you can do with it!

      October 28th

'Pretty Pretty Pretty Lorn'

Pretty Pretty Pretty Lorn
Timid as a haunted faun,
This engaging little rhyme
Merely serves to pass the time,

> Tho' my hands with cold are numb
> Give my love to dear old Mum,
> Also it would make me glad
> Now that dear Almina's mad –
> If you shut her up alone
> Where there was no telephone.
> Dear Virginia Vernon's here
> In my hair and in my ear.
> Hoytie Wilborg too still sits
> Drinking deeply in the Ritz,
> And I've heard from Giraudoux
> That he's sick to death of you.
> Reynaud on the other hand
> Thinks you're absolutely grand,
> Which will prove most sinister
> Should he be Prime Minister.
> Gamelin and Ironside
> Puff and blow and burst with pride
> For I sent a carrier dove
> Saying Lorn had sent her love.

A few days later he heard that his old friend, playwright, painter Clemence Dane (Winifred Ashton), had slipped and fallen in the blackout.

Saturday, November 4th

'Why did you fall, Winnie?'

> Why did you fall, Winnie?
> Why did you fall?
> Were you just drunk, dear,
> Or not drunk at all?
> Were you preoccupied?
> Were you in doubt?
> Or were you merely
> Just bashing about?
> Were you too early,
> Or were you too late?
> Were you in full

Conversational Spate?
Where was dear Olwen [*Davies, her secretary*],
And what was she at?
Letting you hiccup
And stumble like that!
What were you thinking of,
Was it a plot?
Was it a painting,
A sculpture, or what?
Was that which caused you
To fall in the street
Something unpleasant
Or charming or sweet?
What was the cause
Of this fall down the drain?
Was it some quirk
In your functional brain?
Was it your strange
Intellectual strength
Leading you sadly
To measure your length?
Once and for all, darling,
Once and for all
Why did you fall, Winnie?
Why did you fall?
(*Composed and typed personally by Noël Coward amid the horrors of war in Paris 1939*)

'Reply-Reply!'

(*see Shakespeare*, Merchant of Venice)

Noël! A string-and-scissors mind,
One with, and to officialdom cemented,
Ignobly, though bi-lingually, contented
With the Parisian grind.
Cannot conceive how mysticals like me
Can trip it on a lea!

It was economy
That caused the smash –
The old desire for sausages-and-mash
At Bow Street, in a bar
Where once our virgins raised a nunnery
And now policemen are.

Thither I sped to eat;
But, as I made my way down Floral Street,
(A pleasant touch
For one to whom the meanest flower that blows
Does mean so much!)
In the black heavens arose
Balloons,
Those oblong, argent, artificial moons,
And lolloped o'er the sky
Ever so high!

I thought they looked a treat,
So, carelessly, as Olwen trolloped by
I pointed out each separate silken blob.
I carolled: 'Aren't they neat?
Sheer poetry of motion!
They rhyme, they lilt, they scan!'

I did not watch my feet.

I had no notion
They did not know their job.
I trusted them: they failed me: and I fell,
Hurting myself like hell!
Oh – what a fall was there, my countrymen!

       Clemence Dane

There was to be a sequel . . .

A Fallen Postscript

The year has passed with all its joy and pain,
Christmas is nigh and Winnie's down again,
Fresh from a nursing home, of weight bereft,

Words of War

She overlays the little that is left,
Gaily anticipating food and vin,
Our Winnie tumbled down *chez Boulestin*.
Why did she tumble? As I asked before
When in the early months of this drear War,
Indoors or outdoors, in the dark or light,
Winnie was seldom seen to be upright.
Now as the distant drums of Victory sound,
Winnie once more is prostrate on the ground.
Winnie once more, vain Winnie-head-in-the-air,
Goes bashing, hurtling to the bottom stair.
So send your shillings, sixpences and guineas
To help to found a home for fallen Winnies.

To Lorn: Wednesday, November 15th (1939)

'Dearest Mrs Lorn Loraine'

Dearest Mrs Lorn Loraine,
Please allow me to explain
That I'm feeling much much better
Since receiving your sweet letter.
None could say such lyric rhyme
Wasted anybody's time.
Winnie's exquisite reply
Caused me much hilarity.
Now sweet Lornie close your eyes
For a wonderful surprise
Close your eyes and cross your feet
For a fast approaching treat.
MASTER IN A DAY OR TWO
WILL BE COMING BACK TO YOU!
Either Saturday or Sunday
Failing this, at latest Monday
In the quite near 'Avenir'
(French for 'Future', Lornie dear)
You will hear your Master's step
Swift, decisive, full of pep.

You will hear your Master cry
'Lornie Lornie – it is I!'
You will feel the honeyed bliss
Of your Master's welcome kiss.
Just imagine, if you will,
What excitement! What a thrill!
Tell my aged widowed Mum,
Deaf maybe but far from dumb
That her long lost son once more
Is returning from the war.
True the studio will lack
Lovable, dishonest Jack
Also beautiful Natasha
Leaving only you and Smasher.
None the less my heart is light
As a mocking bird in flight
Knowing it so soon will rest
Close to Lornie's largish breast.
I will try to send a wire
So that you can light the fire

Here is her reply:

    Upon my bosom, broad and strong
    As fair Ben Lomond (famed in song)
    The Master, ere much time has passed
    Will lay his noble head at last.

    And I will laugh and I will sing
    And fill the house with carolling
    And toss my pretty curly hair
    Like golden king-cups in the air.

    Oh hurry Master, get here soon
    I cannot wait to start my tune
    I cannot wait to feel you press
    Your head upon my dusty dress.

    So hurry, hurry through the sky
    And wake the love light in my eye.

Occasionally Noël would be able to get a seat back to England on an official plane, although he could never be sure until the last minute. Sometimes the war got in the way . . .

To Lorn: Monday, November 20th (1939)

'Because of the vast political intrigues'

Because of the vast political intrigues
I cannot yet my fond Mama embrace
Nor traverse those uncompromising leagues
To see your pallid and unchanging face
Because of vast political intrigues.

Because of sinister far-reaching plots
And desperate excursions and alarms
I must forgo those twin forget-me-nots
Men call your eyes; I *must* forgo your charms
Because of sinister, far-reaching plots.

Because of my secret work that must be done
I may not hear your loving, heavy tread
Nor see, caught by the early morning sun,
Your shining dentures looming o'er my bed
Because of secret work that must be done.

Because of my unconscionable task
I cannot yet come whirling through the air
Nor yet of Destiny politely ask
To lose myself in your three strands of hair
Because of my unconscionable task.
Next weekend is pretty certain anyhow!

November 23rd (1939)

'Lornie, dear Lornie...'

Lornie, dear Lornie, expect me once more
On Saturday next at a quarter to four
But if on the dot the plane should not arrive,
Expect me once more at a quarter to five.
And if heavy clouds should lie low o'er the sea,
Expect me, my darling, at six-twenty-three.
And if there is wind and the weather is wet,
Expect me, my angel, at *huit heures moins sept*.
Although if they say visibility's bad,
I'll stay here till Sunday and go raving mad.
But still, if *Le Bon Dieu* decides to be kind,
I'll soon be belabouring Lornie's behind.
I'll soon be attacking my Lorn with a cane
And hearing her shrieking with anger and pain
I soon shall be rubbing fish paste on her face
And generally putting her well in her place.
So Lornie, dear Lornie, expect me quite soon
On Sunday or Saturday mid-afternoon.

More than most people Noël needed the stability of his own kind of domestic ritual, which Lorn in particular symbolised. When, for some reason, she wasn't there, such as the Sunday evening early in the war, when he came home on an unexpected weekend leave . . .

'Master's back and all alone'

Master's back and all alone
Gnawing gently Vilma's [the dog] bone
Wondering where Lorn can be.
Is she with the ARP?
Is she stuck as strong as glue
Snug in Sunray Avenue?
Is she, on the other hand,
Reeling down the empty Strand?
Are her rather largish bubs
Resting on the bars of pubs?

> Is she happy? Is she sad?
> Is she sober, drunk or mad?
> How I wonder – all alone
> Gnawing gently on Vilma's bone!

On Christmas Eve his Christmas card to Lorn was another verse letter.

'Dearest sympathetic lovely Lorn'

Dearest sympathetic lovely Lorn
Very many years ago tomorrow
Jesus Christ was definitely born
Into this unpleasant vale of sorrow.
Unpremeditated, this event
Caused a pretty fair amount of chatter.
Later years He adequately spent
Wrestling with mind; disowning matter
Breathing new life into the newly dead
Juggling with loaves and little fishes,
Walking on the water (it is said
Contrary to many people's wishes!)
Working several miracles a week,
Making an enormous lot of speeches;
Telling the conceited to be meek;
Contemplating God on lonely beaches;
Urging local prostitutes to pray;
Blackguarding the rich and aged fossils;
Emphasising every seventh day;
Eating rubber rolls with His apostles
All of this with amiable intent
Hoping against hope the human being
Might succeed in being more content
Not by far, but just by further seeing.
To pursue this story to its end
Might show lack of taste – I'm sure you'd hate it.
Must we watch the human star descend?
'What the hell,' we cry. 'Why celebrate it?'
None the less, in spite of and because

I, with others, must obey convention,
Making in my busy life, a pause
Long enough, my darling Lorn, to mention
That I hope this gay and festive time
(Tho' I fear, without apparent reason)
Might be gladdened by my little rhyme.
Bringing comps of this delightful season.

To Gladys Calthrop, his friend and designer since the 1920s, he was in a less flippant mood.

With All Best Wishes for a Merry Christmas 1939

Back to the nursery. Back to the nursery.
Let us enjoy this sublime anniversary
Full nineteen hundred and thirty-nine years
Let us forget the despair and the tears
Let us ignore all the slaughter and danger
(Think of the Manger! Remember the Manger!)
Let us envisage the star in the East
(Man is a murderer! Man is a beast!)
Let us forget that the moment is sinister
Let us uphold our devout Foreign Minister
Let us not prattle of Simon or Hoare
Or Mr Chamberlain's diffident war.
Let us not speak of Belisha or Burgin
(Think of the Virgin! Remember the Virgin!)
Let us from ridicule turn to divinity
(Think of the Trinity! Think of the Trinity!)
Now as our day of rejoicing begins
(Never mind Poland – Abandon the Finns)
Lift up your voices 'Long Live Christianity!'
(Cruelty, sadism, blood and insanity)
So that the Word across carnage is hurled
God's in his Heaven, all's right with the world!

The year 1939 turned into 1940 – and *still* nothing happened, either in London or in Paris. The Germans were busy overrunning the rest of Continental Europe.

Someone coined the phrase 'The Phoney War'. The French called it *La Guerre Drôle* but they shortly wouldn't have much to laugh at.

It soon became clear to Noël that what he had been asked to do was not as important as he had been led to believe.

Desk-bound as he was, his mind turned to the people he found himself sharing his captivity with. He enshrined some of them in verse and – as his assistant, Cole Lesley, recorded – would take out 'a thick folder' of them, which he would 're-read with reminiscent pleasure' to the end of his life.

There was 'Squadron Leader' Bill Wilson, supposedly a radio expert . . .

Bill

Sing a song to dear kind Bill –
If I don't do it no one will.
Sing a song about his flair
For anything to do with air,
Sing to emphasise the fact
That he leaves nothing quite intact . . .

Dear Bill, may I be rather more *intime*
And call you in our franker moments, Proctor
And compliment you, not on what you seem
(The ideal of some wistful maiden's dream)
But what you really are – a sort of doctor?
A doctor, shall we say, of verbal ills,
A gentle hand to bandage up our phrases,
Correcting grammar, oft against our wills,
Administering small Latin-coated pills,
Making us curse the bloody Greeks to blazes.
But when, dear scholar, you go over far
And spread the substance of your erudition
Mending a radio that's under par,
Mucking about with someone else's car,
Wrecking the carburettor and ignition,
When also, gentle Proctor, you proceed
To play some wild weird sort of table tennis
With all the office objects that we need,
Including light bulbs, you become indeed
Not only trying, but a bloody menace.

Then there was Peter Pitt-Milward, 'an irreverent and cheerful friend of fashion designer Edward Molyneux, who volunteered his services as "Press Scavenger".' . . .

Peter

Peter sits and sits and sits
Tearing newspaper to bits,
Puffing at a filthy pipe,
Gorging journalistic tripe,
Sharpening his acid wits.

Peter dearly loves to vent
Scorn upon the government,
Cursing shrill with claw and brain
Darling Mr Chamberlain
Then subsides, all passion spent.

Peter wears flamboyant ties,
Fondly hoping that he vies
With his chief's more sober taste.
'Diamonds are not cut by paste,
Peter, dear, how e'er one tries.'

Peter argues round and round
Any question false or sound
Standing very much astride
Till his dialectic pride
Brings him crashing to the ground.

Peter has a flair for Art
And is always keen to start
Arguments on these or those
Real or phoney Utrillos
(Always with his legs apart).

Peter sits and sits and sits
In his spiritual Ritz,
Contemplating with distress
The Ungodly bloody press.
Peter sits and sits and sits.

Paul Willert's role was to establish private liaison 'between us (Sir Campbell Stuart Inc.) and various reputable and disreputable refugees with whom it might have been indiscreet for the office to have direct contact'.

Paul

Our Paul is at a rendezvous
With some unpleasant German Jew.
He does this many times a day
We hear him sibilantly say —

'I've had a talk with Oscar Schlinks
Who says our propaganda stinks.
I've also seen Frau Schrudlekraut
Who says that Hitler *can't* hold out
Beyond June nineteen forty-two
(Herman von Rotbaum thinks this, too).
Fritz Wedel, on the other hand,
Assures me the regime will stand
For many, many years to come
(And so does Heinrich Pickelbum).
I also had a beer or two
With Gerhardt Grumpeldorfer, who
You may or may not realise
Once caused the Führer some surprise
By putting on a chiffon dress
And having an affair with Hess!
I'm writing out a long report
On Funsterberg, Hans Block and Kort
Who have been known for years and years
As "Those Disgusting Musketeers".
Who started "Right" and then went "Red"
And finished up in Himmler's bed.
This information, as you know,
Appalled the "Deuxième Bureau"
And also gave a pang or so
To "MI5" and "9FO".
I haven't yet seen Adolph Kuhn
But hope to, Tuesday afternoon,

> I also must, on Monday week
> Find time to contact Otto Scleek,
> So what with this and such and such
> I can't attend the office much.'
>
> And so we say when people laugh
> And ask us questions re our staff,
> 'Our Paul is at a rendezvous
> With some unpleasant German Jew.'

Noël's observations were by no means reserved for his immediate colleagues. A cross-section of military types that would have graced the pages of an Evelyn Waugh or Anthony Powell novel – and duly did – passed through the Paris portals. Several of them owe whatever posthumous posterity they enjoy to a Coward verse letter.

There was Major Leathes . . .

Major Leathes

> In this time of burgeoning and budding
> While the new rich life around me seethes,
> When I hear the chestnut blossoms thudding
> *All* I do is think of Major Leathes.
>
> Major Leathes so debonair and stately,
> Major Leathes so chic and *comme il faut*,
> Speaking to his Colonel so sedately,
> Unlike *other* majors that I know.
>
> Major Leathes whose angry gastric juices
> Give him so so much to rise above,
> Robbing him of Sin's delightful uses,
> Sometimes even robbing him of Love.
>
> Major Leathes, who never, never, never
> Lets a foreign word make him dismayed,
> Ornamenting with his high endeavour
> Campbell Stuart's gay Marine Parade.
>
> Now, dear Major, I will close this poem,
> Evening o'er the sordid city breathes.
> I must go to my small Hoem Sweet Hoem,
> Goodnight and God bless you, Major Leathes.

... and the Colonel Blimp-like figure, ever so slightly redolent of mothballs, of Lord Gerald Wellesley. When he and Lord Reay joined the team, the office was naturally christened the House of Lords. In November 1939 Wellesley was appointed Liaison Officer between the Paris office and GHQ in Arras.

Notes on Liaison

Lord Gerald Wellesley said – 'Now, see here,
I must make liaison with Commandant Reay.
I am also in need of a camouflaged car
And some *laissez-passers* – or whatever they are.
I also *must* have a large box made of tin
To put all my lack of initiative in.
I also require from the dear DMI
The reasons for which and for what and for why
And would someone kindly send off a few wires
Explaining my slightly more private desires?
If Reay or Strathallan would carry my bag
And Noël★ would run to the Ritz like a stag
And ask the day porter to ring up HQ
To ask what the devil they want me to do,
I then would be able to send Wilson back
To bring me the things I'd forgotten to pack.
I really would hate you to think me a bore
But *could* you procure by a quarter to four
A chauffeur-cum-batman to double the jobs;
A file and a safe for my thingamebobs,
A mosquito net and a waterproof (new)
To keep out the rain when I reach GHQ?
I really don't wish to annoy or embarrass
But what sort of car will convey me to Arras?
Or would it be better to go there by train?

★The fleet-footed Noël in question here was Frank Noël Mason-Macfarlane (1899–1953), Director of Military Intelligence for the BEF (British Expeditionary Forces) based in Arras. In his turn he became another subject of a Coward verse after some – fortunately unrecorded – presumably social incident for which he seems to have tried to implicate Noël ... They later became good friends and when, later in the war, he was Governor of Gibraltar, Noël stayed with him during his Middle East travels.

Would somebody make it their job to explain
If when at Headquarters I ever arrive,
The number of miles I'm expected to drive?
And should I send Campbell a detailed report
Of all that I've seen or of what I have thought?
Or would it be better to dictate in code
Or type it myself in my country abode?
In short, will you give me instructions or not
To tell me the whys and the wherefores and what
I'm expected to say should I ever appear
Within sight of Liaison with Commandant Reay?'

A few weeks later there was a progress report of sorts . . .

News Ballad

Lord Gerald Wellesley, now in his stride
Margin for error exceedingly wide.
Lord Gerald Wellesley learning a lot.
Some of it valid but most of it not.
Lord Gerald Wellesley's full of ideas,
Thereby confirming the worst of our fears.
Lord Gerald Wellesley hasn't much hope
Of dropping the droppings just dropped by the Pope.
And still dear Lord Gerald is not really clear
Regarding liaison with Commandant Reay.

Reply-Reply

Dear General, Dear Mason-Mac
Dear Excellence, Sir Noël
How terrible that I've come back
Too late to save your soel!

I'm lacerated to the quick
Knowing the verse you greet us with
Merely provides a moral stick
For your loved ones to beat me with.

How can I happily appear
Before your wife and daughter
Knowing that you, whom they revere,
Have been on such a 'snorter'?

Knowing how freely you imbibe
Without the least contrition
How can I honestly describe
The triumph of your mission?

How can I praise your skill and tact
In dealing with Badoglio
Faced with the miserable fact
Of this obscene imbroglio?

Why have you placed the blame on me
For this wild, alcoholic,
Most shaming and most utterly
Abominable frolic?

When, on the flimsiest excuse
You grab the nearest bottle
What in the world is any use
What'll I tell them, what'll? . . . !

The arrival of Sir Campbell Stuart, the man who had ostensibly posted Noël to Paris, was certainly worthy of verbal celebration:

'Sir Campbell is coming'

Sir Campbell is coming,
Sir Campbell is coming,
The trumpets are blowing,
The drummers are drumming,
Lord Gort is enraptured,
Berlin nearly captured.

The brave Colonel Fraser
Has got out his razor,
The Naval attaché
Is terribly *faché*,

The Group Captain Collyer
Grows jollier and jollier.
Sir Campbell is coming,
Sir Campbell is coming.
The telephone cables
Are joyously humming,
The Lords (our anointed)
Shan't be disappointed.

Clemence Dane was someone Noël held in high regard for her many artistic talents. In her personal life she was an eccentric, living with her long-suffering companion, Olwen Davies, in a crowded and somewhat untidy Covent Garden flat.

Olwen, Olwen

You may talk about your Downing Street and Offices of State
Where the Manhood of Old England is submerged in each debate
You may talk about your Government, your Country and your King
But compared with darling Winnie they don't mean a bloody thing.

And it's: Olwen, Olwen, play a game of chess
And it's: Olwen, Olwen, the kitchen's in a mess
And it's: Olwen, Olwen, make a cup of tea
For Victor, Dick and Gladys and for Noël, Lorn and me.

You may talk about your Shakespeare and your Wordsworth and your Keats
You may talk about your victories and also your defeats
You may talk about the wherewithal of those and this and that
But lift your voice, my darling, when you talk of Winnie's flat.

And it's: Olwen, Olwen, take away the pup
And it's: Olwen, Olwen, help to mix the cup
And it's: Olwen, Olwen, fetch a pound of clay
I wish to model moonlight in an atmospheric way.

You may talk about your Rodins and your Epsteins and your Greeks
You may talk about Surrealists and other modern cliques
But the Germans and Italians and Japanese can come
If you'll give me Art and Letters in a Covent Garden Slum.

And it's: Olwen, Olwen, bring the ice and gin
And it's: Olwen, Olwen, where did I begin?
And it's: Olwen, Olwen, try to learn to spell
And we'll keep our hands in Heaven while we send our foes to Hell.

The frustrations continued to mount for him as the Phoney War dragged on. None of the things he was required to do seemed to make any practical sense to him. There was one exception – Radio Fécamp – and this time the initiative was his own. Fécamp was a small commercial operation, a very insignificant relation of stations such as Radio Luxembourg and Radio Normandie, both of which had long since been taken off the air. What made it important was its location in Normandy, which meant that German bombers could use its signals to give themselves cross-bearings as they crossed the Channel to bomb England's south coast towns. In February 1940 Noël made it his personal crusade to have Fécamp closed down.

Fécamp

Fécamp must not radiate
Though the French prevaricate
Though we all procrastinate
Though the English masturbate
Fécamp must not radiate.

Fécamp shall not operate
Though the Army and the State
Absolutely concentrate
This is our supreme mandate
Fécamp shall not operate.

Fécamp must not radiate
Just because commercial bait
Doesn't quite co-operate
We control the bastard's fate
Fécamp may not radiate.

Fécamp cannot synchronise
Though it tries and tries and tries
Captain Plugge may temporise
Mr Shanks may slap his thighs
Still this place *can't* synchronise.

Fécamp may be a surprise
Planned by our sublime Allies
Ministers may shut their eyes
Still whate'er these swine devise
Fécamp shall not synchronise.

Fécamp so experts advise,
Isn't good and isn't wise
Though dear Monsieur Mistler's spies
Tell such unconvincing lies,
Fécamp MUST NOT sychronise.

Part of the problem was that several members of the French government – who would soon be collaborating with their German occupiers – had a financial interest in the station. It was Noël's personal intervention with his old friend, Anthony Eden – now Head of the Dominions Office – that brought the endless discussions to an end. Eden spoke to some 'friends' and Fécamp went off the air.

In June 1940 France fell. Noël received the news when – on his return from a Ministry of Information visit to America – he had to change planes in Lisbon. The British Ambassador forbade him to use his return reservation to Paris. Had he done so, he would have arrived as the German tanks were rolling into the streets. Since he was already on their 'black list', his return would have been brief.

He was reluctant to relocate to London. Where was the 'real job' he had been promised? But when he did, he found his fellow countrymen and -women as quietly determined as they had always been in times of crisis.

There had been the retreat from Dunkirk. The Blitz had begun. Yet people carried on and a genuine camaraderie was palpable.

For the men and women who would once more get us out of the trouble our statesmen had got us into he had nothing but total admiration.

These Are Brave Men

These are brave men
Who sail the sea in war
But we civilians must never mention it.
There's an unwritten law
That rules one multitude of ordinary heroes
To be prepared

Each minute of each hour
To stay at action stations
Closed in – sweating in the heat
To face too much time
Far too much time
To wonder and to contemplate
In that long waiting,
So many possibilities to fear
To have, in convoying a Merchant fleet,
To move so slowly and to regulate
The engines of the ship, the nerves.
Each man's aware
In each man's secret heart
There lurks, not fright
But some dark premonition of what might
At any second happen.
Suddenly the ship swerves
Sharply to starboard – then again to port.
Submarine alarm
Enemy aircraft – bearing red 3.0
This may be it,
This may be the swift prelude to the slow
And sodden processes of dying.

Lines to a Remote Garrison

When, at long last, this desolate and bloody war is won
And the men who fought in it, lived in it and died in it
Have done their jobs as best they could in rain and sand and sun
Without much time to take excessive pride in it
When these heroic soldiers, sailors, airmen and marines
Are written of in poems, plays and stories
The emphasis will be upon the more dramatic scenes
The sacrifices, tragedies and glories
That this will be, that this should be is right and just and true
A very fitting Anglo-Saxon attitude
But there are many fighting men stuck in one place like you
To whom we owe a lasting debt of gratitude.

It isn't only action, fire and flame that win a War
It isn't all invading and attacking
It takes a lot of guts to keep your spirits up to par
When you know that the essential thing is lacking
The battle area is wide, it stretches round the world
There are islands, deserts, mountains, rocks and crannies
There are many places where the flag of freedom's still unfurled
Where so many men are sitting on their fannies
And they, like you, just sit and wait, eternally prepared
Manoeuvring – parading, doing courses
They haven't even anything of which they need be scared
Except the nightly programme for the Forces!
They write long letters home and then re-write the things they wrote
Remembering the sharp eye of the censor
And sometimes they are stationed in a place that's so remote
That they never even get a smell of ENSA.

Try to remember now and then when browned off and depressed
And when you're feeling definitely out of it
That everybody knows that when it does come to the test
That you're ready and you're steady and you're primed to do your best
And that no one's ever had the slightest doubt of it.

Of course, some of those in which we serve were a lot less admirable and rather more fallible . . .

Notes on an Admiral's Hangover

The Admiral turned over in his dream,
His eyelids fluttered, opened, closed again.
The sky was greying on the starboard beam,
The warm air trembled with a threat of rain.
The Admiral turned over, as the pain
Battered his temples forcing him to leave
The dim-lit caverns of his sleeping brain,
And, as his outraged stomach gave a heave,
He shed a tear on his pyjama sleeve.

This then the price; the hateful reckoning;

The cold, remorseless aftermath; the truth.
How to endure this drained, bleak suffering
Bereft of the resilience of youth?
This shoddy nausea, this drab, uncouth
Submission to infernal punishment
The whip, the flail, the dreaded serpent's tooth
Were easier to bear than this descent
From what, last night, was Man omniscient.

Last night! Last night! His memory awoke
And (sharpened like some iron-barbed harpoon
Wielded by a mad fisherman, whose stroke
Stabs at the floating sickle of the moon)
Made frenzied, futile efforts to impugn
The host of images that would not stay
But swift, like coloured fish in a lagoon,
At every clumsy blundering foray,
Flirted their rainbow tails and slipped away.

The Admiral arose, and, while his hand
Tangled abstractedly his thinning hair,
Gazed through the scuttle at the hated land
No longer glamorous, no longer fair,
No more implicit with the debonair
Potential enchantment of that night,
But grey and dark, the colour of despair.
The Admiral, recoiling from the sight,
Turned to his basin and was sick outright.

For those who were content to let others fight their Battles for them – he had none . . .

'I was in London sitting up in bed one night, listening to the RAF planes going over to bomb Cologne. For two hours there was a steady hum in the sky – and so I wrote this little verse.'

Lie in the Dark and Listen

Lie in the dark and listen,
It's clear tonight so they're flying high

Hundreds of them, thousands perhaps,
Riding the icy, moonlight sky.
Men, material, bombs and maps
Altimeters and guns and charts
Coffee, sandwiches, fleece-lined boots
Bones and muscles and minds and hearts
English saplings with English roots
Deep in the earth they've left below.
Lie in the dark and let them go
Lie in the dark and listen.

Lie in the dark and listen
They're going over in waves and waves
High above villages, hills and streams
Country churches and little graves
And little citizens' worried dreams.
Very soon they'll have reached the sea
And far below them will lie the bays
And coves and sands where they used to be
Taken for summer holidays.
Lie in the dark and let them go
Lie in the dark and listen.

Lie in the dark and listen
City magnates and steel contractors,
Factory workers and politicians
Soft, hysterical little actors
Ballet dancers, 'Reserved' musicians,
Safe in your warm, civilian beds.
Count your profits and count your sheep
Life is flying above your heads
Just turn over and try to sleep.
Lie in the dark and let them go
Theirs is a world you'll never know
Lie in the dark and listen.

And for those who were actively disloyal to the country of their birth he had nothing but contempt.

One of them was Unity Valkyrie Mitford (1914–48), along with her sisters Nancy, Jessica and Diana one of the 'Mitford Girls'. Unity's dubious claim to fame, then notoriety, was her well-published friendship with Hitler and the leading Nazis.

In 1940 family pressure brought her reluctantly home from Germany. Noël was not about to allow her arrival to go unheralded:

Note on Our New National Heroine

Unity, Unity – Daughter of sorrow,
Creature of tragedy, child of distress,
Read her sad tale in the *Mirror* tomorrow,
Learn of her life in the *Daily Express*,
Think how she publicly postured and pandered,
Screeching her views on the Nazi régime.
Weep with her now in the *News* and the *Standard*,
Everything's over, the end of the dream.
Sigh for this amateur social Egeria,
Think how she suffered and suffered in vain,
Caught in the toils of neurotic hysteria,
Ne'er to take tea with her Führer again.
No more photography – no more publicity,
No more defiance and devil may care.
Back to old England and bleak domesticity,
Nothing but decency, truth and despair.
No concentration camps – nothing exciting here,
Nothing sadistic. No national slaves.
Only the freedom for which we are fighting here,
Only Britannia still ruling the waves.
Unity – Unity – Daughter of sorrow,
Sad, disillusioned and pampered and rich
How can she hope for a happy tomorrow?
What is there left for this tiresome bitch?

There were others, supposedly 'on our side', whose credentials he would question.

Unity Unity — daughter of sorrow
Creature of tragedy — child of darkness
Read her sad Tale in the Mirror To-morrow
Learn of her life in the Daily Express
~~Weep with her now in the News and the Standard~~
~~Think how she suffered and suffered in vain~~
Think how she publicly postured and pandered
Screeched her views on the Nazi Regime
Weep with her now in the News and the Standard
Everything over, the end of the dream
Sigh for this amateur social Egeria   Egerie
~~Sigh that the limelight no longer may shine~~
Think how she suffered and suffered in vain
Caught in the toils of neurotic hysteria
Never to ~~be seen with her~~ Take Tea with her Führer again
No more photography — no more publicity
No more defiance and ~~gallant~~ devil may care
Back to old England and bleak domesticity
Nothing but decency, truth and despair
No concentration camps — nothing stirring here
Nothing sadistic. No national slaves
Only the freedom for which we are fighting here
And Britannia still rules the waves.

Noël's MS: thoughts on Unity Mitford, 'daughter of sorrow'

Political Hostess

The Lady Alexandra Innes-Hooke,
Apart from her inherent social grace,
Knew everyone, seldom forgot a face,
Read everything, not just the latest book
And, in her charming house in Seymour Place,
Was shrewd enough to have a perfect cook.

Her luncheons and her dinner parties were
Attended by a 'chic' and motley crew.
There the Gentile rubbed shoulders with the Jew;
Belgravia hobnobbed with Bloomsbury Square,
Writers and Painters, Actors too were there,
Statesmen and Politicians and a few
Foreigners (*Herr Professor – Cher Confrère*).

Politically speaking, Lady A
Was, shall we say, a trifle volatile?
She listened without prejudice or guile
To what her guests, too freely, had to say
On the immediate problems of the day
Then, with a knowing, enigmatic smile,
Misquoted them when they had gone away.

Thus, in those years when all our pride had fled,
When all our policies were misconceived,
The Lady Alexandra soon achieved
A reputation as a fountain-head
Of inside information. What she said
Was widely, and too frequently believed.
(Many of those believers are now dead.)

A long way back, in nineteen twenty-nine,
She hinted darkly that we had misused
The German Nation. Loudly she accused
Both French and British statesmen of malign,
Ungenerous behaviour to a fine
And cultured Race. She later on refused
To comment, when they occupied the Rhine.

During the 'idiotic' Spanish war

Non-Intervention seemed to her to be
Not only right and sensible, but *the*
Only solution. No one could be more
Unprejudiced or democratic nor
Unmindful of the changing world than she,
But 'Reds' were dangerous and worse, a bore.

During the Abyssinian campaign
She was vociferous and rather shrill.
'Why', she exclaimed, 'should we impose our will
On Mussolini? Why should we maintain
This silly "governess" attitude again?
How could he be expected to fulfil
His obligations without more Terrain?'

During the Abdication she was dim
Only when pressed she'd wistfully aver
That tho' she never really cared for 'her'
She'd always been extremely fond of 'him'.
The coming coronation would be grim,
She said, a revolution might occur.
'*Alors, tant pis, il faut baisser* or swim!'

In nineteen thirty-eight she reached her peak
Of bathos. The intolerable strain
Of that degrading year addled her brain
To such a sad extent that she would shriek
At anyone who'd even an oblique
Distrust of Mr Neville Chamberlain.
(This view unhappily was not unique.)

In March when Hitler 'ratified' his pact
By walking into Prague, her mind was clear.
'It really couldn't matter less, my dear,'
She said, 'the tiresome little man attacked
Because he couldn't very well retract.'
She added: 'There will be no war this year
This is not wishful thinking, it's a fact.'

From nineteen thirty-nine to 'forty-two
The Lady Alexandra poured out tea
In various canteens from two 'til three.

Later, an influential man she knew,
(One of the many, *not* one of the Few)
Arranged for her to join the BBC
Only as an adviser, it is true.

A little later she thought she'd try
To see if she could broadcast on her own.
Altho' she'd never seen a microphone
They let her do three Postscripts in July
And when some beast in Parliament asked why
In an exceedingly sarcastic tone,
Her friend transferred her to the M. of I.

Thus Lady Alexandra Innes-Hooke,
Altho' her house in Seymour Place has gone,
Still bravely serves Perfidious Albion
And, like Lord Tennyson's annoying brook,
Goes on and on and on and on and on.

The year 1941 brought 'London Pride', one of the songs that would get his fellow Britons through the war – his equivalent to Ivor Novello's 'Keep the Home Fires Burning', which had done just that in the first 'war to end all wars'.

In that same period – as he says in 'Personal Note':

> Feeling the world so shadowed . . .
>
> . . . I have sought
>
> Relief by those excursions into rhyme

Sing of the Shepherd's Night

Sing of the shepherd's night
And the flickering cottage lamp,
The meadowsweet in the shallow fen
And the lonely gypsy camp.
Sing of the Neon light,
The motor car and the city square,
Hampstead Heath and the Naphtha flare,
Parliament and twilight and Big Ben
And all the women and the men
Of England's day and yesterday.

I'll sing of home and love and work,
Of Magna Carta and Dunkirk
And Christmas bells and charity and pride.
Put us in mind to watch and pray
That the glory abides
With us – and the story.

There were lighter moments. Having never been a fan of Neville Chamberlain and His Appeasers (far removed from a rock group), he had little faith in bureaucrats . . .

We Must Have a Speech from a Minister

We must have a speech from a minister,
It's what we've been trained to expect.
We're faced with defeat and despair and disaster,
We couldn't be losing our Colonies faster,
We know that we haven't the guns to defend
The 'Mermaid' at Rye, or the pier at Southend;
You have no idea how we've grown to depend
In hours of crisis
On whacking great slices
Of verbal evasion and dissimulation,
A nice Governmental appeal to the Nation
We'd listen to gladly with awe and respect,
We know that the moment is sinister
And what we've been earnestly trained to expect,
When such moments we reach,
It's a lovely long speech,
(Not a comment or chat
About this, about that)
But a really long speech,
An extremely long speech,
An ambiguous speech from a minister.

We must have a speech from a minister,
We don't mind a bit who it is
As long as we get that drab lack of conviction,
That dismal, self-conscious, inadequate diction.

We find Mr Churchill a trifle uncouth;
His ill-represented passion for telling the truth.
His 'Eye for an Eye' and his 'Tooth for a Tooth'
Is violent, too snappy,
We'd be far more happy
With some old Appeaser's inert peroration,
We'd give ourselves up to complete resignation,
Refusing to worry or get in a frizz.
We know that the moment is sinister,
We've already said we don't mind who it is,
We'd fight on the beach
For a really long speech,
(Not a breezy address,
Or a postscript on Hess)
But a lovely long speech,
A supremely long speech,
An embarrassing speech from a minister.

(Spring 1941)

There was to be another lighter moment in darkest Denham.

Noël was there in 1941 to shoot his film about his beloved Royal Navy – *In Which We Serve*. His friend and designer, Gladys Calthrop, was given leave from her wartime assignment in the MTC (Mechanised Transport Cargo) to assist Noël by designing the film's sets and clothes. In peacetime she was notorious for her somewhat multi-coloured personal apparel. This she had now had to exchange for an unrelieved khaki, causing Noël to write her another of his verse letters. (For some time her nickname had been 'Blackheart', commonly reduced to 'Blackie'.)

'Where are the bright silk plaids...'

Where are the bright silk plaids of happier years
And all those prawns that used to deck your ears?
Where, in the mists of yesterday, oh where
Is that small watch that formed a *boutonnière*?
Where is the twist of Mechlin lace you had
And called a hat before the world went mad?
Where's the harpoon that fastened up your coat,
Where those gay *mouchoirs d'Apache* for your throat?

All, all are gone. The leopard skin, the sheath
Of striped percale. But perhaps beneath
Your blue and khaki, so austere and cold,
My Blackheart is my Blackheart as of old,
With shoulder-straps of shagreen and maybe
A *brassière* of lapis lazuli.

In the Coward 'family' you had to get used to this kind of affectionate teasing. Sadly there was a lot less to laugh about when later in the year Gladys received news that her son, Hugo, had been killed.

The film successfully behind him, 1942 saw Noël touring the provinces with three of his plays in repertory – *Present Laughter*, *This Happy Breed* and *Blithe Spirit*. The first two had been written in 1939 and were actually in rehearsal when war was declared and London's theatres temporarily closed.

If people couldn't come to the theatre – Noël decided – the theatre would come to them. The long tour, which also took in factory and hospital visits and troop concerts, proved too much for him towards the end and he was forced to take a brief break in Tintagel.

Tintagel

There's nothing much here but sky and sea
Of varying blues and greys,
Primroses if you care to look,
English Nostalgia (*see Rupert Brooke*).
Soft springy turf,
The pounding surf,
There's nowhere else that I'd rather be
And it's lovely beyond all praise.

There's not much here but sky and sea
And cliffs and different birds,
Seamews, cormorants, Cornish chaffs,
King Arthur's Castle (*see photographs*)
A small golf course,
A lot of gorse.
The sun goes down and the seagulls cry
And it's lovely beyond all words.

Convalescence

To have been a little ill
To relax
To have Glucose and Bemax
    To be still.

To feel definitely weak
On a diet
To be ordered to be quiet
    Not to speak.

To skim through the morning news,
To have leisure,
The ineffable, warm pleasure
    Of a snooze.

To have cooling things to drink,
Fresh Spring flowers,
To have hours and hours and hours
    Just to think.

To have been a little ill
To have time
To invent a little rhyme
    To be still.

To have no one that you miss
    This is bliss!

        (April 1943)

The Americans had entered the war in December 1941 after 'the day of infamy' that was Pearl Harbor.

They invaded Britain in 1942.

In the First World War George M. Cohan (the 'Yankee Doodle Dandy') had given the doughboys a catchy song to march to:

    Over there,
    Over there,
    For the Yanks are coming . . .
    . . .
    And we won't be back
    Till it's over over there.

This time – much as the American contribution was needed and appreciated – there was, it must be admitted, a certain culture clash. In a phrase current at the time the Brits felt that Yanks were 'Over-paid. Over-sexed. And over here'.

Noël tried to put things in context:

Lines to an American Officer

These lines are dedicated to a man
I met in Glasgow, an American.
He was an army officer, not old,
In the late twenties. If the truth were told
A great deal younger than he thought he was.
I mention this ironically because
After we'd had a drink or two he said
Something so naïve, so foolish, that I fled.
This was December, nineteen forty-two.
He said: 'We're here to win the war for you!'

Now listen – I'm a Britisher
I love America and know it well.
I know its fine tradition, much of its land
From California to Maine. I know the grand
Sweep of the Colorado mountains; the sweet smell
Of lilac in Connecticut; I close my eyes
And see the glittering pageant of New York
Blazing against the evening sky; I walk
In memory, along Park Avenue, over the rise
Before Grand Central Station; then Broadway
Seared by the hard, uncompromising glare
Of noon, the crowded sidewalks of Times Square
So disenchanted by the light of day
With all the sky-signs dark, before the night
Brings back the magic. Or I can wait
High on a hill above the Golden Gate
To see a ship pass through. I could recite
All the States of the Union, or at least
I think I could. I've seen the Autumn flame
Along the upper Hudson. I could recite
So many memories. I know the East,

Words of War

The West, the Middle West, the North, the wide
Flat plains of Iowa; the South in Spring,
The painted streets of Charleston echoing
Past elegance. I know with pride
The friendship of Americans, that clear, kind,
Motiveless hospitality; the warm,
Always surprising, always beguiling charm
Of being made to feel at home. I find,
And have found, all the times that I've returned,
This heartening friendliness. Now comes the war.
Not such a simple issue as before.
More than our patriotism is concerned
In this grim chaos. Everything we believe,
Everything we inherit, all our past
Yesterdays, to-days, to-morrows, cast
In to the holocaust. Do not deceive
Yourself. This is no opportunity
For showing off; no moment to behave
Arrogantly. Remember, all are brave
Who fight for Truth. Our hope is Unity.
Do not destroy this hope with shallow words.
The future of the world is in our hands
If we remain together. All the lands
That long for freedom; all the starving herds
Of tortured Europe look to us to raise
Them from their slavery. Don't undermine
The values of our conflict with a line,
An irritating, silly, boastful phrase!
Remember – I'm a Britisher.
I know my country's faults. Its rather slow
Superior assumptions; its aloof
Conviction of its destiny. The proof
Of its true quality also, I know,
This lies much deeper. When we stood alone,
Besieged for one long, agonising year,
The only bulwark in our hemisphere
Defying tyranny. In this was shown
The temper of our people. Don't forget
That lonely year. It isn't lease or lend,

> Or armaments, or speeches that defend
> The principles of living. There's no debt
> Between your land and mine except that year.
> All our past errors, all our omissive sins
> Must be wiped out. This war no nation wins.
> Remember that when you are over here.
> Also remember that the future peace
> For which we're fighting cannot be maintained
> By wasting time contesting who has gained
> Which victory. When all the battles cease
> Then, if we've learned by mutual endurance,
> By dangers shared, by fighting side by side,
> To understand each other, then we'll forgo a pride,
> Not in ourselves, but in our joint assurance
> To the whole world, when all the carnage ends,
> That men can still be free and still be friends.
>
> (Glasgow, December 1942)

'These are the times that try men's souls.' – Thomas Paine.

Noël was an admirer of America and of many things American but – knowing England and America as well as he did by this time – he frequently felt frustrated by some of the oblivious attitudes he encountered there during the war years.

Sent to gauge sentiment there in 1941, he had written a play on the subject, *Time Remembered*, which attempted to show Americans that, although they were presently neutral, the war Britain was already fighting was inevitably going to be their war too. The play was never produced. It was upstaged later that year by Pearl Harbor.

In it he gave a speech to his heroine, Lelia – an Englishwoman who brings her children to the safety of America, then changes her mind and returns to play her part in the conflict: 'This war's making most people feel bloody in one way or another – apart from the actual, immediate horror of it, it's planting a fine crop of neuroses in all of us. God knows what we shall be like when it's over.'

The Culture Gap had revealed itself again in a small but significant way that same year, when he was on his way home from a goodwill visit to Australia and New Zealand. The technical limitations of air travel meant that the Clipper bringing him back over the Pacific had to land and refuel on a tiny atoll called Canton Island. There he found the stark contrast of Mr and Mrs Frank Fleming, the British Resident, living alone in their run-down house but still religiously raising and lowering the Union Jack every day of their lives, while a few yards away was a state-of-the-then-art American hotel. (The island was divided by treaty between the UK and the US.)

There was little doubt on which side of the island Noël's sympathies lay:

Canton Island

Accept this testimonial from one
Who's travelled far, who's travelled fairly wide
Who's sought for many a changing tropic tide
Who, in the varied course of his career,
Has journeyed North and South and West and East,
Sharing with pleasure, not unmixed by fear,
The diverse habitats of man and beast.
This testimonial need not be scorned,
Idly dismissed or casually ignored
Especially as he who writes was warned
That here on Canton Island he'd be bored.
Bored! On this self-sufficient coral reef?
Bored with this fascinating personnel?
Bored with the luxury beyond belief
Of this irrelevant and strange hotel?
Where every meal provides a different thrill
Of gay anticipation; where each dish,
No matter how it's listed on the bill,
Tastes doggedly of oranges or fish.
Where modern science has so deftly brought
Refrigeration to the finest art
That even a Red Snapper freshly caught
Smells unmistakably of apple tart!
Where all the bedrooms are equipped with showers
With, written on the faucets, Cold and Hot
So that the passengers can pass the hours
Endeavouring to find out which is what.
Where, when you find your bed has not been made,
Little avails your anger or your sorrow,
Swiftly you learn to let emotion fade
Then ring the bell and wait for a Chamorro.
(Chamorros! Children of the Southern Seas,

Noël in Imphal, north-east India, to reassure the 'Forgotten Army' waging the Burma campaign that they were not forgotten back Home (his accompanist, Norman Hackforth, is on his right) (1944)

Natives of Guam, incapable of crime,
Uncertain, coy but striving hard to please
So vague, so blissfully unaware of time.
How they have guessed, these innocents abroad,
That service, in a Democratic State
Has in its nonchalance – its own reward?
They also serve who only ring and wait.)
Who could be bored when each new day brings forth
Some psychological or cosmic twist,
Rain from the West; a cyclone from the North;
A new bug for the Entomologist;
A Clipper zooming down out of the night,
Discharging passengers of different sorts;
Elderly Bankers blinking at the light,
Ladies in strained, abbreviated shorts,
Fat men and thin men, quiet men and loud
Out of the sky they come to rest below
Then when they've fed and slept, unshaven, cowed,
At crack of dawn, into the sky they go.
What sort of man is he who on this dot;
This speck in the Pacific; this remote
Arena full of plot and counterplot,
Could not be interested – could fail to note

The vital dramas, comedies, burlesques,
The loves, the hates, the ceaseless interplay;
The posturing, the human arabesques
Performed interminably day by day?
Who, if he's human, would not almost swoon
With pleasure as he dives from off the dock
Into the limpid depths of the lagoon
And meets an eel advancing round a rock?
Where is the witless fool who could deny
The fun of swimming gently in the dark
And wondering if that which brushed his thigh
Was just a sting-ray or a six-foot shark?
The man who could be bored in this strange place,
The man unable to appreciate
The anguished look on everybody's face
When told the North-bound clipper *isn't* late.
The man too unreceptive and too slow
To be responsive to the vibrant beat,
The pulse, the Life-Force. Throbbing just below
The surface of this coral-bound retreat,
Dear God, that man I would not care to know!
Dear God, that man I would not wish to meet!
                              (March 6th, 1941)

A somewhat different tone from his Thank You letter to the hotel managers, Jack and Lordee Bramham:

Postscript

Dear Lordee. Dear Jack, How delightful it's been
    To have stayed in this lovely hotel.
The food was delicious. God, what a 'cuisine'!!
    (The drink was delicious as well.)
The beds were so soft and the weather so fine,
    The water so fresh in the showers.
The service indeed was completely divine
    I could go on about it for hours.
And as for those wonderful movies we saw

(You didn't because you were busy –
Remember you left us just outside the door
    Complaining you felt a bit dizzy?)
And as for the time when the plane was delayed
    What fun we all had with the Flight-Crew,
I'm glad that they only drank iced lemonade
    For Clippers can't fly with a tight crew.
I'll always look back on these halcyon days
    And a sigh of regret I shall utter
When I think of the many and various ways
    You managed to flavour the butter!
Dear Lordee. Dear Jack. When I get to New York
    I'll discuss the whole thing with Ward Morehouse
For the Waldorf, in spite of the way people talk,
    Compared with this place, is a whorehouse.
So thank you, dear Lordee and thank you, dear Jack
    With my head and my heart and my soul
This is but 'au revoir' for I'm bound to come back,
    Your affectionate 'stop-over' NOËL
               Canton Island, March 6th, 1941

The end of 1943 found him briefly in New York again and some of those earlier concerns recurred . . .

Happy New Year

'Happy New Year' the fifth year of war.
'To Victory' – 'To Nineteen Forty-Four'
'To all our fighting men' 'To their release
From carnage' – 'To a world at last at peace'
These were the words we said. The glib, confused
Hopelessly hopeful phrases that we used.
Then we had more champagne – somebody sang
Supper was served – outside we heard a gang
Of revellers gaily carousing by
Blowing their foolish squeakers at the sky.
'Happy New Year' – Happy New Year for whom?
How many people in that scented room?

How many people in that drunken crew
Squealing and swaying down Fifth Avenue
Thought for a moment; felt the faintest doubt;
Wondered what they were being gay about;
Here in New York, with shrill conviviality
Toasting their lack of contact with reality.
Lifting my glass, I sadly bowed my head
Silently to congratulate the Dead.

As the war went on, so did Noël. He travelled wherever the powers-that-be decided on missions that were part covert fact gathering, and increasingly visiting and entertaining the armed forces in every theatre of war.

He found the experience humbling. Whatever everyone did, it seemed such a very small contribution . . .

I've Just Come Out from England

I've just come out from England, and I feel
Foolishly empty-handed, for I bring
Nothing to you but words. But even so,
Even mere words can now and then reveal
A little truth. I know, or think I know,
If only I had had the chance to go
To all your homes and talk to all your mothers,
Wives and sweethearts, sisters, fathers, brothers;
What they'd have said and wanted me to say.
Those messages, unspoken, wouldn't ring
With sentimental pride, they'd be restrained.
We British hate to give ourselves away,
All our traditions have firmly trained
Our minds to shun emotional display.
Our people always under-state with such
Determined nonchalance, whether it's praise
Or blame, anger or joy or woe;
However moved they are, or may have been,
They'll very very seldom tell you so.
But still, beneath the crust we feel as much,
If not a great deal more than those who sob

And weep and laugh too easily. My job,
Being a writer, is to read between
The lines that others write; to look behind
The words they string together and to find
The right translation, the right paraphrase
Of what they feel rather than what they say.

What they would say, those patient people who
So very lovingly belong to you,
Would be extremely simple, almost off-hand:
'Give Jack my love' 'Tell Bert to come home soon'
'Tell Fred Aunt Nora's gone, he'll understand'
'Tell Jimmy everybody's doing fine'
'Give George our love and tell him Stan's had leave
And Elsie's doing war-work nine till nine'
'Tell Billy that last Sunday afternoon
We saw a newsreel and we recognised
Him on a tank – we weren't half surprised' . . .
It wouldn't take a genius to perceive
What lies beneath these ordinary phrases
But on my own responsibility
I'd like to tell you what I know to be
Deep in the hearts of all of us in Britain.
The war's been long, it's had its tragic phases
Its black defeats, its violent ups and downs,
But now, in all the villages and towns
Hope is restored, new faith in victory,
New faith in more than victory, new pride
In something that deep down we always knew,
Thus, at long last, through you and all you've done,
We have been proved again. Much will be written
In future years. Historians will spew
Long treatises on your triumphant story,
They'll rightly praise your gallantry and glory
And probably embarrass you a lot.
They'll make exhaustive military notes,
Argue each battle fought, from every side,
But maybe they'll forget to say the one
Important thing. Four simple words are not

Unlikely, 'midst so much, to get mislaid:
For once I feel I need not be afraid
Of being sentimental. I can say
What those at home, who miss you and have such
Deep pride in you, would wish me to convey,
In four short words – note the true English touch –
The words are simply: 'Thank you very much.'

Bread and Butter

Wherever he went on his wartime travels, Noël, being conventionally brought up, never failed to write a 'Thank You' letter to his temporary hosts. It was quite often a verse letter. After a visit to Malta, for instance . . .

'Dear Admiral . . .'

Dear Admiral, a Bread and Butter letter
To writer and receiver is a curse
And so this time I feel it would be better
To write to you in lilting, lyric verse.
Permit me to express appreciation
Of all your charming hospitality,
Allow me, with poetic inspiration,
To further your remembrance of me.
Remember me not as a sharp annoyance,
Not as an irritating, nagging pest,
Rather recall the swift, gay, verbal buoyance
Of your departed and distinguished guest.
Try to forget my frequent interference
When you saw fit to reprimand your staff,
Rather recall my exquisite appearance
Wearing a spotted Yugo-Slavian scarf.
Try to forgive your clumsy Flag Lieutenant,
Try not to spill the vials of your hate,
When inadvertently he hoists your pennant
Upside down and very much too late.
Try to remember when that bleating heifer,
Jasper, appears to have a morning chat
That it invariably makes it deafer
When unexpectedly he's shouted at!
When your domestic staff have disobeyed you,
Try, in conclusion, to remember, please,
God, who with such terrific wisdom made you
Made with less wisdom also the Maltese.
And thus admitting that we're all God's creatures,

Gently look back in sweet humility.
Try to recapture my elusive features
And when I'm far away, remember me.
Yours in affectionate adieu – NC

To Admiral Sir James Somerville

If some Magician should come to me
And ask me what I should like to be
I'd shout my choice
In a ringing voice.
'A really popular C-in-C!'

For C-in-Cs are a varied breed
And many rapidly run to seed
And very few
Can beguile the crew
Of caustic sailors they have to lead.

And only one that I've ever met
Can, spurning disciplined etiquette,
Select with care
And unerring 'flair'
The perfect, apposite epithet.

So could I choose of my own free will
To take on somebody else's drill
I'd shout 'Hey Hey'
In a naval way
And be like Admiral Somerville!

Bread and Butter Letter to Lord and Lady Killearn

My dearest Miles and Jacqueline
It is now and always has been
The most enchanting joy to me
To come back to this Embassy
And rest my weary bones awhile
Soothed by the gentle, turgid Nile.

　　　　　Also to feel though worlds have changed
　　　　　That life can *still* be well arranged.
　　　　　To start each lovely, lazy day
　　　　　With an abundant breakfast tray,
　　　　　To swim and frolic in the cool
　　　　　And admirable bathing-pool
　　　　　(Which though an angry shade of green,
　　　　　Norman assures me is *quite* clean).
　　　　　To find that luxury endures
　　　　　In spite of changing temperatures,
　　　　　In spite of all that science brings
　　　　　Including air conditionings!
　　　　　And best of all to prove again
　　　　　That friends are friends and friends remain.
　　　　　　　　　　　　August 1944, Cairo

In *Future Indefinite* Noël recalls the time he spent entertaining the troops in the Indian subcontinent. It was a trip he had not planned to take.

　　Lengthy tours of Australia, New Zealand, the Middle East and now South Africa had tired him but when his old friend, Mountbatten, contacted him in South Africa with an urgent personal request to break his journey home with a side trip to the area for which he was now responsible, Noël felt he could not refuse. It was now his job to help the 'Forgotten Army' realise that, in fact, they were not forgotten back home.

　　The Mountbatten friendship went back to the 1930s and they would seek each other out, wherever in the world they happened to be: 'I spent one of the gayest months I have ever spent with him and Edwina in Malta . . .'

Casa Medina

　　　　　I'll sing you a song of the days that I passed
　　　　　With dear Dickie and darling Edwina,
　　　　　Of the whistling wind and the skies overcast,
　　　　　Of each moment at sea that I thought was my last,
　　　　　And the pains that I suffered from eating too fast
　　　　　At the dear little Casa Medina.

　　　　　I'll sing you a song of the days that were spread
　　　　　With an exquisite social patina

How I laughed at the jokes that the C-in-C said
How the sandflies and the horseflies disfigured my head
How I twisted and writhed in my rickety bed
In the dear little Casa Medina.

I'll sing you a song of the days that I spent
In that conjugal battle arena
When Edwina wrote letters that never were sent
And Dickie gave orders of vital content
And we tried for three days to find out what he meant
In the dear little Casa Medina.

I'll sing you a song of the picnics at sea
During which we got greener and greener.
When Dickie devoured fourteen eggs for his tea
And then very firmly decided to ski
While we prayed between retches, Dear God, let us be
In the dear little Casa Medina.

There was not too much to smile about on this trip. Noël arrived at Dickie's HQ in Ceylon and was soon on his way with Norman Hackworth (his accompanist) and Mike Umfreville (one of Mountbatten's ADCs) to criss-cross the battle zones.

Noël recorded that they were frequently 'bogged down in mud, cowering in trenches during a Jap air raid, or strapped to our seats in a bucketing plane during an electric storm'. Many of the concerts took place in appalling conditions. On one occasion a sudden change of wind brought 'a most horrible, nauseating stink, which emanated from several hundred rotting Japanese bodies stacked in a clearing a quarter of a mile distant. After the concert I was discreetly sick in a bucket before going on to the next show some miles away. Norman remained unmoved and captain of his soul.'

There was a brief return to civilisation: 'At a place called Digboi we stayed in the house of a Scottish planter and his wife, Bill and Jean Fleming, who accepted the invasion of Norman, Mike, me and the two batmen without even wincing.'

Bread and Butter Letter to Jean and Bill Fleming
(*Digboi, Upper Assam*)

The travellers came to a bungalow.
A bungalow on a hill.
All three of them were muddy

And one was bloody
Ill.

They walked right in and they lounged about
And they stayed and stayed and stayed
While the monsoon rain came tumbling out
Of a sky like grey brocade.

They teased the cat and they pulled the plait
Of the uncomplaining Jane,
They ordered this and they ordered that
And joked in bawdy vein.

Instead of staying a brief two days
And going off in a hurry
They lived for a week on mayonnaise
And whisky and rice and curry.

They requisitioned that bungalow.
That bungalow in Assam
As gin flowed like a river
They didn't give a
Damn!

That bungalow was over-run
(As we were once by the Dane)
And five days after they should have done
They beetled off again.

They ate and ate and they drank their fill
Those war-scarred travellers three
Consisting of Major Umfreville
And Norman H. And me.

Dear hospitable Bill and Jean
Although your larder's depleted
Please, please believe we've never been
So well and tenderly treated.

The travellers left that bungalow
Where so much fun had been had.
All three of them were muddy
And all were bloody
Sad.

Then it was back to Calcutta, where he stayed with Richard Casey, the Australian he had met in Washington in 1940 who had persuaded him to set off on his overseas travels.

Bread and Butter Letter to Mr and Mrs R. G. Casey

Government House, Calcutta

To come from the Indo-Burma mud
From the land of the leech and the louse
From monsoon weather and fire and flood
To the peace of Government House.
(A resonant 'Hallelujah' boys, for the peace of Government House!)

There to be welcomed by Dick and Maie
And a bevy of ADCs,
Whose pleasant function by night and day
Are ruled by the verb: 'To Please'.
(A rousing and grateful cheer my boys, for those amiable ADCs!)

To be able to rest and stretch the legs
And relish the food before us
And guzzle the ice-cold 'Chota pegs'
The affable bearers bore us.
(A silent prayer for the 'Burra pegs' those wonderful bearers bore us!)

To order at will a streamlined car
(Whose driver speaks Hindustani)
And come back laden from the Bazaar
To lashings of 'Nimbu-Pani'.
(The coolest drink in the world my boys, is the G.H. 'Nimbu-Pani'!)

To come from a land of trucks and tanks
And roughing it in Assam
To pass through servants in serried ranks
Acknowledging each salaam.
(There's nothing goes to the head so much as a properly done salaam!)

To come from the Front as I said before
Where we lived less like men than pigs
And find respite from the sounds of war
In dear Mrs Casey's digs.
(From Inverness to Penzance, my boys, there's nothing to touch these digs!)

It's nice to be able to enlarge
(With never a groan nor grouse)
On the fact that the good old British Raj
Still reigns at Government House.
(A rollicking cheer for the British Raj and Three for Government House!)

In Delhi we stayed in the Viceroy's house with Lord and Lady Wavell . . . I had heard that Lord Wavell was taciturn and difficult to talk to and that Lady Wavell was inclined to be remote and unapproachable. I found them both exactly the contrary. Lord Wavell's passion for poetry alone would have been enough to endear him to me; his memory was remarkable and his own anthology, *Other Men's Flowers*, was selected with taste and imagination except, in my opinion, for a preponderance of Macaulay. I remonstrated with him about this and, far from being taciturn, he merely laughed and said he found Macaulay the most satisfactory of all for reciting out loud in a noisy aeroplane.

To His Excellency
Field Marshal Viscount Wavell, GCB, CMG, MC

My dear Lord Wavell, being as you are
A gentle man, whose strange divergencies
Of mind are rare in this beleaguered star,
Racked with its wars and modern urgencies
How, as a soldier born and bred and trained;
Hardened in battle; wedded to the sword,
Have you so very stubbornly maintained
Your lyric passion for the written word?
This 'Flair', apart from Viceregality,
Suggests that you will think me none the worse
For thanking you for hospitality
In most sincere but undistinguished verse.
In spite of any clichés I may utter,
Thank you for kindness, grace and bread and butter.

Finally, they returned to Kandy in Ceylon and the long, long trail was over. 'Then what I had been dreading for a long time happened. I collapsed finally and knew that I had come to the end of my rope.'

After a lengthy period of recuperation he was at last on his way home. It only remained to send Dickie's bread and butter letter . . .

To Admiral the Lord Louis Mountbatten

It isn't for me
To bend the knee
And curtsey and cringe and pander
Because my JUNIOR happens to be
A really SUPREME Commander.
But nevertheless
I must confess
Dear Dickie, my stay in Kandy,
Apart from being a great success
Has made me feel fine and dandy.
It's been the peak
Of a rather bleak
And perilous undertaking
To lie in state for nearly a week
While history's in the making.
The food we had
(Though the films were bad)
Was definitely nutritious
And nobody but a graceless cad
Could say it was not delicious.
The roguish chaff

Of the Chief of Staff
On any official question
While never failing to raise a laugh
Was dicing with indigestion.
To joke with glee
With a C-in-C
When only a drab civilian
Could never really happen to me
Except in the King's Pavilion.
When all is done
And the war is won
How happy these days will seem – O
I'll shed salt tears for the games and fun
I shared with the dear SUPREMO.

NOËL COWARD

Bread and Butter, Ceylon, July 1944

On those wartime travels there was another endangered species – though, fortunately, it was blissfully unaware of the fact. Many a military or other matron must have dined out on stories of how they had recently had the good fortune to meet 'that charming Mr Coward'. Little did they realise how his sharp pen had pinned then down like butterflies on his private page:

Reflections

I often wonder why Commander Fyffe
Chose such a noisy, unattractive wife.
It seems quite inconceivable to me
That such a man of such fine quality
Should, out of all the world, have fixed his choice
On anyone with such a rasping voice,
The thickest ankles and the smallest eyes
And when undressed, wide corrugated thighs,
Who quite consistently wrecks every party
By being so abominably hearty.
Whose hearty, hoydenish idea of fun
Is so embarrassing to everyone,
Whose loud determination to impress

Meets with such very very small success,
Whose prowess on the tennis courts or links
Is so much less effective than she thinks,
Whose only contribution to a dance
Is, if her hostess gives her half a chance,
To keep suggesting in a piercing squeal
That everyone should do a Scottish Reel.
I cannot quite forgive Commander Fyffe
For choosing such a really horrid wife.
Oh, why did Captain H——, RN
Display so little acumen
In picking for his better half
A girl with such a silly laugh?

It was an old habit that died hard. As far back as 1930, when he and Jeffrey Amherst – his friend and travelling companion – were in the Far East, they stopped off in Singapore as the guests of the Consul-General, Lord Clementi. Noël's subsequent verse commemorated his spouse, who clearly did not strike a responsive chord in him . . .

'Oh Lady Clementi!'

Oh Lady Clementi!
You must have read a lot of G. A. Henty
But you've not read Bertrand Russell
And you've not read Dr Freud.
Which perhaps is the reason
You look so unenjoyed.
You're anti-sex in any form,
Or so I've heard it said
You're just the sort who would prefer
A cup of tea instead.
You must have been a riot
In the Matrimonial Bed.
Whoops! Lady Clementi!

There was a P.S.:

> Whoops, Lady Clementi,
> Not *dulce* but extremely *fermiente*
> A little dull at 35,
> A bore at 44,
> You really are a fountainhead of fun in Singapore.

Germany surrendered on 7 May 1945. The Allies had won the war but Noël was by no means certain who would win the peace.

But at least the boys who had won it for us could now come home to a hero's welcome, couldn't they? *Couldn't* they?

Reunion
(originally 'POW')

'It's so lovely to have you back,' she said
But the tone was pitched too high.
He, sitting opposite, crumbled a roll
Made like a crescent with black seeds on it,
Lit a cigarette and tried to smile;
A gesture devastating in its hopelessness,
A gallant effort, gallantly designed
To reassure her, an abortive, brave attempt
To cut at least a temporary clearing
In the surrounding jungle. She smiled back
Seeing him, for an instant, suddenly
Clearly and vividly as he once had been
Before the cruel, separating years
Had altered everything. She turned away
And fumbled in her bag to hide her tears.
Outside the open window, light summer rain
Had left a sheen on the Soho street
Reflecting stars and moon and neon lights
At the feet of stranger characters
Shuffling back and forth, pausing at corners
To whisper in alien tongues and then retire
Back into the shadows.
Inside the restaurant the customers sat

Encased in impersonal, synthetic cosiness.
There were small red lamps on all the tables
And rather untidy vases of anemones,
Whenever the service door swung open
There was a smell of garlic and frying fat
And the noise of banging crockery in the kitchen.
When the *Maître d'Hôtel* brought the menu
The atmosphere eased a little
Because there was something to say.
He was sallow and swarthy, the *Maître d'Hôtel*,
With sadness in his chocolate-coloured eyes.
Suddenly she longed to catch at his coat tails and cry
(In Italian of course) 'Cheer up – cheer up
You'll be going home some day
Home to your own place, your own familiar unhygienic village
With olive groves rolling up to the sky
And the Campanile and the Piazza
Where the people you really know pass by.'
But he took their order and went away
And at their table the silence lay
And the evening stretched before them
Bleak, desolate and grey
With so much so much so much to think
And so little, so little to say.

Twenty years later he was even less sure who had won what . . .

The Battle of Britain Dinner, New York, 1963

I have been to the 'Battle of Britain' dinner,
Held at the Hotel Shelbourne on 37th Street and Lexington
And there they were, a few survivors
Of that long dead victory
And there they were too, the non-survivors
Somewhere in the air above us,
Or at any rate in our hearts
The young men who died, humorously, gaily, making jokes
Until the moment when swift blazing death annihilated them.

And there we were, raising our glasses to them
Drinking to their intolerable gallantry
And trying to make believe that their sacrifice
Was worthwhile.
Perhaps it was worthwhile for them, but not for us.
They flew out of life triumphant, leaving us to see
The ideal that they died for humiliated and betrayed
Even more than it had been betrayed at Munich
To those conceited, foolish, frightened old men.
Today in our country it is the young men who are frightened
They write shrill plays about defeat and are hailed as progressive.
They disdain our great heritage. They have been labelled by their dull
Facile contemporaries as 'Angry Young Men'
But they are not angry, merely scared and ignorant,
Many of them are not even English
But humourless refugees from alien lands
Seeking protection in our English sanity
And spitting on the valiant centuries
That made the sanity possible.
These clever ones, these terrified young men
Who so fear extinction and the atom bomb
Have little in common with the men we were remembering tonight.
Whatever fears they had remained unspoken. They flew
    daily and nightly into the sky
Heavily outnumbered by the enemy and saved us for
    one valedictory year
Gave us one last great chance
To prove to a bemused and muddled world
Our basic quality. All that was done
The year was lived alone and then
Conveniently forgotten and dismissed
Except for just one night each long year
We raised our glasses sentimentally
An Air Vice-Marshal made a brief, appropriate speech
And then we chatted a little, oppressed by anti-climax
And finally said good-night and went our ways.

Yes, the country he loved was in a mess all right, but it would pull through. It always had. London Pride was still in the air and anyone who couldn't feel it – well, they could do the other thing.

Let the People Go
(*The Intellectual*)

I wish the intellectuals,
The clever ones,
Would go to Russia.
Those who have University Degrees,
Those 'Leftist' boys and girls
Who argue so well
About the 'Workers' Rights'
And 'Man's True Destiny' and the delights
Of equal independence, State controlled.
Let them leave England, please.
If our traditions hold
No magic for them; if new Gods compel
Their very new allegiance, let them go.
Those ardent intellectuals
Were never ones
To do much more than analyse,
Very meticulously, our defects
Of Government and Empire. They're too wise
To care about our Past: 'England Expects
Each man to do his duty.' Theirs is clear,
To go to Russia.
Why should they linger here?
Where they can hardly flush a
Toilet without explaining carefully why,
And how, such bourgeois actions signify
Capitalistic greed and retrogression
And oppression.
Their place is overseas.
Not where the British Raj
The hated flag unfurls;
Perish such thoughts!
Not where the natives cringe,
Bullied and crushed wherever British rule is
And where the bloated Englishman, half drunk, in shorts,
Forces the gentle, uncomplaining coolies
To do all sorts
Of most degrading things, including Sports.

No. No. Russia is large.
England is very small
And we have little space
For those who can only perceive disgrace
In our achievements. As they seem to know
So very clearly
That our Empire's tottering on the fringe
Of final dissolution
(Rightly of course),
A just and fitting punishment for all
Our unregenerate displays of force,
We must pay dearly
For those uncouth, dishonourable deeds
Long live the Revolution!
Our Grenvilles, Raleighs, Drakes,
Our Good Queen Besses,
Our braggart Marlboroughs, Wellingtons and Clives
Were those who brought us low,
And though
The shameful memory of them still survives,
The Soul of Man, the Human Spirit, bleeds
At their excesses
God! Let these people go.
Not for their own so much as for our sakes.
We don't require them,
Nor can we much admire them
Measured against our much less enlightened
Unflurried and unfrightened
True citizens. Far better they should be
Proving their theories amidst alien snow
Where men are free
And equal with each other. Let them trot
Off to that other earth, that other plot,
That demi-Paradise, that teeming womb
Of other values. There till the crack of Doom
Let them remain
And multiply contentedly. And when in
The years to come, if they should entertain
A doubt or two

> All they have to do
> To reassure themselves and find again
> Their lost illusions, is to join the queue
> Standing in snow before that foreign tomb,
> And reverently have a look at Lenin.

'I am England', Noël once said in an interview, 'and England is me.'

And as Frank Gibbons confides to his baby grandson in *This Happy Breed*, 'The people themselves, the ordinary people like you and me, know something better than all the fussy old politicians put together – we know what we belong to, where we come from, and where we're going. We may not know it with our brains, but we know it with our roots.'

Noël grew up in Edwardian England at a time when there was an accepted place for everything and everybody – and everybody 'knew their place'. More than that, most people felt comfortable with it. You knew where you were. You didn't get uncomfortable ideas above or below your 'station'.

Though few were willing to contemplate it at the time, the status quo couldn't last – and didn't. The First World War made cracks in the social edifice. Men who had been to war came back with a different perspective and the subsequent Depression caused them to question many of the fundamentals they had grown up with.

The Second World War shattered the already shaky structure. The Welfare State. Social equality (at least in theory). Sexual equality (in all too visible evidence). Anything apparently went – but what to make of it all?

> We British are a peculiar breed
> Undemonstrative on the whole.
> It takes a very big shock indeed
> To dent our maddening self-control.

In one of his two long narrative verses – the other being 'P&O 1930' – Noël looks at this bravura Brave New World through the eyes of an elderly upper-class couple, General and Lady Bedrington, whose comfortable, predictable world has been turned upside down by these social changes, by seeing so many of the things 'one doesn't do' being casually done. Conservative – with both a large and a small 'c' – now facing chaos. Somehow the Bedringtons and their like will survive. After all, they're not quite dodos yet – and they *are* British.

The Bedringtons over their married years
Had learned to accept defeats . . .

Mutely they realised that here and now
It was essential for them both to face
Some of the facts of life which, hitherto,
Their inbred reticence had stowed away,
With other fixed taboos of various kinds,
Down in the depth of their sub-conscious minds.

Just as in his own world Noël is determined to outlast the Angry Young Men of the theatre and their kitchen sinks – and *did*.

In his case the Dodo was a Phoenix – born to be reborn.

Not Yet the Dodo

In the countryside of England
Tucked snugly beneath the Sussex Downs
Or perhaps a mile away or two away
From gentle cathedral towns
There still exists to-day
A diminishing few
A residue
Of unregenerate characters who
Despite two wars and the Welfare State
And incomes sadly inadequate
Still, summoned by Sunday morning chimes,
Walk briskly to church to say their prayers
And later, in faded chintz arm-chairs,
Read of divorces, wars and crimes
And, shocked by the trend of world affairs,
Compose,
In a cosy post-prandial doze,
Tart letters of protest to *The Times*.
These people still tap the weather-glass
And prune their roses and mow their grass
Representative
For so long as they live
Of the English upper middle-class.

General and Lady Bedrington
Lived on the borders of Cornwall and Devon
In a red-brick, weather-bleached Georgian house
With a distant view to the sea,
They drove into Plymouth twice a week
In an ancient Austin Seven
And in summer, on rather a sloping lawn,
Played croquet after tea.
The thirty years of their married life
Had been lived in faraway places,
Before and during and after the war
They'd always been on the move.
Alien climates and tropical suns
Had sallowed their English faces
And now, at long last, their elderly ways
Were set in a tranquil groove.
The household staff which should have been six
Was reduced to one and a 'daily'.
The 'one' was Maggie Macdonald who'd been Lady Bedrington's maid
In the early, hurly-burly days
When they'd settled themselves so gaily
In that 'barracky' house in the compound
Of the Garrison at Port Said.
Later, when Priscilla was born
And so sadly and swiftly died,
It was Maggie who coped with everything,
Efficient beyond belief.
It was Maggie who, in the desolate hours,
Stayed by her mistress's side
And with dour, stubborn Scottish sense
Blunted the edges of grief.

It was Maggie also who, some years after,
When Barry was born in Delhi,
Nursed Lady B through the merciless heat
And ultimately contrived,
On a breathless morning at six o'clock
While the bugles were sounding Reveille,
To deliver the baby an hour and a half
Before the doctor arrived.

And later still, when war had come,
She brought the boy home to his Granny
In a crowded troop ship that sailed for England
Under a brazen sky.
She fluttered a handkerchief from the deck,
Proud of her role as a 'Nanny',
While Lady Bedrington, blinded with tears,
Waved the convoy 'good-bye'.

Maggie Macdonald was old and grey
But far from full of sleep
She had rheumatism in hip and knee
And her eyes were not what they used to be
But she woke with the morning every day
As though she'd a tryst to keep.

She ran the house like an oiled machine,
She did the marketing, cooked the meals:
On afternoons off, in her Sunday black
She walked three miles to the village and back
With a vast, asthmatical Aberdeen
Lumbering at her heels.

Maggie saw no indignity
In the fact that she worked for others.
She returned to Scotland once a year
For a fortnight's family atmosphere
In a little grey house outside Dundee
With one of her married brothers.

There were lots of relatives,
Brusque but kind;
Grand nephews and nieces to see
She brought them presents and gave them treats
And walked with them through the Dundee streets
But always, at the back of her mind,
Were the General and Lady B.

But even more than the Bedringtons
It was Barry who claimed her heart,
She wept each time he left for school,
Upbraiding herself for a doting fool

And stuffed him with cream and saffron buns
And apple and blackberry tart.

And when, as an undergraduate,
He came home for long week-ends,
She washed his shirts and pressed his slacks
And lied for him and covered his tracks
And was ready with soda-bi-carbonate
For him and his Oxford friends.

The problem of Barry's future career
Blew up at his coming-of-age.
He chose his moment and seized his chance
And, in the library after the dance
Announced, in a voice quite firm and clear,
That he meant to go on the stage.

The General went purple in the face,
Lady Bedrington kept her head.
They both of them tried to talk him round
But the boy inflexibly held his ground
Until at last, with unhappy grace,
They surrendered and went to bed.

Maggie was told the news the next day
And felt she might easily faint
But she pursed her lips and packed his bags,
Gloomily tied on the luggage tags
And waved the pride of her life away
To his world of powder and paint.

General and Lady Bedrington
With inward excitement but outward calm
Arrived, as usual, at Paddington
Where Barry was waiting, efficient and kind,
Though the General noticed, with vague alarm,
That his hair was rather too long behind.
With him was standing a tall young man
Wearing corduroys and an open sweater
Who, Barry explained, was Danny Hoag
With whom he was sharing a two-room flat
In a cul-de-sac off the Earls Court Road.

He added, impressively, that Dan
Quite frequently drew designs for *Vogue*
And Lady B, with a private sigh,
Ardently wished she could like him better.
Barry procured a cab outside
And off they drove through the London rain
Danny dripping with Irish charm
Caressing them with his gentle brogue,
Barry, voluble, chatting away,
Telling them with self-conscious pride,
About the theatre, about the play,
About some pompous old Blimp who wrote
Explosively to the *Telegraph*
Protesting against the author's use
Of four-letter words and his abuse
Of England's quality, England's pride
England's achievement past and present.
The General stared at the street outside
And thought the play sounded damned unpleasant.

When they had reached the De Glenn hotel
And the boys had taken the taxi on
General and Lady Bedrington,
After their welcome from the staff,
Walked upstairs to their double room
Both thinking thoughts best left unsaid
Both of them trying valiantly,
Sitting together on the bed,
To help each other to vanquish gloom.
'I didn't think that much of that Irish bloke!'
The General murmured unhappily.
His wife, as though he had made a joke,
Laughed indulgently, patted his knee
And telephoned down to order tea.

They went to the theatre
Sat through the play
And were shocked, bewildered and bored,
And, during the final curtain calls,
Numb, in their complimentary stalls,

They looked at each other, looked away
And forced themselves to applaud.

The audience straggled up the aisle
And vanished into the mews
But both the General and Lady B,
Frozen in hopeless apathy
Sat on in silence for a while
Like people who've had bad news.

Stunned, inarticulate and deeply tired
They finally were led resignedly
Up four steep steps and through an iron door
To meet the cast and author of the play.
 The odd young woman who escorted them
 Wore, with a skin-tight jumper, denim slacks,
 Black stockings, grubby plimsolls and a beret
 From under which curtains of greasy hair
 Descended to her shoulders. On the stage
 Barry received them and presenting them
 With filial pride and touching eagerness
 To all his strange colleagues who stood around
 Proudly upon their consecrated ground.
 Poor Lady Bedrington, with social grace,
 Managed to conquer her embarrassment
 And murmur some polite but empty phrases.
 The General, mute before his only son,
 Finally cleared his throat and said, 'Well done!'

The supper party after the play
In Barry and Danny's flat
Could not be accurately called
An unqualified success.
The cast were all invited
And some other cronies appeared
Including a sibilant gentleman
In velvet slacks and a beard
And a sullen Lesbian in evening dress
Who brought a Siamese cat.

 General and Lady B were received

With cautious politesse.
A tall girl offered them sandwiches
And a whisky and soda each.
They sat on a sofa side by side
And longed to be home in bed.
There was little ham in the sandwiches
And a great deal too much bread
But they chewed them bravely, bereft of speech,
Encased in self-consciousness.

The party, after an hour or two,
Abandoned its formal endeavour.
A sallow youth with enormous ears
Was coaxed to do imitations.
The people he mimicked obviously
Were known to everyone there
But the Bedringtons rather missed the point
For they didn't know who they were
And Barry's hissed explanation
Bewildered them more than ever.

A girl with slightly projecting teeth
Agreed, after much persuasion
To tell the story of how she'd been
Seduced in 'digs' in Hull.
The present company evidently
Had heard it often before
And when she'd finished, vociferously
Demanded an encore
To which she at once assented
And told an equally dull,
Long, complicated anecdote
Which was even more Rabelaisian.

The Bedringtons, over their married years,
Had learned to accept defeats.
So, at the same moment, they both got up
Still smiling with frozen eyes.
A hush descended upon the group
While politenesses were said
And Lady Bedrington's cloak was fetched

From Barry and Danny's bed.
Barry got them a taxi
And, muttering swift 'good-byes'
They drove back to the De Glenn hotel
Through the bright, deserted streets.

That night they lay, restless, in their thin twin beds
And Lady B discreetly wept a little.
The General, equally wretched, bravely tried
To reassure her, soothe her with platitudes.
'Youth will be served,' he said. 'We can't expect
Old heads on young shoulders, this is a passing phase,
He'll soon grow out of it. Cheer up my dear,
It's dangerous to take up moral attitudes.
Let the young idiot and his ghastly friends
Enjoy themselves and go their foolish ways.'
He got out of his bed to kiss her cheek
As he had done for nearly forty years.
'Silly old thing,' she said, and dried her tears.
The General, having got back to bed,
Switched off the light and, turning on his side,
Tried, unsuccessfully, to sleep.
Lady B also, in the oppressive dark,
Waited unhopefully for oblivion.
Again, entirely soundlessly, she wept,
Again it was almost dawn before they slept.

To royal garden parties every year
Vast numbers of loyal subjects are invited
From South and West and East and North they come,
Some from the country, some from the suburbs, some
(On leave from Zanzibar or the Seychelles)
From inexpensive Kensington hotels.
Matriarchs in large hats and flowered prints,
Ebony delegates from far Dominions,
One or two sharp-eyed ladies from the Press,
Tiny green gentlemen in native dress,
Colonial Governors with eager wives
Jostling in line for when the Queen arrives.
Bright debutantes quite recently presented,

Actresses of impeccable repute,
A novelist or two, bishops galore,
Plus members of the diplomatic corps,
A smattering of ancient admirals
And matrons from the London hospitals.
Cabinet ministers, some rural deans,
Newly created knights and peers and Dames,
Field marshals, air marshals, a few VCs
Sauntering beneath the royal trees
Every mutation of the middle-class
Proudly parading on the royal grass.

The Queen, surrounded by her retinue,
Graciously moves among her varied guests.
Curtseys are made, heads are correctly bowed
And as she makes her progress through the crowd
Pauses are organised for conversation
With those marked on the list for presentation.
Following her, forming their separate groups,
Some other members of the royal family,
Sharing with affable, polite mobility,
Part of the afternoon's responsibility.
After an hour or so of this routine,
Either in blazing sun or gentle rain,
The royalties, by mutual consent,
Withdraw themselves to an exclusive tent,
Weary of bobbing head and bended knee,
And thankfully sit down to have their tea.

The porter at the De Glenn hotel
Having procured a hired limousine,
Stood to attention as the Bedringtons
Set proudly forth to keep their regal tryst.
The General, in top hat and morning-coat,
Lady B, in floating chiffon dress,
Climbed with unhurried calm into the car
Though Lady B's enormous cartwheel hat
Needed to be manoeuvred with some care.
Walter, the valet, Rose, the chambermaid,
Ernest, the waiter on the second floor,

Waved from the landing window, while Miss Holt,
Her pince-nez glinting in the morning sun,
Forsook the cashier's desk and with a cry,
Rushed down the hotel steps to say 'good-bye'.

We British are a peculiar breed
Undemonstrative on the whole.
It takes a very big shock indeed
To dent our maddening self-control.

The slow decline of our Island Race
Alien prophets have long foreseen,
But still, to symbolise English grace,
We go to London to see the Queen.

Our far-flung Empire imposed new rules
And lasted a century or so
Until, engrossed with our football pools
We shrugged our shoulders and let it go.

But old traditions are hard to kill
However battered about they've been.
And it's still, for some, an authentic thrill
To go to London to see the Queen.

The car moved very slowly through the traffic.
Its occupants sat still, preserving elegance,
The General would like to have crossed his legs
And smoked a cigarette, but he refrained;
His trousers were well-pressed and must remain
Well-pressed until he got back home again.

Sense of Occasion and the Royal touch
Wakened in their reactionary hearts
Old memories of less disturbing years
When social values were more specified.
Before the proletariat, en masse,
Reversed the status of the ruling class.

For them the afternoon (until the end)
Was beautiful and somehow reassuring.
They saw the Queen pass by and Lady B
Executed a most successful curtsey:

Then the Queen Mother, with her lovely smile,
Chatted to them both for quite a while.

Past friends appeared, perhaps a little changed:
Emily Blake who'd made that awful scene
With Boy Macfadden on the polo ground;
Both of the Granger girls, now safely married;
Isabel Pratt, whose face had grown much larger,
Still with her rather dubious Maharajah.

The Hodgsons, alas, in mourning for poor Hilda;
Vernon and Hattie Phillips from Madras,
Everyone welcoming, everyone pleased to see them,
But typically it was Ella Graves
Wearing a hideous hat and sharp with malice,
Who pounced upon them as they left the Palace.

Eleanor Graves, née Eleanor Walker,
Has always been a compulsive talker,
A fact
Which combined with her monumental lack of tact
Caused quite a lot of people to avoid her.
This might conceivably have annoyed her
Very much indeed
If she'd
Possessed enough humility to perceive it,
Or believe it,
But Oh no – Oh dear me no!
Her sense of superiority was so
Deeply ingrained
That she remained
Garrulous, mischievous and indiscreet,
Blandly protected by her own conceit.
'I'd no idea you were here!' she shrieked,
Inserting herself between them,
And 'It seemed like centuries', she wailed,
Since the last time she'd seen them,
She said they *must* see her sweet new flat,
'Just pop in for drinks, or dine'
And added with shrill irrelevance,
That Lady B's hat was divine.

They were trapped there, waiting for their car
Without a hope of escape.
The General wished she could be tied up
And gagged with adhesive tape.
It wasn't until they'd both agreed
To lunch on the following day
That at long last their car appeared
And they thankfully drove away.

It was after lunch on the next unhappy day,
When her other guests had said their 'good-byes' and left,
That Eleanor, insufferably mysterious,
Seized on the moment she'd been waiting for.
'There's something I just must warn you about,' she hissed,
'And if you weren't such old and valued friends,
I wouldn't interfere or say a word,
But as I'm so fond of you and this is serious,
I thought I'd take my courage in both hands
And tell you, straight from the shoulder, what I've heard
About your Barry and that Irish character
Who, judging from all accounts, are quite inseparable.
As yet the situation's not irreparable,
But action must be taken, something done,
To salvage the reputation of your son.'

The General's eyes became cold and bleak.
He set his jaw and his face was grim.
He opened his mouth, prepared to speak,
But Lady B was too quick for him.
She rose to her feet and swiftly turned
With smiling lips and a heart of lead.
'How kind of you to be so concerned,
We're both devoted to Dan,' she said.

On leaving Eleanor's flat they took a bus
And sat in silence, worried and unhappy.
They left the bus at Prince's Gate and walked
Into the Park, still without speaking, still
Struggling to evade the implications
Of Eleanor's malign insinuations.

Sitting on two green chairs beneath the trees
They absently surveyed the London pastoral:
Nurses and children, governesses, dogs,
Two lovers sleeping in each other's arms,
A young man with his coloured shirt undone
Profiting from the unexpected sun.

Mutely they realised that here and now
It was essential for them both to face
Some of the facts of life which, hitherto,
Their inbred reticence had stowed away,
With other fixed taboos of various kinds,
Down in the depths of their sub-conscious minds.

Their self-protective innocence of course
Was not as valid as it seemed to be.
They both of them, within their private thoughts,
Knew things that neither of them would admit.
Lady B traced patterns on the ground,
With her umbrella-tip. The General frowned.

Sitting there quietly on their painted chairs
Aware that they were together, yet alone,
They watched, without noticing, the changing scene:
The brilliant sunlight of the afternoon
Softening and merging into early evening,
The shadows lengthening under the London trees,
Staining with grey the brownish, trodden grass.
The summer noises seemed to be changing too
Becoming less strident as the day wore on:
The hum of traffic, buses grinding gears,
Children's shrill voices, sharp staccato barks
From those alert, exclusively London dogs
Which seemed indigenous to London Parks.
Finally, stiffly, they got up and walked,
Still without speaking, back to the hotel.
In both their minds decisions had been made,
Mutually arrived at, without discussion,
And when they reached their bedroom Lady B
Took off her hat, stared in the looking-glass
And searched her face with anxious scrutiny

Discovering with relief that all the strains
And inward conflicts of the last few hours
Had left no outward traces to betray her.
Her eyes perhaps did look a trifle tired
But then, all things considered, that was not
Entirely to be wondered at. She sat
Decisively upon the bed and took
The telephone receiver from its hook.

Barry and Danny got back to the flat at six
After a rather aimless afternoon
Searching for antiques in the Brompton Road.
Barry was hot, irritable, conscious of guilt,
Because he hadn't made the slightest effort
To find out if his parents were all right
And if their glum little Kensington hotel
Was comfortable. He could have sent some flowers
If he had thought of it. He mooched about,
Took off his clothes and flung himself on the bed.
Danny looked at him quizzically and said,
'Why don't we call your rather frightening mother
And ask them both to dine somewhere or other?'

The telephone, at that moment, rang.
Barry lifted it to his ear
And suffered a further guilty pang
When his mother's voice said, 'Is that you, dear?'
At any rate the evening went off well.
The Bedringtons were fetched from their hotel,
Squeezed into Danny's second-hand MG
And driven, perhaps a thought erratically,
To dine in a converted Wesleyan chapel
Called, rather whimsically, 'The Golden Apple'.

The room was tiny, lit by flickering candles.
The waiters wore canvas trousers, vests and sandals,
The menus, although very large indeed,
The General found difficult to read,
Poor Lady B in her self-conscious flurry
Rather unwisely plumped for chicken curry.

The noise was deafening, the service, slow.
Danny, resolved to make the party go,
Laid himself out, with Irish charm and wit,
To loosen up the atmosphere a bit.
And Lady B was vaguely mortified
To see the General laugh until he cried.

Later that evening, General and Lady B,
Preoccupied with their eventful day,
Slowly prepared themselves to face the night.
Lady B pensively took off her rings
And put them in the dressing-table drawer.
The General went stumping down the passage
As usual, to the bathroom, with his sponge-bag.
Lady B rubbing her face with a cleansing cream,
Could hear him in the distance, gargling.
Suddenly she remembered Ella's words:
Her bland, unwarranted impertinence,
'That Irish character' 'Something must be done'
'To save the reputation of your son!'
Lady B conscious that her hands were shaking,
Made a tremendous effort at control
And, with a slight, contemptuous grimace,
Finally continued massaging her face.

On the fourth day of their dejected holiday,
Breakfasting in the hotel dining-room,
General and Lady B, without discussion,
Inspired by age-old mutual telepathy,
Arrived at the same conclusion. Lady B
Absently took some toast, then put it back.
'I think,' she said, 'I'll go upstairs and pack.'

It was Danny who answered the telephone,
Barry was still asleep.
Lady B's voice was icily polite,
'I really must apologise,' she said,
'For calling you so early in the morning.
I'd like to have a few words with my son
However if he isn't yet awake
Please don't disturb him – You could perhaps explain,

Words of War

We've had a tiresome telegram from home
Which means that we must leave immediately
And so we are leaving on the mid-day train.'
Danny, completely taken by surprise,
Tried, unsuccessfully, to sound dismayed
But Lady B cut short his protestations
Quite firmly, still implacably polite.
'Please tell him', she went on, 'that we will write
The moment we get back. It was *such* fun',
She added, 'dining with you both
At the strange restaurant the other night.'

Maggie Macdonald had second sight
A loving, instinctive flair.
The telegram Lady B had sent
Confirmed her growing presentiment
That trouble was in the air.

She waited grimly to meet the train
Though her welcoming smile was gay
And while they greeted her normally
And chatted away informally
She searched their faces for signs of strain
And the signs were as clear as day.

At dinner, outwardly serene,
The General praised the salmon.
Afterwards he and Lady B
Sat for a while and watched TV
Then, gallantly loyal to routine,
Played three games of backgammon.

Maggie, knowing her mistress very well
Was certain she would not go up to bed
Without some hint, some sort of explanation
Of why they had so suddenly returned.
So, busying herself with little chores,
She put the cat out, tidied the dresser drawers,
Ironed some handkerchiefs and wound the clock,
Pottered about, arranged the breakfast tray,
Put on the kettle for a cup of tea

And finally, with nothing else to do,
She sat down in her creaking cane arm-chair
And waited for a footstep on the stair.
She heard the front door slam and knew the General
Had gone out for his customary stroll;
Silence enclosed the house, silence so deep
That the bland ticking of the kitchen clock
Sounded presumptuous, a loud intrusion,
Confusing more her heart's dismayed confusion.
Edward miaowed outside, she let him in
And, stalking before her like a conqueror,
He jumped into his basket, washed his face,
Shot her a glance and delicately yawned.
She gently massaged him behind the ears
And, unaccountably, burst into tears.

Of course, at this moment, Lady B appeared
Catching poor Maggie red-eyed and betrayed.
She paused for a moment at the door and then
Swiftly advanced and took her in her arms.
'Don't Maggie dear, please please don't cry,' she said,
'It isn't all that bad, really it's not.
Nothing appalling's happened, nothing sad,
Merely a tiresomeness, let's just sit down
Quite calmly and discuss it, you and me,
And, while we're at it, have a cup of tea.'

They sat there in close conference
With their crowded years behind them
Both bewildered and both distressed
But both determined to do their best
Not to allow their innocence
And prejudice to blind them.

They both knew more and they both knew less
Than either of them admitted.
To them, the infinite, complex
And strange divergencies of sex
Were based on moral capriciousness
And less to be blamed than pitied.

They both agreed that there'd always seemed
A 'difference' about Barry.
He'd never plagued them with sudden scares
Involving dubious love affairs;
Preserving himself, so they fondly dreamed,
For the girl he would finally marry.

But here they were guilty of sophistry
For, with deep, unspoken dread,
Their minds rejected the ghastly day
That would whisk their paragon away
Beyond their possessive idolatry
To an alien marriage bed.

Their earlier fears having been replaced
By faintly embarrassed relief,
They tried, with mutual urgency,
To cope with this new emergency;
Like storm-tossed mariners suddenly faced
With a strange, uncharted reef.

For more than three hours they sat there in the kitchen.
Maggie made sandwiches and brewed fresh tea.
Out in the quiet night the world was sleeping
Lulled by the murmur of the distant sea.
Finally Maggie, with shrewd common sense,
Embarked upon her speech for the defence.

'If you want my opinion,' she said, 'I think
We're both of us wasting our breath.
You can't judge people by rule of thumb
And if we sit gabbling to Kingdom Come
We'll neither of us sleep a wink
And worry ourselves to death.
People are made the way they're made
And it isn't anyone's fault.
Nobody's tastes can quite agree,
Some like coffee and some like tea
And Guinness rather than lemonade
And pepper rather than salt.

'If Mr Barry had got caught out

By some little teenage whore
And brought her home as his blushing bride
Not only would we be mortified,
But we'd have a real problem to fuss about
And worry a great deal more.

'Being a "spinster" as you might say
Not overburdened with looks,
I never went in for much romance
Though I had some fun when I got the chance
And whatever knowledge has come my way
Has come through people and books.

'I don't know what this is all about
But Barry's the one I care for.
I don't mind whether he's strange or not
Or goes to bed with a Hottentot.
It's no good us trying to puzzle out
The what, the why and the wherefore.'

When Maggie's tirade came to an end
She suddenly bowed her head.
Lady B rose and kissed her cheek
And, when she could trust herself to speak
Said, 'Now, my most loyal and loving friend
It's time we went up to bed.'

During the next few days the weather held.
The russet Devon cliffs cast purple shadows
Staining the edges of the quiet sea.
The General played golf, Lady B pottered
About the garden, old Mrs Macklehenny
Drove out from Saltash with her married niece,
Ate a vast luncheon and remained for tea.
On the fifth morning Lady B sat down
Purposefully at her writing desk,
Unscrewed her fountain pen, stared at the view,
Absently noting an old cargo ship
Lumbering across the shining bay.
The dark smoke from its funnel twisting high
Scribbled a question mark in the sky.

'My darling boy,' she wrote. 'You really must
Forgive me for not writing days ago
To thank you for our little jaunt to Town.

'You can't imagine how Papa and I
Enjoyed ourselves, you really were so sweet
To give your aged parents such a treat.
The weather here is perfect, not a cloud
You'd almost think you were in Italy.
The garden's drying up of course, no rain
For nearly two whole weeks. Old Mrs Drew,
The one who used to help you with your stamps,
Suddenly died last Saturday, so sad
But still, all things considered, a release,
When one is ninety-four one can't complain
At ceasing upon the midnight with no pain.
The Hilliard girls are back from Switzerland
Looking, Papa says, commoner than ever.
Hilda, the one who's said to be so clever,
Met some professor in the Engadine
And got engaged to him all in a minute!
And he's apparently quite mad and drinks,
Perhaps she's not so clever as she thinks.
That's all my news and so I'd better stop
And not go rambling on like poor Aunt Jane
Who, incidentally, fell down again
Just outside Gorringe's, the poor old duck
Seems to be really haunted by bad luck.'
Lady B paused, and, nibbling her pen,
Frowned for a moment and then wrote, 'P.S.
Please give our love to Danny and remember
That we expect you *both* in mid-September.'

General and Lady Bedrington
Lived on the borders of Cornwall and Devon
In a red-brick, weather-bleached Georgian house
With its distant view of the sea.
They still drove to Plymouth twice a week
In their rattling Austin Seven
And still, if the weather was feasible

Played croquet after tea.

Maggie still tramped to the village
With Black Angus, the Aberdeen.
The sun still rose and the sun still set
And the Eddystone light still shone.
Lady B and the General both
Encased in their daily routine
Began insensibly to forget
Their excursion to Babylon.

Drawing by Lynne Carey

5.

SHALL WE JOIN THE LADIES...?

Ladies – whether real or fictional in verse, story or lyric – loomed large in Noël's work. He appeared to be mesmerised by determined ladies or wilful women.

There was 'Mrs Worthington' (who entertained theatrical ambitions for her daughter); 'Mrs Wentworth-Brewster' (she of the Bar on the Piccola Marina); the movie star 'Louisa' (whose fate was to be 'terribly lonely all over again'); 'Josephine' (who was courted by Napoleon 'in a coarse, rather Corsican way'); 'Alice' (who always seemed to be 'at it' again) . . .

And then there was 'Mrs Mallory' . . .

Mrs Mallory

Mrs Mallory went to a Psychiatrist
On the advice of Mrs Silvera
Who had been twice divorced
And considered herself to be mal-adjusted.
Mrs Mallory who had never been divorced at all,
Considered that she was also mal-adjusted
Not for any specific reason, really
Nothing you could put your finger on
But a definite feeling of dissatisfaction
With life in general and Mr Mallory in particular,
And Deirdre too who was no comfort and solace to her mother
Though at her age she should have been
But she was an unpredictable character
Who devoted too much time to 'Rock-n-Roll'
And none at all to domestic science
And helping in the house and keeping a wary eye open
For Mr Right to come along and sweep her away
To a series of social triumphs
In Washington possibly, or at least Baltimore,
Which Mrs Mallory could read about in the gossip columns
And then send the cuttings to Irma in Minneapolis
Who would have to read them whether she liked it or not.

Mrs Mallory lay on the Psychiatrist's sofa
With her arms relaxed at her sides
And her feet sticking up, one to the right and one to the left
Like a mermaid's tail.
The Psychiatrist sat behind her out of range

And waited politely for her to begin to talk
Which she was only too eager to do
After the first shyness had worn off,
And he had asked her a few routine questions.
But she talked and talked and talked and talked.
So much, so much came tumbling out of her,
More than she would ever have believed possible,
But then, of course, unlike Mrs Silvera, he didn't interrupt
And say things like 'That reminds me of when I went to Atlantic City
With my first husband' or 'I feel exactly the same, dear, naturally,
But I have to control my feelings on account of being so strictly raised.'
The Psychiatrist didn't seem to be reminded of anything at all.
He sat there so quietly that once Mrs Mallory looked round
To see if he had dropped off, but he hadn't;
There he was scribbling away on a pad and occasionally nodding his head.
She told him all about Deirdre
And Mr Mallory coming home from the Rotarian lunch
And taking his pants off on the landing
And shouting 'Everything I have is yours, you're part of me!'
So loudly that Beulah had come out of the kitchen
And seen him with his lower parts showing
And his hat still on.
She also told the Psychiatrist about the man in the subway
Who had pressed himself against her from behind
And said something that sounded like 'Ug Ug'
Which was the one thing she had never told Mrs Silvera
Perhaps on account of her having been so strictly raised.
She told him as well about the extraordinary dream she had had
On the night following the Beedmeyers' anniversary party
But when she was in the middle of it,
Before she had even got to the bit about the horse,
He suddenly rose and smiled and said that he hoped to see her next Friday.
At the same time.
She got up from the couch
Feeling a little dizzy and aware that her left foot had gone to sleep
But when she stamped at it it was all right.
She felt much better when she got home
And much less mal-adjusted
And when Mr Mallory came home from the office

She had put on her new hostess gown
Which she had only worn twice
Once at the Beedmeyers and the other time at the Palisades Country Club
On Christmas Eve.
Also she had rubbed some 'Shalimar' behind her ears
And greeted him with an all embracing welcoming smile
But it was none of it any use really
When dinner was over they looked at television as they always did
Until it was time to go to bed.
Mr Mallory spent longer in the bathroom than usual
And the 'Shalimar' began to wear off.
But when he did come back in his pyjamas
It didn't seem to matter much anyway
Because he merely belched and said 'Excuse me' automatically,
Blew her a perfunctory kiss and got into his own bed.
Later on, after he had read *McCall's* for a little,
He switched off the light.

Mrs Mallory lay in the darkness
With her arms relaxed at her sides
And her feet up, one to the right and one to the left
Like a mermaid's tail
And a tear rolled down her face all the way to her chin.

And for every insensitive Mrs Worthington or overly sensitive Mrs Mallory there were those innumerable – not to say unmentionable – ladies who would corner him on social occasions. Of which there were all too many.

Social Grace

I expect you've heard this a million times before
But I absolutely adored your last play
I went four times – and now to think
That I am actually talking to you!
It's thrilling! Honestly it is, I mean,
It's always thrilling isn't it to meet someone really celebrated?
I mean someone who really does things.
I expect all this is a terrible bore for you.
After all you go everywhere and know everybody.

It must be wonderful to go absolutely everywhere
And know absolutely everybody and – Oh dear –
Then to have to listen to someone like me,
I mean someone absolutely ordinary just one of your public.
No one will believe me when I tell them
That I have actually been talking to the great man himself.
It must be wonderful to be so frightfully brainy
And know all the things that you know.
I'm not brainy a bit, neither is my husband,
Just plain humdrum, that's what we are.
But we do come up to town occasionally
And go to shows and things. Actually my husband
Is quite a critic, not professionally of course,
What I mean is that he isn't all that easily pleased.
He doesn't like everything. Oh no, not by any means.
He simply hated that thing at the Haymarket
Which everybody went on about. 'Rubbish,' he said
Straight out like that, 'Damned Rubbish!'
I nearly died because heaps of people were listening.
But that's quite typical of him. He just says what he thinks.
And he can't stand all this highbrow stuff –
Do you know what I mean? – All these plays about people being miserable
And never getting what they want and not even committing suicide
But just being absolutely wretched. He says he goes to the theatre
To have a good time. That's why he simply loves all your things.
I mean they relax him and he doesn't need to think.
And he certainly does love a good laugh.
You should have seen him the other night when we went to that film
With what's-her-name in it – I can't remember the title.
I thought he'd have a fit, honestly I did.
You must know the one I mean, the one about the man who comes home
And finds his wife has been carrying on with his best friend
And, of course, he's furious at first and then he decides to teach her a lesson.
You must have seen it. I wish I could remember the name
But that's absolutely typical of me, I've got a head like a sieve,
I keep on forgetting things and as for names – well!
I cannot for the life of me remember them.
Faces yes, I never forget a face because I happen to be naturally observant
And always have been since I was a tiny kiddie

But names – Oh dear! I'm quite hopeless.
I feel such a fool sometimes
I do honestly.

It was undoubtedly innumerable evenings such as this that took Noël to his typewriter, where he could express his true feelings about the inevitability of even more . . .

I've Got to Go Out and Be Social

I've got to go out and be social,
I've got to go out and be social,
I've got to be bright
And extremely polite
And refrain from becoming too loose or too tight
And I mustn't impose conversational blight
On the dolt on my left
And the fool on my right.
I must really be very attractive tonight
As I have to go out and be social.

I have to go out and be social,
I've got to go out and be social,
I have to forget
The Bohemian set
And discuss with the flower of *Burke* and *Debrett*
The fall of the *franc* and the National Debt,
I have to regret
That the weather is wet
There's so much that I can't afford to forget –
As I have to go out and be social.

There was that sub-species – the Lady Journalist:

'I have a great friend who is a journalist,' I said. 'She's a darling.'
  'Then she must be a very bad journalist,' snapped Buddha. 'No good journalist could go on being a darling, even if she started as one.'

Pomp and Circumstance (1960)

The Lady at the Party

Look at her sitting there
A little way apart; her tortured hair
Twisted and bullied into brittle curls
Ape-ing the more flamboyant 'Glamour Girls'.

Notice her beady eyes
In action, as her sordid trade she plies.
Watch her lean forward smiling, strained to hear
Some note of discord in the atmosphere,

Some little private sigh
Uttered unconsciously in passing by,
A 'nuance' normal ears might well have missed
But not those of a lady columnist.

What was the circumstance?
What freak of destiny, what horrid chance,
What disillusionment, what venom'd spur
Goaded this wretched human scavenger

Drearily to decide
To jettison all decency and pride
And choose a life whose livelihood depends
Upon the private sorrow of her friends?

See how polite they are!
Bringing her this and that, going too far,
Showing too clearly in their votive flights
How much they fear the column that she writes.

Where does the answer lie?
Is the demand creating the supply
Enough excuse for pandering to dead,
Decaying minds, to earn your daily bread?

What is it worth in gold?
This sale of human dignity, this cold,
Ignoble, calculating, drab descent
Into the drains of social excrement?

When, in the future years
(Beyond publicity, beyond the tears
Her cheerful, base betrayals caused to flow)
She's near to death, will she that instant know

How much despair and pain
Was wrought by her salacious, vulgar brain
Or will she, in the shadow of the hearse,
Suspect the priest of flirting with the nurse?
Pity her if you can
This haunted, mediocre harridan
Haunted by fear; a puzzled sense of loss,
And all the lives she's nailed upon the cross.

Morning Glory

'There's something rather sad', she said,
'In seeing a great big ship go down.'
She languidly shook her lovely head
And plucked the edge of the eiderdown.
Her hands were white and her nails were red
Her marble brow wore a pensive frown
'It's really terribly sad', she said,
'To see a beautiful ship go down.'
The breakfast tray lay across her knee

A dusty beam of sunlight shone
And fruit and silver and China tea
And a crumbled, half-devoured scone.
The thin blue smoke of her cigarette
Wove, above us, a tangled skein,
The end of it, where her lips had met,
Proudly boasted a scarlet stain.
As though appalled by her own surmise
She gave a shudder and then a stretch
And turned her empty, lambent eyes
To have a look at the *Daily Sketch*.
The front page headlines were large and black
The pictures under them blotched, obscene
A few dark heads in the swirling wrack
'Survivors' stories on page sixteen'.
She read a little and sipped her tea
'Fifty passengers safe and sound'
Then she brightened perceptibly
'Fourteen hundred and fifty drowned'
She read the glutinous journalese
That smeared the names of the lost and dead
Then, rather neatly, controlled a sneeze.
'That was sheer agony,' she said.
I looked at the lissom, graceful line
Her body made 'neath the silken sheet
Her heart so far so far from mine
Yet I could almost hear it beat.
I wandered back over hours of sleep
To try to catch at the night gone by
To see if morning would let me keep
At least a fragment of memory.

In Masculine Homage

She was as pretty as she could be,
A terribly charming lady.
She wore her hat like a bridal wreath,
And flashed her small American teeth;

Shall We Join the Ladies . . . ?

Demanding of men an awed submission,
Polite obeisance to her Tradition.
Which was, for those who had eyes to see,
The age old feminine fallacy
That women live strange, mysterious lives,
With intuitions as sharp as knives.
With streaks of innocence, pure as snow,
And small, sly secrets, men mustn't know.
Her neck was white, and her hands were slim,
And she had a son, and seemed fond of him.
He was ten, or twelve, so of course she'd been
A married woman at seventeen.
She used her eyes to arouse a man,
But she lacked the warmth of a Courtesan.
She was as pretty as she could be.
A tediously charming lady.

Tenyo Maru
Yokohama
December 20th, 1929

Open Letter to a Mayor

Dear Mr Mayor, I feel myself impelled
By some strong impulse which will not be quelled
To ask you, just for once, to put aside
Your urban dignity, your civic pride
And answer me a question fair and square.
Now, man to man, or rather man to Mayor:
What evil circumstances; what obscene desires;
What aberration; what witches' fire;
What hidden complex in your early life
Caused you to choose quite such a horrid wife?
Were you ensnared? If so, with what? And how?
To what bleak magic did your spirit bow?
How could she, even in her younger years,
Ever have *not* bored everyone to tears?
How, e'en when dandled on her mother's arm,
Could she have shown the slightest sign of charm?

Could I but see in this her present mould
Some remnant of beauty since grown old,
Could I imagine, in some vanished Spring,
This squat, unlissom figure gambolling,
Could I, for just one instant, find a trace
Of erstwhile kindness in that metal face
Then Mr Mayor, I would have held my peace,
But as it is I find I cannot cease
To ponder, wonder, query, question why?
(Considering the adequate supply
Of women amiable, of women kind,
Of women clever, flexible of mind,
Of women glamorous, of women smart,
Of women sensuous and warm of heart)
Why, why, why, why dear Mayor did you select
A woman so determined to reject
All canons of politeness, every grace.
A woman so determined to efface
From social life all pleasantness and tact
A woman so unfitted to enact
A role quite obviously not designed
To suit a paltry soul, a meagre mind?
A role in fact of graciousness and charm,
Of kindliness to strangers and of calm,
Untroubled manners. Mr Mayor, I hate
So unequivocally to have to state
That she to whom you gave your honoured name,
With whom you proudly from the Altar came
With whom you cheerfully agreed to share
The arduous travail of being Mayor,
This creature whose exaggerated sense
Of her importance, whose grotesque, immense
Conviction that she's witty, worldly wise,
Unfailingly attractive in men's eyes,
Outspoken, frank, unmatched in repartee,
Bewilders me. What can the basis be
For these delusions? Is she stricken blind
Before her mirror? Has God been too kind
And cunningly contrived her inner ear

So that each time she speaks she cannot hear
The cliché and the antiquated quips
That fall with such assurance from her lips?
Oh! Mr Mayor, forgive me if you can
Reply to me quite frankly, Mayor to man.
Why did you marry her, what bitter fate
Led you towards so sinister a mate?
What siren's call, what shrill malignant voice
Lured you to such a miserable choice?
What devil's angel with dank wings outspread
Persuaded you to share your civic bed
With such a dull, unprepossessing, rude,
Unequalled Queen of social turpitude?
Why did you do it and thus let her loose
Upon the city? What was your excuse?
Answer me please, pray set my mind at ease
What did you do it for? Please tell me – please.

With curiosity my mind's devoured
I am, yours most sincerely, Noël Coward.

Quiet Old Timers

I love to think of Mr Stamps
Whose supercilious prattle
Which, like a strange celestial coup
Inspired by the Oxford Group,
Can spread the Word of God to tramps
Who wish to reach Seattle.
I love to think of Mrs Stamps
At one time faintly flighty
Who, changing from a draggled dove
Into a paragon of love,
In these days one really vamps
Her boy friend The Almighty.
I love to think of both the Stamps
In conjugal seclusion
Tightly encased in thought sublime

> Having a dreadfully quiet time
> Bearing with pride the mental cramps
> Of mystical illusion.

And then there was the Lady Poet.

A fugitive fragment of Coward verse turns up in his one and only American film – *The Scoundrel* (1935).

Noël as Anthony Mallaré, the scoundrel-y publisher, greets the all-too-gullible Cora Moore (Julie Haydon) with the ultimate seduction line for a lady poet. He's *read* her poems. He wants to *publish* them. He's even *memorised* three of them.

He then proceeds to quote from one of them – a typical outpouring of young female yearning . . .

> I am a stranger wandering always
> Only the dark trees know me
> And the dark sky
> And the cold wind
> That comes to warm itself in my heart . . .

Although the screenplay is nominally by Ben Hecht and Charles MacArthur, it was generally accepted that Noël rewrote his own lines. So here he is, speaking his own words as if someone else had written them! (And no, he does *not* publish Ms Moore's work. He dies instead and spends the rest of the film seeking forgiveness for a life ill led.)

Probably because of the influence of his mother, Noël was always fascinated by – but by no means always enamoured of – dominant women.

Mary Baker Eddy

A particular *bête noire* he would refer to frequently over the years was Mary Baker Eddy (1821–1910), the founder of the Christian Science movement. 'I have little reverence for the teachings of Christian Science; as a religion it has always seemed to me to induce a certain arid superiority in its devotees, as well as encouraging them to swish their skirts aside from many of life's unspiritual, but quite unquestionable realities.'

'She surveyed the house with a bright smile, the sort of smile you receive from a Christian Scientist when you announce that you have a toothache.'

Beyond These Voices (unpublished novel)

What a Saucy Girl

Steady, steady, Mary Baker Eddy,
You've got to play the final scene.
Admit that it's distasteful
To say that pain ain't painful
What about some more morphine?
In your great fight with sin, come
Admit you made an income
Far greater than your friend the Nazarene.
Steady, steady, Mary Baker Eddy,
What a saucy girl you've been!

And should someone of his acquaintance admit to being a Christian Scientist, there was every possibility that they would find themselves enshrined in Coward verse.

To Evelyn Russell Layton on her birthday – 4 August 1961 (the wife of Joe Layton, the choreographer/director who was directing *Sail Away*).

Midst the Hustle and the Bustle . . .

Midst the hustle and the bustle,
While the dancers swirl and sway,
Kindly note Miss Evelyn Russell
Centre stage in *Sail Away*.
Note her posture, calm and steady,
Note her amiable disdain.
Thanks to Mary Baker Eddy,
Evelyn Russell feels no pain.

Every tendon, every muscle
Tensed to keep 'Wavy Thought' at bay.
Hallelujah, Evelyn Russell,
Hail to this, your Natal Day.

Marie Stopes

Then there was Marie Stopes (1880–1958), the noted feminist and leading advocate of birth control. Noël met her as a fellow passenger on the SS *Cedric* on his way back to England from his first visit to America.

'She had, appropriately, the eyes of a fanatic, but the rest of her was dim, excepting her conversation which was surprisingly vivid and almost exclusively concerned with the theatre.'

She saw herself as a novelist and playwright, and managed to cajole him into spending weekends with her and her husband in the country, where she could assail him with her own literary efforts. After the success of *The Vortex*, she even suggested they collaborate on a sequel – a suggestion to which Noël replied: 'Psychologically speaking, there is no sequel – unless, of course, the gardener's boy found the box of cocaine and gave it to his younger sister, who took a boat to Marseilles and went into a bad house, one of those particularly bad houses for which Marseilles is justly famous.' That effectively ended the discussions but caused Noël to elect the good doctor to his personal pantheon of Formidable Ladies . . .

If Through a Mist

If through a mist of awful fears
Your mind in anguish gropes,
Dry up your panic stricken tears
And fly to Marie Stopes.

And if you have lost life's shining goal
And mixed with sex perverts and dopes,
For Normal soap to cleanse your soul
Apply to Marie Stopes.

And if perhaps you fail all round
And lie among your shattered hopes,
Just raise your body from the ground
And *crawl* to Marie Stopes.

Ella Wheeler Wilcox

When Noël was growing up there can hardly have been a newspaper to open or a calendar page to be turned without coming across a whimsical verse or homily from Ella Wheeler Wilcox (1859–1919). And no family bookshelf was complete without a copy of *Drops of Water* or *Poems of Passion*.

In later years Noël chose to pretend to believe that beneath the saccharine there lurked . . .

Whoops! Ella Wheeler Wilcox

Whoops! Ella Wheeler Wilcox,
You were certainly a cultured little pearl
And for all your dissertations
On the orthodox sensations,
I gather that at times you've
Been a rather naughty girl!

Oh, Ella Wheeler Wilcox,
How you raised your lover's hopes quite high.
When they went from bad to worse,
You just wrote a little verse.
Ella Wheeler Wilcox. Fie!!

'It was just that she had a complete set of Ella Wheeler Wilcox that prejudiced you.' One of many lines intended for plays that were never used.

Beatrice Eden

Fortunately there *were* strong women that Noël liked. One of them was Beatrice Eden, first wife to Tory politician Anthony Eden, waiting in the wings at the Foreign Office to be Prime Minister (although he was not destined to win golden opinions when he finally stepped into the part).

'Oh, Beatrice dear, what a superb weekend'

Oh, Beatrice dear, what a superb weekend,
What sybaritic luxury was ours.
How nice that your old man's Russian friend
Not only sides against the Axis powers,

But sends to us such treasure from afar,
Such blowing-out but exquisite champagne,
Such absolutely spiffing caviar.
Oh, Beatrice darling, let me come again.

Let me once more in tepid water dip
And huddle frozen by the fireplace grate;
Let me again on polished parquet slip;
Let me retire, exhausted, far too late.

Let me once more escort you to a rout
And stand in tears amid the alien corn,
Watching my colleagues one by one pass out,
While you, dear, stay unvanquished till the dawn.

From early dusk I waited patiently
Till night, star-spangled, put her gown of ebon on.
Where was my saviour, where was Anthony?
The answer, darling Beatrice, was a Lebanon.

Letter to Beatrice Eden

Oh, Beatrice dear, allow me please to utter
My heartfelt, loving and undying gratitude
Not only for that lovely bread and butter
But for a weekend of such sweet beatitude.
The eminent gay gentleman you married
Thus rurally detached from life political
Was so benign, relaxed and quite unharried
That even I for once could not be critical.
You rose above the harsh discordant feature
I foisted on your gentle aristocracy.
You treated Joyce, that flaunting, painted creature,

> With all the graciousness of true democracy.
> In fact, my measle-ridden peacherino,
> The weekend was a jolly decent beano.

Beatrice divorced Eden in 1950 and died in 1957. Eden himself – humbled by the Suez fiasco of 1956 – sought refuge in Jamaica at Ian Fleming's Goldeneye.

Noël wrote to Lornie: 'I'm afraid that what I once wrote in a bread and butter poem to Beatrice years ago is only too true. The verse ended with the gaily prophetic phrase, "The answer's a Lebanon".'

6.

INDEFINITE THOUGHTS ON THE INFINITE

In a 1946 letter to Lillian Gish: 'I think I'd like to live to be 150 if I could see how the Brave New World works out' . . .

When asked by David Frost in a TV interview about his attitude to God, Noël replied, 'We've never been intimate – but maybe we do have a few things in common.'

> Ah me! This growing old! . . . I wonder how long it will be before I make my last exit . . . I am resigned. There is no sense in rebellion. I suppose I should envy the afterlife believers, the genuflectors, the happy-ever-after ones who know beyond a shadow of a doubt that we shall all meet again in some celestial vacuum, but I don't. I'd rather face up to finality and get on with life, lonely or not, for as long as it lasts. Those I have really loved are still with me in moments of memory – whole and intact and unchanged. I cannot envisage them in another sphere. I do not even wish to.
>
> Diary 1961

Noël never quite made up his mind about the hereafter. In his early verse he took the fashionable and romantically morbid view of Death (with a capital 'D'):

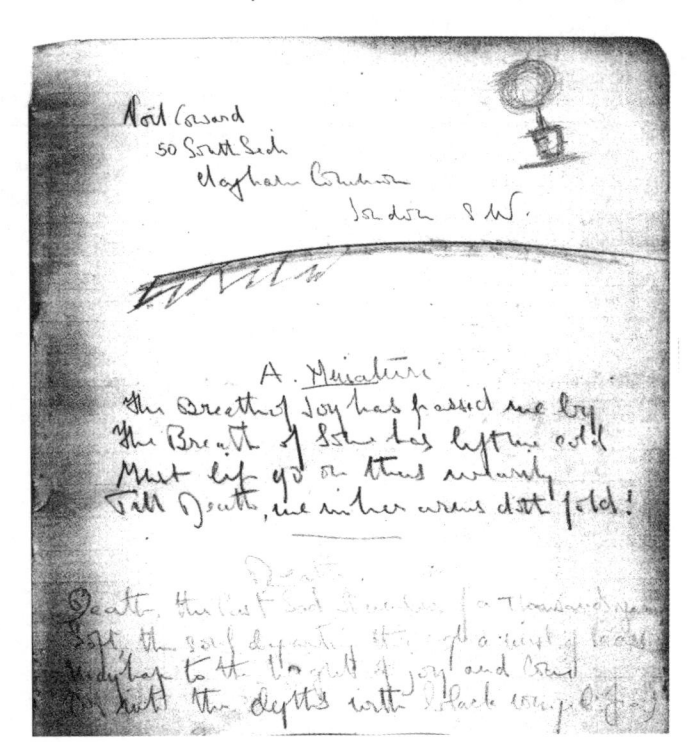

A Miniature

The Breath of Joy has passed me by,
The Breath of Sorrow has left me cold.
Must life go on this wearily
Till Death me in her arms doth fold!

Death

Death, the last sad slumber of a thousand years,
Soft, the soul departing through a mist of tears,
Mayhap to the light of joy and laughter
Or into the depths with black whipped fears.
> (*Written c.1914 at 'Ben Lomond', 50 South Side,
> Clapham Common, London SW*)

In 1916 he was touring with *Charley's Aunt*:

In Bristol I had a religious mania lasting exactly one day and based upon an inexplicable fear of death, which descended upon me abruptly in the middle of a matinée . . . I felt definitely that I should never see my home again . . . there was thunder in the air as well, and during that night a terrific storm broke, convincing me that this was my destined finish. I wept thoroughly at the vivid picture of Mother's face when she heard how the sharp lightning had struck her darling through the window of the second floor back. I murmured incoherent prayers, vowed many vows and promised many promises, if only I might live a little longer. They were apparently granted, for I woke up the next morning, as bright as a button and rapidly forgot the entire episode, promises and all.

When, in 1917, his friend John Elkins suddenly died of spinal meningitis while serving in the Royal Flying Corps, Noël expressed the depth of his feelings in verse.

Lines to God

If I should ultimately meet my God,
He will not be the God of love or battles,
He'll be some under God whose job it is

To organise sharp sounds and things that rattle.
He'll be the one who, all my life on earth
Can most sadistically my spirit shatter
With little hammerings and sudden shouts
And hollow ricochets of empty mirth.

Meditation on Death

I can meditate on Death for quite a while without being scared and then suddenly I realise fears are creeping through my reasoning – not perhaps fears of the actual death but premonitions of the unsuitable loneliness immediately preceding it. However suddenly it comes, can it ever be suddenly enough? Will the close-packed hours of two moments equal the more extended agony of two days or two weeks or two months? Which would you choose of these, knowing the infinite elasticity of Time? One can only hope for enough strength of intellect to be able to stand that craven last minute rush to salvation, that pitiful clutching at the fact of some smug, ambiguous Deity. Death bed repentances seem to me to be pretty small potatoes.

Someone (writer *William Bolitho*) once said to me: 'Be careful when you write about Death. It's a serious thing, big and important. None of your damned flippancy. You can't go sauntering towards Death with a cigarette lolling from your mouth.' And then, if you remember, you said – 'Look at the people in the French Revolution. They laughed and were flippant up to the very last moment.' But that was so very different; they were performing beautifully. Extenuating circumstances permit the flippant cigarette. If I were dragged out into the square by a mob that I despised, I'd give a good performance, I'm sure. It's very easy when you don't have to do anything about it, when everything's arranged for you and your line of conduct, so definitely and dramatically worked out.

(c. 1930)

Which led him to ask rhetorically:

Do I Believe?

Do I believe in God?
Well, yes, I suppose, in a sort of way.
It's really terribly hard to say.
I'm sure that there must be, of course,
Some kind of vital, motive force,

Some power that holds the winning cards
Behind life's ambiguous façades
But whether you think me odd or not
I can't decide if it's God or not.

I look at the changing sea and sky
And try to picture Eternity
I gaze at immensities of blue
And say to myself 'It can't be true
That somewhere up in that abstract sphere
Are all the people who once were here
Attired in white and shapeless gowns
Sitting on clouds like eiderdowns
Plucking at harps and twanging lutes
With cherubim in their birthday suits,
Set in an ageless, timeless dream
Part of a formulated scheme
Formulated before the Flood
Before the amoeba left the mud
And, stranded upon a rocky shelf
Proceeded to sub-divide itself.'
I look at the changing sea and sky
And try to picture infinity
I gaze at a multitude of stars
Envisaging the men on Mars
Wondering if they too were torn
Between their sunset and their dawn
By dreadful, night engendered fears
Of what may lie beyond their years
And if they too, through thick and thin,
Are dogged by consciousness of Sin.
Have they, to give them self-reliance,
A form of Martian Christian Science?
Or do they live in constant hope
Of dispensations from some Pope?

Are they pursued from womb to tomb
By hideous prophecies of doom?
Have they cathedral, church or chapel
Are they concerned with Adam's apple?

> Have they immortal souls like us
> Or are they less presumptuous?
>
> Do I believe in God?
> I can't say No and I can't say Yes
> To me it's anybody's guess
> But if all's true that we once were told
> Before we grew wise and sad and old
> When finally Death rolls up our eyes
> We find we're in for a big surprise.

Surprisingly, perhaps, tucked away among some miscellaneous correspondence, is an undated prayer:

A Prayer: Most Merciful God

> Most merciful God, grant we pray thee, that we may never forget that as followers of Christ we are the observed of all men, and that our failures may cause others to stumble; that in a measure God places his honour in our hands.
>
> Help us that we may be true and loyal to the best and highest we know and that we may show truth and loyalty in every activity of our daily life.
>
> Grant to us the Royal gift of courage.
>
> Give unto us a keen sense of honour, that we may never give ourselves the benefit of the doubt.
>
> And finally we pray thee for a true sense of humour; may its kindly light and its healing power relax life's tension.

All this, O God, we ask in the
Name of Jesus Christ, Thy Son, Our
Lord.

AMEN

. . . and a surprisingly emotional verse dedicated to Elaine Stritch, herself a devout Catholic:

This Is the Moment

This is the moment
I wish I could fill it
With someone I love
But God didn't will it.

So much fun I have had
Besides which I am glad
To have given or taken
Something good, something bad.

But 'lights out' now and then
I will wake up again
And try very hard so . . .
Amen.

There were moments when the Father and Son appeared to break through . . .

If I Should Ever Wantonly Destroy

If I should ever wantonly destroy
This mechanism which is all my world
All other worlds beyond my world – all stars
All things remembered; unremembered; lost;
Imagined; dreamed of; calculated; loved;
Hated; despised; looked forward to; desired –
If I should ever wilfully escape
From what my conscience calls responsibility

From this strange, unexplained necessity
Of living life. If I should fail,
Run whimpering to death because some fear,
Because some sudden sharp neurotic dread
Some silly love, some moment of despair
Loosens me from the purpose that I hold
This sense of living life until the end
Then, only then, please pity me, my friend.

Condolence

The mind, an inveterate traveller,
Journeys swiftly and far
Faster than light, quicker than sound
Or the flaming arc of a falling star
But the body remains in a vacuum
Gagged, bound and sick with dread
Knowing the words that can't be spoken,
Searching for words that must be said.
Dumb, inarticulate, heartbroken.
Inadequate, inhibited.

Nothing Is Lost
(Originally 'Deep in Our Sub-Conscious')

Deep in our sub-conscious, we are told
Lie all our memories, lie all the notes
Of all the music we have ever heard
And all the phrases those we loved have spoken,
Sorrows and losses time has since consoled,
Family jokes, out-moded anecdotes
Each sentimental souvenir and token
Everything seen, experienced, each word
Addressed to us in infancy, before
Before we could even know or understand
The implications of our wonderland.
They there all are, the legendary lies
The birthday treats, the sights, the sounds, the tears

Forgotten debris of forgotten years
Waiting to be recalled, waiting to rise
Before our world dissolves before our eyes
Waiting for some small, intimate reminder,
A word, a tune, a known familiar scent
An echo from the past when, innocent
We looked upon the present with delight
And doubted not the future would be kinder
And never knew the loneliness of night.

. . . but most of the time one eyebrow was firmly raised:

Father and Son

I knew a man who believed in God
And Christian ethics and Right and Wrong
In Life Hereafter and angels' wings
And all the other beguiling things
That lure the tremulous soul along
From infancy to the final sod.

This pious creature believed as well
That every sparrow that fell to earth
Was duly noted by 'One Above'
In ecstasies of paternal love;
And babes that weren't baptised at birth
Were briskly fried in a tinsel hell.

He disapproved, I need hardly say,
Of carnal pleasures and bawdy jokes
And all the accoutrements of sin
(Including dancing and Gordon's gin)
And no inducement could ever coax
Him out of church on the Sabbath day.

He viewed the chaos and tears of war
As just a whim of the 'Will divine'
When youth was shattered and cities razed
He murmured smugly 'The Lord be praised'

Indefinite Thoughts on the Infinite

And shot a rather annoying line
About the sins we were punished for.

He married early and took his wife,
In doleful wedlock, to Ilfracombe
Performing dutifully every rite
Appropriate to a bridal night
While no gleam pierced the pervading gloom
Of life or passion or joy of life.

He later bred, with the passing years,
Some insignificant progeny
Who genuflected and prayed and squirmed
And ultimately were all confirmed
And set in a mould of sanctity
To forge ahead with their dim careers.

But one of them (by some chance unkind;
Some strange deflection on Nature's part;
Some ancient heritage, or perhaps
Some lost, irrelevant cosmic lapse)
Showed early signs of an eager heart
And, worse than ever, a questing mind.

This unregenerate malcontent,
This septic thorn in parental flesh,
Grew up to query the Holy Writ
And, far from being ashamed of it,
Entwined his family in a mesh
Of theological argument.

He scorned the Testaments new and old,
Was unimpressed by the Holy Grail,
He scoffed at bishops and Father Knox
And every biblical paradox
He seized upon as a useful flail
To knock all mystical dogma cold.

His father shuddered, his mother cried,
His married sister knelt down and prayed
And one stayed down for the whole of Lent
Thereby creating a precedent

Which, though not budging the renegade,
Suffused her ego with holy pride.

He grew and flourished, this Green Bay Tree,
He used his body and used his mind,
He looked on life with a cheerful eye
And when war came and he had to die
He seemed remarkably disinclined
To compromise with the Deity.

He'd lived his time and his time was done.
He'd made the most of his brief, gay years.
He'd suffered lightly his growing pains
And revelled in suns – and in winds and rains –
And loved a little and shed some tears
Without embarrassing anyone.

The funeral came, and the retinue
Of mournful relatives did their stuff.
The vicar loaded the church with prayer
And no one noticed a stranger there,
A flashy creature; a 'bit of fluff'
Who sat alone in an empty pew.

Her face was set in a stony smile.
Her hat was saucy and over smart.
She didn't weep and she didn't kneel
And though her eyes couldn't quite conceal
The misery that was in her heart,
She walked quite perkily down the aisle.

The dismal, lustreless caravan
Pursued its way to the rightful place.
The father's head was correctly bowed
But suddenly in the shuffling crowd
He saw, with horror, the brazen face
And scarlet lips of a courtesan.

His soul was seared with a burning flame;
His heart contracted with righteous wrath;
His nostrils twitched at the scent of sin
And, marching up to the Magdalene,

Indefinite Thoughts on the Infinite

He barred her way on the grave-lined path
And asked her why and for what she came.

She first looked down and then raised her head.
She met his eyes and then turned aside
To where the family huddled round
That blatant hole in the sacred ground.
Her body stiffened as though with pride.
'Your son was a pal of mine,' she said.

The Christian gentleman lost control
For there before him, personified,
Were aching memories, youthful tears,
The doubts and dreams that had plagued his years,
Frustrated passions and loves denied
And all the fears that had damned his soul.

He lost control and he lost his head.
His thin lips parted as though in pain
And while he quivered in every limb
It really never occurred to him
That what tormented his throbbing brain
Was a bitter jealousy of the dead.

He lost control in a mist of hate,
He also forfeited Christian grace.
His chin was slavered with beads of sweat
As, with a scurrilous epithet,
He struck her brutally in the face
And thrust her roughly towards the gate.

She staggered slightly and stood at bay
Unsteadily in her high-heeled shoes.
She made a movement as though to speak,
Thought better of it and touched her cheek
Caressing gently the shameful bruise,
And then, quite quietly, walked away.

Disposing thus of the alien guest
He closed his mind to the whole affair
And, kneeling down with his kith and kin,
Soon cleansed his soul of the stink of sin.

And while he joined in subservient prayer
The son he hated was laid to rest.

I knew a man who believed in God
And Christian ethics and Right and Wrong,
But not in Nature's sublime bequest
Of fearless, passionate, human zest
That bears adventurous souls along
From infancy to the final sod.

Ignatius Hole

The Reverend Ignatius Hole
Refused to sanction Birth Control,
Declaring it, in brief, to be
A crack at Christianity.
Regardless of pre-natal taints,
Oblivious to those complaints,
Which economically must
Occasionally be discussed,
A member of the League of Youth,
An ardent seeker of the truth,
A man compassionate and kind
Whose amiable and virile mind
Could be described at any rate
As relatively adequate.

Onward Christian Soldiers

Now we have it on impeccable authority
(Without a trace of irony or mirth)
That when the Day of Judgment comes, the meek will take priority
And set about inheriting the earth.
In so far as I'm concerned
They can have it if they've earned
So dubious and thankless a reward
For if all that moral sanctity and snug superiority
Can seriously gratify the Lord,

Let 'em have it – let 'em keep it
Let 'em plough it – let 'em reap it
Let 'em clean it up and polish it and garnish it and sweep it.
Let 'em face up to its puzzling complexities
And, to their gentle, diffident dismay,
Discover what a crucible of hate and crime and sex it is
And start reorganising right away.
But when they begin to fail
It will be of small avail
For them to turn the other silly cheek
For the Lord will smile remotely on their worries and perplexities
And serve them damn well right for being meek.

So, *was* there a God? *No* God? More than *one* God?

Noël was never quite prepared to put his money down. The only thing he was reasonably sure of was that Somebody – if there *was* a Somebody – needed to do a lot better job of running things.

It seemed to him that in all probability one God had more on His hands than He could deal with and seemed to have delegated a few underemployed archangels to handle the small stuff – and make rather a hash of it on the whole. So while he continued to ponder the imponderable, he'd like a few words with one of those Little Gods.

Lines to a Little God

There's just one little God I'd like to meet,
Not a Big-Shot, not the All Highest Head Boy.
I've quite a few complaints with which to greet
My Judges on the day that I'm a dead boy.
The God that I particularly itch
To say just one vituperative word to,
Is that sardonic, mean son of a bitch
Whom no religious sect has yet referred to,
That under-God whose whole-time job it is
To organise our minor miseries.

Not our great sorrows; not the bitter pain
Of anguished last good-byes; not death; nor blindness;
Nor yet the agonising mental strain

Imposed on us by pious loving-kindness.
Not melancholia; not sex-frustration;
Not hope abandoned; not the toll of war;
Nor the unutterable desolation
Of an illusion dead for evermore.
But each and every little sting that serves
To agitate and lacerate our nerves.

The little pig; that sly, sadistic Goebbels
Who makes the windows rattle in the night,
Who shrewdly times the intermittent burbles
Of water pipes when I am trying to write.
Who so arranges that my next door neighbours
Elect to have some friends in for a drink
When, wearied by my histrionic labours,
I snatch an hour in bed to rest and think.
Who also, at five-thirty in the morning,
Sets off an accidental air-raid warning.

This beastly little God, this misbegotten
Smart-Aleck whose whole livelihood depends
On fixing that the one song I've forgotten
Should be demanded loudly by my friends.
Who also plans for hotel maids to call me
Briskly with cups of tea at half-past seven.
Whatever dire punishments befall me
When I meet this rat at the bar of Heaven
I'll rip his star-spun, butter muslin frock off
And knock his sneering, bloody little block off.

Having got that off his chest and all things considered, he was left with the feeling that

> When finally Death rolls up our eyes
> We find we're in for a big surprise.

Let's hope it was a pleasant one.

7.

THE THEATRE: 'A TEMPLE OF DREAMS'

'The theatre must be treated with respect. It is a house of strange enchantment . . . a temple of dreams.'

Despite his many other interests and accomplishments, the Theatre was Noël's abiding love.

One begins to wonder why he didn't write more about it – before remembering how much he wrote *for* it.

From a very early age he was a Boy Actor, 'dreaming of the future, reaching for the crown' which was so soon to be his. Auditions, stage mothers – his own being an early Mrs Worthington, who at least had talent to put on the stage.

His youthful eye was unsparing of the types that shared the stage with him and in subsequent plays such as *Red Peppers* he would pin them down like ageing butterflies. Nonetheless, his criticism, though accurate, had kindness at its core. 'Talent must prevail', of course, but commitment was what counted: the need to perform and to give it one's all – even if the 'all' was sometimes less than enough.

The Theatre was 'a temple of dreams' and everyone was entitled to his or her dream.

Noël had his theatrical heroes and heroines – Novello, Dietrich, Lillie, the Lunts – many of whom he celebrated in verse. There were others – like Mary Martin – who fared less well. And then there were the Leading Ladies who were no longer leading – and who shall be blessedly nameless. ('God preserve me in future from female stars. I don't suppose He will.')

Critics were always the bane of Coward's professional life. ('I think it is so frightfully clever of them to go night after night to the theatre and know so little about it'.) The doyen of British critics offended and paid the price.

Opera was another *bête noire* to be shooed into place. He knew he *should* like it – but he didn't. And that was that.

And then there was Mr Graham Greene, an adversary who turned into an admirer. But while he was on the wrong side of the Coward fence he became an adversary in verse.

The Boy Actor

I can remember, I can remember.
The months of November and December
    Were filled for me with peculiar joys
So different from those of other boys.
    For other boys would be counting the days
Until end of term and holiday times
    But I was acting in Christmas plays
While they were taken to pantomimes.

I didn't envy their Eton suits,
Their children's dances and Christmas trees.
　My life had wonderful substitutes
For such conventional treats as these.
　I didn't envy their country larks,
Their organised games in panelled halls;
　　While they made snow-men in stately parks
I was counting the curtain calls.

I remember the auditions, the nerve-racking auditions:
Darkened auditorium and empty, dusty stage,
Little girls in ballet dresses practising 'positions'
Gentlemen with pince-nez asking you your age.
Hopefulness and nervousness struggling within you,
Dreading that familiar phrase, 'Thank you, dear, no more.'
Straining every muscle, every tendon, every sinew
To do your dance much better than you'd ever done before.
Think of your performance. Never mind the others,
Never mind the pianist, talent must prevail.
Never mind the baleful eyes of other children's mothers
Glaring from the corners and willing you to fail.

I can remember. I can remember.
The months of November and December
　　Were more significant to me
Than other months could ever be
　　For they were the months of high romance
When destiny waited on tip-toe,
　　When every boy actor stood a chance
Of getting into a Christmas show,
　　Not for me the dubious heaven
Of being some prefect's protégé!
　　Not for me the Second Eleven.
For me, two performances a day.

Ah those first rehearsals! Only very few lines:
Rushing home to mother, learning them by heart,
'Enter Left through window' – Dots to mark the cue lines:
'Exit with others' – Still it *was* a part.
Opening performance; legs a bit unsteady,
Dedicated tension, shivers down my spine,

Powder, grease and eye-black, sticks of make-up ready
Leichner number three and number five and number nine.
World of strange enchantment, magic for a small boy
Dreaming of the future, reaching for the crown,
Rigid in the dressing-room, listening for the call-boy
'Overture Beginners – Everybody Down!'

I can remember. I can remember.
The months of November and December,
    Although climatically cold and damp,
Meant more to me than Aladdin's lamp.
I see myself, having got a job,
    Walking on wings along the Strand,
Uncertain whether to laugh or sob
    And clutching tightly my mother's hand,
I never cared who scored the goal
    Or which side won the silver cup,
I never learned to bat or bowl
    But I heard the curtain going up.

In 1911 the Boy Actor found himself a part-time pupil of the legendary acting teacher, Miss Italia Conti (1873–1946). At this time Miss Conti was working closely with the famous actor-manager, Sir Charles Hawtrey (1858–1923), the man who was to teach Noël so much about comedy technique. Noël was cast in two of Hawtrey's plays that year – *The Great Name* and *Where the Rainbow Ends* (a child's play which, in its day, rivalled *Peter Pan* for popularity).

He couldn't help but notice the lady's high-handed behaviour and the memory stayed with him. A decade later he recalled his impressions in an 'Ode', which he sent to Violet:

Ode to Italia Conti

Oh, Italia, with thy face so pale
Why must you float about the Stalls
Where Mr Hawtrey sits?
Dost think that passing thus thou wilt prevail
Upon him to cut out the finest bits
Which we poor principals in our parts must speak?
We often hear the hapless ballet tremble

When they're corrected by your raucous squeak.
To principals you like not you will serve
Out contracts in which cheek and guile are blended
And then you have the most appalling nerve
To say they must be yours till world is ended.
In vain you've tried to lure us to your classes –
We are not such unmitigated asses.

'A Principal'

A young Noël as the Page with Sir Charles Hawtrey at the piano in *The Great Name*

Concert Types

His youthful touring days exposed Noël to a cross-section of available talent in both provincial theatre and concert hall. In 1917 he wrote a series of verses on 'Concert Types':

No. 1   The Pianist

A figure of uncertain age
And some amount of regal grace
Is always first upon the stage
In imitation Brouxelles lace.
With elephantine touch she thumps
Out bits from Wagner's *Parsifal*
She ought to have been cut in lumps
And buried quietly when small.

No. 2   The Tenor

The next upon the programme is
A thin young man intensely sad
Who swears that steadfast love is his
Because he throbs with passion mad –
'My heart is lighter than a bird!'
He screams in accents piercing shrill.
I think that even if interred,
This man would go on singing still.

No. 3   The Contralto

Contraltos are a cheerful band
Of women, all immensely fat,
Who wave aloft a podgy hand
And warble down to low A flat.
When launched upon their favourite song,

They never seem inclined to stop.
I feel, if prodded with a prong,
They probably would go off 'Pop'.

No. 4   The Humorist

This roguish man with face ablotch,
A made up bow and button boots
Whose boring anecdotes in Scotch
Invariably start with 'Hoots',
I think should quickly be interned
In some unpleasant smelling cell!
Or, if not that, he might be burned
And emptied down a disused well!

No. 5   The Child Prodigy

An infant prodigy of nine
I shoved upon the stage in white.
She starts off in a dismal whine
About a Dark and Stormy Night,
A burglar whose heart is true,
Despite his wicked looking face!
And what a little child can do
To save her Mama's jewel case!
This may bring tears to every eye.
It does not set my heart on fire
I'd like to stand serenely by
And watch that Horrid Child expire!

No. 6   The Soprano

A woman in insipid pink
Will start off with a ditty
Which nearly all the audience think
Quite the reverse of pretty.

> She sings at length of Love Divine
> In many am'rous phrases
> And whilst I listen, I consign
> Her and her song to Blazes!

From time to time he would find himself on the same bill as the kind of act that could most kindly – and euphemistically – be called a 'trouper':

When Babsie Got the Bird

> Babsie's on the stage. She's only forty!
> Babsie's got a grown up girl and boy –
> She tries her very hardest to be naughty
> And thinks it looks alluring to be coy
> Babsie's sung in all the halls round London West
> She still hopes that in time she'll reach them
> From what I know about her
> Ability to give them what is best.
> Then poor old Babs'll get the bird again,
> The Bird again once more
> And for a week or two she won't be heard of again
> But she won't be off for long, you may be sure.
> Then one fine day she will appear again
> At some outlandish place, you bet
> And when we're dead and gone,
> As the years go rolling on Babsie still the bird will get.
> Babsie's first engagement was a failure.
> Babsie's second also was a frost.
> Babsie toured for years in South Australia
> With a song, the theme of which she always lost.
> Once she sang it in a Nature Village
> In the middle of the vast Australian scrub.
> She said, 'It seems to strike me
> That these people don't quite like me.'
> Another thing that struck her was a club.
>
> Then poor Babsie got the bird again,
> The bird again much worse.
> I don't think that song e'er will be heard,

They had to fetch a doctor and a nurse
But soon Babsie got all right again
And lately she's been singing quite a lot
And even when I'm dead,
I'm sure I'll hear it said
That Babs again the bird has got.

Noël with Madge Titheradge

Over the years Noël would pay tribute in verse to a number of his colleagues. There was MADGE TITHERADGE (1887–1961), an Australian actress whose career was in London. She was associated with Noël for many years and starred in his 1926 play, *The Queen Was in the Parlour*.

To Meg Titheradge

The lyric tribute is addressed to Meg's
Enthusiastic, hardy little legs
And also, as we're handing out awards,
To her supremely vocal vocal-cords.
How strange that so minute a throat could nurture

A larynx clearly made of gutta-percha.
And how more strange (and jolly nice, of course)
That so much harnessed locomotive force
Should be condensed in so 'petite' a creature
Whose charm is not her least distinctive feature.
And so this band; this company; this group;
This happy breed of vagabonds; this troupe;
This Noël Coward galaxy; this Rep;
Await with pleasure your unfailing step
And fondly hope, when Judgment Day befall us
That you, dear Meg, will not omit to call us.

HELEN HAYES (1900–93) was one of his favourite American actresses. He had accepted his first starring role in a film *The Scoundrel* in 1935 on the understanding that she was to co-star. This didn't happen but they did become lifelong friends.

Noël wrote a verse to her daughter Mary, born in 1933. Hayes's husband was Charles MacArthur who (with co-writer Ben Hecht) had produced *The Scoundrel*.

Sadly, Mary died in 1949.

To Mary MacArthur

With pleasure Miss MacArthur dear
I venture to inscribe
The following polite, sincere
And gentle diatribe.

To one face pray be reconciled
Admit no 'ifs' nor 'buts'
Your mother is an Actress, child
And consequently, 'Nuts'.

There's one more face that you must list
And face for good or bad,
Your father is a Dramatist
And obviously mad.

Whichever way your fortune bends
And circumstances change
Your mother's and your father's friends
Are certain to be strange.

In all this odd eccentric clan
Just one exception shines
The *talented and witty* man
Who wrote these *charming* lines!
(May 1933)

IRENE VANBRUGH (1872–1949) was literally a Grand Dame of the English theatre in the early decades of the twentieth century. On 6 November 1950 – a year after her death – a Memorial Matinée was held for her. Noël contributed this Epilogue:

Irene Vanbrugh Memorial Matinée: The Epilogue

Your Majesty, Ladies and Gentlemen.
A little while ago a lady died
A lady who, for many of us here
Eptomised the dignity and pride
Of our profession. Over fifty years
Have passed since young Vanbrugh's quality
Was stamped indelibly upon the hearts
Of Londoners. During those changing years
We were most privileged, not only us
Her colleagues who so loved and honoured her
But you as well, you on the other side.
Perhaps you took for granted (as you should)
The lightness of her touch in comedy;
The note of hidden laughter in her voice;
The way she used her hands to illustrate
Some subtle implication. She could charge
An ordinary line with so much wit
That even critics thought the play was good!
They, too, took her for granted (as they should).
Then on the other hand, the other mask
The mask of tragedy; she could wear that
With such authority that even we,
Her fellow actors could perceive
Through her most accurate and sure technique
Her truth, which was her talent, shining clear.
Your Majesty, Ladies and Gentlemen,

A little while ago this lady died
Apparently, only apparently,
For even though the art that she adorned
Must in its essence be ephemeral,
Players of her integrity and grace
Can never die. Although we shall not hear
That lyrical, gay voice again, nor see
The personal inimitable smile
That she bestowed on us at curtain calls
The theatre that she loved will still go on
Enriched immeasurably by the years
She gave to it. This epilogue is but
A prelude to the future she endowed
With so much legend, so much memory
For all the young beginners who will learn
Their intricate and fascinating trade
And owe perhaps, some measure of their fame
To the undying magic of her name.

IVOR NOVELLO (1893–1951) was invariably depicted by the English press as a bitter rival to Noël. Rivalry there certainly was but it was of the friendliest sort and both of them thoroughly enjoyed fanning the media flames. Noël once joked: 'The two most beautiful things in the world are Ivor's profile and my mind.'

Ivor was so impressed with what Noël achieved in *Bitter Sweet* (1929) that he determined to try his own hand at this kind of operetta. A series of box-office successes – *Glamorous Night, The Dancing Years, Perchance to Dream* – followed and now it was Noël who had to try to compete and replicate his original success.

Ivor died suddenly after a performance in what was perhaps his most successful show – *King's Rhapsody*. There was a Memorial Performance for him on 7 October 1951 at which Noël delivered this Tribute:

Tribute to Ivor Novello

Dear Ivor. Here we are, your world of friends
The Theatre world, the world you so adored
Each of us in our hearts remembering
Some aspect of you, something we can hold
Untarnished and inviolate until
For us as well the final curtain falls.

For some of us your talent, charm and fame
The outward trappings of your brilliant life,
Were all we knew of you and all we'll miss.
But others, like myself, who loved you well
And knew you intimately, here we stand
Strangely bewildered, lost, incredulous,
That you, so suddenly, should go away.
Those of us here to-night who have performed
And sung your melodies and said your words
Professionally, carefully rehearsed
Have felt, I know behind their actor's pride
In acting, a deep, personal dismay –
A heartache underlying every phrase.
The heartache will eventually fade
The passing years will be considerate,
But one thing Time will never quite erase
Is memory. None of us will forget,
However long we live, your quality;
Your warm and loving heart; your prodigal,
Unfailing generosity, and all
Your numberless, uncounted kindnesses.
I hope, my dear, that after a short while
There'll be no further sorrow, no more tears.
We must remember only all the years
Of fun and laughter that we owe to you.
Mournfulness would be sorry recompense
For all the joy you gave us all, all the jokes
Your lovely sense of humour let us share.
Gay is the word for all our memories
Gay they shall be for ever and a day
And there's no greater tribute we can pay.

A monolith of the English theatre during the professional careers of both Noël and Ivor was impresario HUGH ('BINKIE') BEAUMONT (1908–73), head of the all-powerful theatrical agency, H. M. Tennent. Immensely shrewd but somewhat unpolished, Binkie was a diamond in the rough and at one point during the war Noël and Lorn thought a gentle hint or two might be in order . . .

Hugh 'Binkie' Beaumont: theatrical impresario and 'diamond in the rough'

'Dearest Binkie, dearest Bink'

Dearest Binkie, dearest Bink,
Lorn and I sincerely think
You have been for long enough
Both illiterate and rough
And in fact for many a year
Very, very common, dear
So accept from this address
Hints on gentlemanliness.

That which warns of Luftwaffe spleen
Is a *siren*, not a *sireen*
Soldier's furlough, sweet but brief,
We call *leave* and never *leaf*
Use grammatical restraint
Is *not* is correct . . . not *ain't*
Words like 'nothing' may we say,
End with G and not with K.
Napkins, in the smarter sets,
Are not known as *serviettes*
Also, these are not tucked in
Neatly underneath the chin.

> May we add that *opposite*
> Is pronounced to rhyme with 'bit'.
> Should you belch at lunch or tea
> *Never* mutter 'Pardon me'.
> Mark these rules and, if you can,
> Be a little gentleman.
> (With love from Mr Noël Coward and Mrs Lorn Loraine)
> (Nancy Mitford anticipated)

Binkie died just a few days before Noël himself and was very much on his mind at the time.

Thoughts on Beatrice Lillie

Total adoration and utter irritation were present in equal measure in Noël's relationship with BEATRICE LILLIE (1898–1989).

In 1938 he was to direct a Broadway revue, *Set to Music* – a revised version of his 1932 hit *Words and Music*. Bea Lillie was to star in it. It was generally accepted that she was one of the funniest ladies ever to grace the stage but – as Noël was painfully aware – there was a price to be paid. The lady tended not to remember the lines as written. As she was making her own eccentric way to New York, he cabled her:

> OCTOBER 1938
> LADY PEEL
> QUEEN MARY
> PRETTY WITTY LADY PEEL
> NEVER MIND HOW SICK YOU FEEL
> NEVER MIND YOUR BROKEN HEART
> CONCENTRATE AND LEARN YOUR PART

To which she replied:

> THANKS MUSTY DUSTY NOËL C
> FOR BEASTLY WIRE TO LADY P
> TO CONCENTRATE IS HARD I FEAR
> SO NOW SHE'S CRYING IN HER BEER

More than twenty years later Bea was to star as Madame Arcati in *High Spirits* – Martin and Gray's musical version of *Blithe Spirit*, which Noël was directing. By now the problem was even worse. In sheer frustration Noël wrote to Lorn from the Boston try-out:

> Beatrice Lillie is a cunt
> No matter what you've heard
> Beatrice Lillie is a cunt
> And doesn't know a word.
> Beatrice Lillie is a Twat
> Whatever news you've had
> Beatrice Lillie is a Twat
> Who's driving Master mad.

He did not realise until much later that what she was experiencing was not wilful unprofessionalism but the early signs of Alzheimer's disease that would effectively rob her of the last twenty years or so of her long life.

Fortunately, there were happier occasions.

Noël had met the Lunts – ALFRED LUNT (1892–1977) and LYNN FONTANNE (1887–1983) – during his first impoverished visit to New York in 1921. They became immediate friends and Noël's ('Junior') friendship (with 'Grandma' and 'Grandpa') lasted for the rest of Noël's life. Because continents invariably separated them, the cable became a convenient, if extravagant, way to bridge the gap. A typical post-visit greeting might be . . .

> GRANDPA AND GRANDMA TO LEAVE YOU IS SARD
> DON'T BE TOO HARD
> ON THE SILLY OLD BARD
>
> (10 March 1935)

> UPON THIS DATE BY A HAPPY STAR
> DEAR GRANDPA WED DARLING GRANDMAMA
> AND TO SALUTE THESE YEARS OF WEDDED BLISS
> THEIR LOVING JUNIOR SENDS A LOVING KISS
>
> (26 May 1947)

Mutual teasing was always an important element. On Alfred's fiftieth birthday Noël would cable:

HALF A CENTURY HAS SPED
OVER GRANDPA'S SILVER HEAD
SILVER HAIR IS GRANDPA'S SORROW
HERE TODAY – BLACK TOMORROW

Back in 1921 – when they were all just beginning to establish themselves – they had taken a vow that, when they were all stars, Noël would write a play for the three of them to appear in together. In 1933 they fulfilled that ambition with *Design for Living*. At the end of its sold-out New York run Noël sent Alfred and Lynn a farewell cable:

'Darling Alfred, dainty Lynn'

DARLING ALFRED, DAINTY LYNN,
NOW THE HOLIDAYS BEGIN.
THREE SUPERB BUT WEARY HACKS
COMFORTABLY MAY RELAX.
NO MORE SLAPS TO KEEP THE CHIN UP,
NO LONG TRAINS TO TRIP OUR LYNN UP.
LET US THANK BENIGN JEHOVAH
THAT THE LONG, LONG TRAIL IS OVER!

After the superb professionalism of the Lunts, the MARY MARTIN (1913–90) experience came as a dash of cold water.

Mary Martin and Graham Payn in *Pacific 1860*

She'd never left her native America before she came to London in 1946 to star in Noël's first post-war musical at Drury Lane, *Pacific 1860*.

The sweet Texas exterior concealed a tough lady who never understood the character of Elena, the worldly diva she was meant to be playing, who tried to insist on wearing clothes only a Victorian trollop would have worn and whose knowledge of English social etiquette was inadequate at best. On one occasion Noël had to tell her that 'One does *not* say to Princess Margaret – "Give my best to your sister. Bye-bye for now!"'

He got a measure of satisfaction by venting his frustration in verse. ('Sylvia' was actress Sylvia Cecil, who played the diva's companion and confidante.)

I Resent Your Attitude to Mary

I resent your attitude to Mary.
It betrays a very ugly sort of mind.
She is innocent and pure
And her husband, I am sure,
Would consider your behaviour rather crude and most unkind.

He resents and I resent
And all the passers-by resent
Your hideous attitude to Mary.

I resent your attitude to Mary,
You only send her flowers once a day
Tho' her voice is apt to jar,
She's a very famous star
And she's only taking ten per cent for acting in your play.
Tho' her husband's heel is rather hairy,
He does very nicely on her pay.
He resents and she resents
And even Sylvia resents
Your beastly attitude to Mary.

'Our legendary, lovely Marlene'

But perhaps the most enjoyable tribute he ever wrote was the one he delivered to MARLENE DIETRICH (1904–92) on her cabaret debut at London's Café de Paris on 21 June 1954. Their paths had first crossed when – after Noël had made *The Scoundrel* – she phoned him at Goldenhurst, his home in Kent. Thinking it was someone playing a practical joke, he hung up but the next day a cable arrived: 'I SEE YOU EVERY NIGHT AND TALK OF YOU ALL DAY STOP MARLENE'. Hard to resist.

She proved to be a creature of moods. When he sent her a bottle of champagne for her birthday in 1951, he accompanied it with:

> To celebrate your birthday, most adorable Marlene
> I have been to an immense amount of trouble
> To get you this expensive bottle of champagne.
> Please remember that my love's in every bubble.

The lady drank the champagne there and then and dropped the verse in the bin! But three years later she must certainly have appreciated:

Tribute to Marlene Dietrich

> We know God made trees
> And the birds and the bees
> And the seas for the fishes to swim in.
> We are also aware
> That he has quite a flair
> For creating exceptional women.
> When Eve said to Adam
> 'Start calling me Madam'
> The world became far more exciting
> Which turns to confusion
> The modern delusion
> That sex is a question of lighting
> For female allure
> Whether pure or impure
> Has seldom reported a failure
> As I know and you know
> From Venus and Juno
> Right down to la Dame aux Camélias.

> This glamour, it seems,
> Is the substance of dreams
> To the most imperceptive perceiver.
> The Serpent of Nile
> Could achieve with a smile
> Far quicker results than Geneva.
> Though we all might enjoy
> Seeing Helen of Troy
> As a gay, cabaret entertainer
> I doubt that she could
> Be one quarter as good
> As our legendary, lovely Marlene.

Introducing the lady became a virtual alternative career:

I am so happy to be home again and particularly happy to have got back in time for this special occasion, because I have got myself into an absurd habit which, try as I may, I cannot break – the habit of introducing Marlene.

Glamour is an overworked word. Like so many other evocative words, it has been isolated and debased by enthusiastic journalists until today it is used, monotonously and inaccurately, to describe every protuberant starlet who leers at us from the pages of a movie magazine. Nevertheless, authentic glamour is still rare and exciting. It is an abstract quality, evanescent and indefinable, and Marlene possesses more of it than anyone else I know. It endows the brilliance of her technical performance and everything she does with special extra magic.

In all the many years I have belonged to the Theatre I have seen many great stars give many great performances. It is not their performances I remember in detail but certain detached glamorous moments that they emblazoned on my memory for ever and a day.

I can remember when I was very young seeing Gertie Millar flitting across a moonlit stage singing 'Tony from America', Lily Elsie dancing, with ineffable grace, the staircase waltz in *The Count of Luxembourg*, Anna Pavlova flying on to the stage like a living flame in *The Bacchanal* and, in later years, my beloved Gertrude Lawrence, sun-tanned and radiant in a white Molyneux dress, moving towards me across the stage of the Phoenix Theatre in *Private Lives*.

These, and many other moments, I shall always treasure and I like to think that today in London there are young people, and middle-aged ones, too, for that matter who, many years hence, will suddenly say – with a note of fond nostalgia – 'Ah yes – but I remember seeing Marlene Dietrich walk down the stairs of the Café de Paris!'

Marlene apart, Noël often claimed to be metaphorically hag-ridden by actresses of 'a certain age'. For all too many of them it was *Anno Domini* – or at least the perception of it – that brought down the final curtain.

Epitaph for an Elderly Actress

She got in a rage
About age
And retired, in a huff, from the stage.
Which, taken all round, was a pity
Because she was still fairly pretty
But she got in a rage
About age.

She burst into tears
It appears
When the rude, inconsiderate years
Undermined her once flawless complexion
And whenever she saw her reflection
In a mirror, she burst into tears
It appears.

She got in a state
About weight
And resented each morsel she ate.
Her colon she constantly sluiced
And reduced and reduced and reduced
And, at quite an incredible rate,
Put on weight.

She got in a rage
About age
But she still could have played Mistress Page
And she certainly could have done worse
Than *Hay Fever* or Juliet's Nurse

But she got in a terrible rage
About age.

And she moaned and she wept and she wailed
And she roared and she ranted and railed
And retired, very heavily veiled,
From the stage.

(January 15th, 1961)

Critics

'O you chorus of indolent reviewers.'

Tennyson (after Catullus)

'Criticism and Bolshevism have one thing in common. They both seek to pull down that which they could never build.'

Routine for a Critic (Dirge)

Night after night my weary body slumps
Into my usual complimentary seat,
Hedged in by those I envy and detest,
The rich, the 'chic', the fashionably dressed,
The over-publicised, effete, elite,
Shrill-voiced young introverts,
Authors and actors reeking with success,
Earning ten times my income more or less
And stumbling, as they pass, across my feet.

Night after night when I have judged the play
And sent 'collect' a cable to New York on it,
Stated my opinion, burnt my boats,
Typed out my notice from my programme notes
And maybe written out a broadcast talk on it,
I then go home to my suburban wife,
Still querulous, still having 'change of life'.
Still in the pink kimono with a stork on it.

Night after night I go to sleep and dream
My latest play has been a huge success,
I see myself, a flower in my lapel,
Returning to my luxury hotel,
Wearing, as usual, my faultless evening dress.
The lift boys bow to me, the waiters beam,
They know and I know that soon I'll be knighted.
Also they're all aware I've been invited
To champagne supper with a Duchess.

There was one, however, who committed the cardinal critical sin. Mr JAMES AGATE (1877–1947) was the legendary critic of the London *Sunday Times* . . .

To Mr James Agate

(to an eminent critic)

Mr James Agate
Arrived late
As a matter of fact
He missed half the first Act.
Then, in the Circle Bar,
Whence Bacchus beckoned,
He missed most of the Second,
Discussing Milton's blindness,
Thus going too far
From which I reckoned
That he would skip the Third
But I was wrong, far worse occurred,
He fell asleep!
There in his seat on the aisle
He dozed awhile,
Authors may weep
At such unkindness
But other than author's tears;
The ghosts of earlier years,
His own shades, his proprietary ghosts
Whom he reveres;
All those of whom he boasts
Of having seen, remembered; those would cry
More bitterly, more sorrowfully than I.
His Sarah, his Réjane and his Rachel,
(He can't remember her but he can tell
Many an anecdote
About her, and can quote
From *Phèdre*
Alas, he never quotes from *Cavalcedre*!)
How these would sob
To see so 'vrai' a critic,

> So 'blasé' a critic,
> So 'gonflé' a critic
> Let down his job!

Nor were his comments confined to the footlights. The silver screen also inspired his occasional ire:

Lines to a Film Censor (1940)

> I do not care for Mr Green,
> I think his mind must be obscene.
> His moral muscles only flex
> At phrases relevant to sex.
> He may be old. He may be young,
> But to his ears the English tongue
> Is not important in the least –
> The man is palpably a beast.
> To him, the movie world's misuse
> Of English words is no abuse.
> He shudders not at 'lounge' or 'phone'
> But if illicit love be shown
> With all of its sad, frustrated dreams,
> He wriggles, squirms and yells and screams.
> He does not flinch – as who would not? –
> At 'Pardon me' and 'Thanks a lot',
> His dull, unpleasing mind forgives
> A stream of split infinitives
> But should you show the facts of life,
> A secret love, a faithless wife,
> And should you, by a word, imply
> The truths that often underlie
> The surface of our mortal span,
> This mediocre little man
> Gives vent to his unpleasant spleen
> And absolutely cuts the scene.
> The reason British pictures are
> From Uruguay to Zanzibar
> From the Antipodes to Hull

Renowned for being slow and dull
And famed as well for their uncouth
Evasion of the slightest truth
Can, I am sure, be swiftly traced
To the dishonest, double-faced
Most prurient and most obscene
Licentious mind of Mr Green.
Can no one quench the moral fire
Of Thomas Bloody Green, Esquire?

In the scheme of things it should not be overlooked that there was a time when Noël was himself a critic – albeit a young one and in verse . . .

Novel by Baroness Orczy
(1865–1947)

In Revolutionary times
The thriller plot is laid.
The mob commit appalling crimes,
Entirely undismayed.
The things they do are awfully mean,
They rob, they burn, they guillotine.
In blood and anything obscene
They positively wade.

The hero gets in awful scrapes
And then from every scrape
Miraculously he escapes
With charming *savoir-faire*.
In many ways he's quite a lad,
His oaths are often frightfully bad.
He even says 'Zounds!' and 'Egad!'
And never turns a hair.

If ever he is in a fix,
He's but to raise a hand
When there, before you've counted six,
Appears his gallant band.
Tho' some are big and some are small
And some are short and some are tall,

There's no denying one and all –
They are a gallant band.

His wife, the Heroine, is sweet
But through her having blabbed
And generally been indiscreet,
She gets her husband nabbed.
Then, stricken with immense remorse,
She quickly sees her only course
Is to deliver him by force!
Thus, she gets also grabbed.

They put her in a prison cell
And tell her she must die.
She screams – 'The Scarlet Pimpernel
Will do you in the eye.'
These words make all the gaolers gape.
Meanwhile, her husband with some tape
Assists her to make her escape.

When back in their Ancestral Halls
Her fluttering heart he calms.
He strokes her lily hand and falls
A victim to her charms.
She tells him that the wrong she's done
Was only meant for girlish fun.
He playfully says – 'You are a "one"'
And takes her in his arms.

The Garden of Allah
(after Robert Hichens 1864–1950)

The Heroine's delightful,
She's never terse or spiteful.
Her blood's a most artistic shade of blue.
She seldom kicks her mother
Or ill-treats her younger brother,
Things more vulgar-minded people
Often do.

She has distinguished ideals,
She never sups off Fried Eels
(A dish that her relations often guzzle).
She reads a lot of books on
Hygienics, and she looks on
This life as an enigma, or a puzzle.

(*The Scarlet Pimpernel* was first a play, then a best-selling novel [1905] that spawned several sequels. *The Garden of Allah* [1904] was another romantic potboiler that caught the popular mood of the time.)

Words...

Noël could never be accused of being a literary snob. A great reader all his life – as his library attests – he had eclectic taste. He always claimed that his favourite writer was E. Nesbit, the Edwardian writer of children's books and, indeed, a much-thumbed copy of her *The Enchanted Castle* was on his bedside table when he died.

Nonetheless, there were certain writers who made their appearances in supporting roles over the years in the Coward canon.

RUDYARD KIPLING (1865–1936) crops up surprisingly often. Something in Kipling's unquestioning jingoism had a great appeal from the start and when the sun finally began to set on writer and Empire alike, Noël found the adjustment a difficult one to make.

In the beginning, though, since the foundations were rock solid, there was no harm in a little parody . . .

Tarantella
(Re: Kipling)

There's a funny little temple
On a sultry Indian road
Where the *Jugarees* are waving in the breeze.
There's a dusky dark-eyed *Dowli*
In a *Raigyput* abode
And she sings amid the humming of the bees.
Midst the humming of the bees
And the rustling of the trees
This passion loving *Dowli*
Sits a-singing cross the seas.
She has washed her old chemise
And hung it on the trees
And the sight of it has only
Stilled the humming of the bees.

I had loved her very madly
When in India's sunny clime
And she worshipped only
Dowli's will.
But altho' I know she wants me,

Now I do not care a damn,
For the memory of her husband makes me ill,
Makes me absolutely ill.
How I panted down that hill
And that horrid man pursuing me
With all intents to kill.
So I hid myself until
He had passed the sugar mill
And to all intents and purposes
He's running down there still!

The author adds the following explanations:

Jugarees – plants which give forth strong odour
Dowli – a female hippopotamus or a slave girl – in the above case it is the latter
Raigyput – dilapidated, odorous, spicy!

Boots
(Re: Kipling)

We're foot-slog-slog-slog-slogging over Africa
Foot-slog-slog-slog-slogging over Africa
Boots-Boots-Boots-Boots moving up and down again
There's no discharge in the War.

Seven-six-eleven-five-nine-and-twenty mile today,
Four-eleven-seventeen-thirty-two the day before.
Boots-Boots-Boots-Boots moving up and down again,
There's no discharge in the War.

Don't-Don't-Don't-Don't look at what's in front of you.
Boots-Boots-Boots-Boots moving up and down again,
Men-Men-Men-Men go mad with watching 'em,
There's no discharge in the War.

We-can-stick-out hunger, thirst and weariness
But not-not-not-not the chronic sight of 'em
Boots-Boots-Boots-Boots moving up and down again,
There's no discharge in the War.

T'ain't-so-bad-by-day because of company
But night brings long strings of forty thousand million
Boots-Boots-Boots-Boots moving up and down again,
There's no discharge in the War.

I-have-marched-six-weeks in 'Ell to certify
It-is-not-fire-devils, dark or anything
Boots-Boots-Boots-Boots moving up and down again,
There's no discharge in the War.

And then, of course, there was the Bard ('my colleague Will') . . .

A Question of Values

Christopher Marlowe or Francis Bacon
   The author of *Lear* remains unshaken
Willie Herbert or Mary Fitton
   What does it matter? The Sonnets were written.

One of the great loves of Noël's life, it seems, was the first Queen Elizabeth – closely followed by ER II! He read everything about her he could lay his hands on and said (according to Cole Lesley): 'I think we should have got on, don't you? I don't think I should have been frightened of her, I should have stood up to her and I think I could have made her laugh.'

His interest extended to people who surrounded her, particularly those who seemed able to combine their courtly duties with the penning of lyrical poetry. There were, however, occasions when he felt he had over-indulged and it drove him to rhymed parody of what he had just read:

After a Surfeit of Sir Philip Sidney

Oh womb from which hath 'merged
My true love chaste
By love hath not begat
My old time's waste.

... and Music

It would be true to say that Noël was not an enormous fan of classical music.

Gilda   People are wrong when they say that opera isn't what it used to be. It is what it used to be – that's what's wrong with it.

Design for Living (1933)

'I can't bear Mozart. I know I'm missing a lot, but that can't be helped . . . all too often it sounds like a Pekinese peeing on a mink rug.'

'Not a tremendous Wagnerian on account of getting fidgety . . . I wish he'd get on with it.'

'There has never yet been composed a piece of classical music that was not too long.'

He summed up his feelings in:

Opera Notes

I feel inclined to send a teeny-weeny
Admonishment to dear Signor Bellini
For having seriously tried to form a
Coherent opera from *Norma*.
I think we must face the fact that the *Carmen* by Bizet
Is no more Spanish than the Champs-Elysées.

Should I desire to be driven mad
I'd book a seat for *Herodiade*
Which, although it's by Massenet who wrote *Manon*,
Is really not a good thing to plan on
And gives me, by and large, more claust-
 rophobia than *Faust*.

I often say, for which opera lovers attack me,
That if I were a soprano I'd let them sack me
Before I'd sing *Lakmé*.

Nobody could bear to read a
Detailed synopsis of *Aida*
And we all know the plot of *La Gioconda*
Is apt to wander.
But neither of these so arch and sticky is
As *Gianni Schicchi* is.

Though Wolfgang Mozart wrote *The Magic Flute* he
Alas, alas, composed *Cosí Fan Tutte*
The roguishness of which is *piu piu male*
Than *Don Pasquale*
But then poor Donizetti
Was likewise not
Too hot
At choosing libretti.

Then there are those *Rosenkavaliers* and *Fledermauses*
Written by all those Strausses
Which play to crowded houses
And, to me, are louses.
There couldn't be a sillier story
Than *Il Travatore*.
And yet, and yet, and yet Oh
Just think of the libretto
Of *Rigoletto*!
Both of these were set to music by Verdi
How dared he?
On the other hand we must admit that *Thaïs*
Is more concaïs
And fairly naïs.

We must also admit that every Victorian hurdy-gurdy
Owes a deep debt of gratitude to Giuseppe Verdi.

...and a Literary Footnote

Noël's friendship with GRAHAM GREENE (1904–91) was a late flowering. In the 1940s – when Greene was a theatre and film critic for the *Spectator* – Noël wrote the following after 'two very unpleasant attacks on me and my work':

The Ballad of Graham Greene

Oh there's many a heart beats faster, lads,
And swords from their sheaths flash keen
When round the embers – the glowing embers –
Men crouch at Hallowe'en.
And suddenly somebody remembers
The name of Graham Greene.
(A literary disaster lads
The fall of Graham Greene.)

Oh, there's many a Catholic Priest, my boys,
And many a rural Dean
Who, ages later – long ages later
When all has been, has been –
Will secretly read an old *Spectator*
And pray for Graham Greene.
(Let's hope its sales have decreased, my boys
Because of Graham Greene.)

One asks oneself and one's God, my lads,
Was ever a mind so mean,
That could have vented – so shrilly vented –
Such quantities of spleen
Upon a colleague? Unprecedented!
Poor Mr Graham Greene.
(One's pride forbids one to nod, my lads
To Mr Graham Greene.)

Oh there's many a bitter smile, my boys
And many a sneer obscene
When any critic – a first-rate critic,
Becomes a 'Might have been'

Through being as harsh and Jesuitic
As Mr Graham Greene.
(Restrain that cynical smile, my boys,
To jeer is never worth while, my boys.
Remember the rising bile, my boys,
Of Mr Graham Greene.)

. . . and in a private communication:

'Dear Mr Graham Greene, I yearn'

Dear Mr Graham Greene, I yearn
So much to know why you should burn
With such fierce indignation at
This very fact that I exist.
I've been unable to resist
Sitting up later than I need
To read in the *Spectator* what
Appears to be no more, no less
Than shocking manners. I confess
Bewilderment. I've seldom seen
Another brother-writer press
Such disadvantage with such mean
Intent to hurt. You must have been
For years, in secret nourishing
A rich, rip-snorting, flourishing
Black hatred for my very guts!
Surely all these envenomed cuts
At my integrity and taste
Must be a waste of your own time?
What is my crime, beyond success?
(But you have been successful too
It can't be that) I know a few
Politer critics than yourself
Who simply hate my lighter plays
But do they state their sharp dispraise
With such surprising, rising bile?
Oh dear me no, they merely smile.
A patronising smile perhaps

But then these journalistic chaps
Unlike ourselves, dear Mr Greene,
(Authors I mean) are apt to sneer
At what they fear to be apart
From that which they conceive as art.
You have described (also with keen,
Sadistic joy) my little book
About Australia, one look
At which should prove, all faults aside,
That I had tried, Dear Mr Greene,
To do a job. You then implied
That I had run away, afraid,
A renegade. I can't surmise
Why you should view your fellow men
With such unfriendly, jaundiced eyes.
But then, we're strangers. I can find
No clue, no key to your dark mind.
I've read your books as they appear
And I've enjoyed them. (Nearly all.)
I've racked my brains in a sincere
But vain endeavour to recall
If, anytime or anywhere,
In Bloomsbury or Belgrave Square,
In Paris or Peking or Bude,
I have, unwittingly, been rude,
Or inadvertently upset you.
(Did I once meet you and forget you?
Have I ever been your debtor?
Did you once write me a letter
That I never got – or what?)
If I knew, I shouldn't worry.
All this anguish, all this flurry,
This humiliating scene
That I'm making, Mr Greene,
Is a plea for explanation
For a just justification
By what strange Gods you feel yourself empowered
To vent this wild expenditure of spleen
Upon your most sincerely
Noël Coward.

8.

'I Travel Alone'

'I have never liked living anywhere all the year round.'

'My body has certainly wandered a good deal, but I have an uneasy suspicion that my mind has not wandered nearly enough.'

Present Indicative (1937)

> 'Why oh why, do the wrong people travel
> When the right people stay back home?'
> *Sail Away* (1961)

> Travel, they say, improves the mind.
> An irritating platitude
> Which frankly, entre nous
> Is very far from true . . .

Noël himself was an inveterate traveller from his twenties on. In many ways he benefited from the fact that travel meant ocean travel. You got on a ship and you stayed on a ship. The other passengers became your neighbours for a predetermined period and an object study for an observant writer.

In an era of air travel it's hard to imagine something similar.

He was also able to explore areas of the world that were presently unspoiled by 'sun tan oil and the gurgle of Coca-Cola'. But as the years went by a certain self-doubt crept in . . .

> Was this the ship that lauched a thousand faces
> Upon the bosom of the seven seas?
> Was this the ship that bore to far off places
> The scum of culture-keen democracies?

The 'wrong people' were beginning to outnumber the 'right people'. Perhaps it was time to 'stay back home'. Nonetheless, he carried on almost to the end in his search for 'that distant shore'.

On Leaving England for the First Time

> When I left England first, long years ago,
> I looked back at the swiftly fading shore
> And suddenly, quite without warning, knew
> That I was sad at leaving. It is true
> That I was on holiday, no war
> Was dragging me abroad, but even so!
> How strange it was. How strange it is, this strong,
> Deep-rooted feeling, for one's native land.
> When is it born? Why should it come to flower
> So inconveniently just at the hour
> Of parting? I have grown to understand
> In later years, after so many long,
> Far journeyings. But on that distant day

When first I felt that unexpected, gentle
Tug at my heart, I tried to keep at bay
Such foolishness and, as I turned away,
Laughed at myself for being unsentimental.
(1942)

An ocean cruise in the 1930s was a cosmos. You met the world and his wife – if, indeed, she was his wife. All human life was there.

In the second of his verse odysseys Noël takes us aboard that floating village, a P&O liner on its voyage from Shanghai to London's Tilbury docks, and shares the comings and goings of its villagers in their 'appointed places' forced to rub shoulders and rub along in ways they would go to infinite social pains to avoid back in the Old Country.

Even now there are hints of what is to come, 'remembering other voyages long ago'. A world in which social distinctions will become blurred – but not yet, not quite yet . . .

P&O 1930

The siren hoots three times its final warning
The first one long, the second two much shorter.
The passengers at the rail are suddenly stunned
Staring disconsolately at the Shanghai Bund
As the widening gulf of yellow river water
Between the ship and the shore
Presses its back upon its usual day
Painted kites fly in the windy morning,
The ceaseless bustle and the ceaseless noise
The clanking trams, the cries of rickshaw boys
Grow faint. But long before
The black and khaki ship is underway
The aggressive bugles bray
Announcing 'Tiffin', while the passengers
Obedient and docile
Regardless of where he or she prefers
To sit, politely file
Like gentle horses entering their stables
To their appointed places at the tables.

Lines of chairs on the promenade deck,
Smell of engine room rising through hatches,
Mrs Blake, with a sunburnt neck,
Organising Shuffleboard matches,
Missionaries with pale, kind eyes,
Drained of colour by savage skies,

Strumming militantly glum
Hymns on a harmonium.

Flying fish from the bow waves skittering,
Mrs Frobisher's endless tittering
And at night the great stars glittering.

Bugles blowing, deafening, instant,
The Governor's Lady amiable but distant,
Returning home for six months' leave
A necessary all too brief reprieve
From State Receptions, Women's Federations,
Official visits to remote plantations,
From garden-parties under alien trees
And mocking, inefficient ADCs.
Again the bugle's unrelenting blast,
Brown-sailed junks and sampans sailing past,
Clanging of ship's bells signalling the Watches,
Poor Mrs Vining's unbecoming blotches;
All her own fault, when all is said and done,
For sleeping on the boat-deck in the sun.
Mrs Ashpole, tremulously eager,
To poor out the minutiae of her meagre
Unreflective, imperceptive mind.
Major Morpeth, coarse and unrefined,
Mrs Morpeth, timid and retiring,
Both their daughters earnestly perspiring.
Colonel Wintringham, supreme at sports,
Tremendous knees beneath tremendous shorts,
Tremendous hands, tremendous calves and thighs
And small, submissive, vulnerable eyes.
Soup and water-biscuits at eleven,
Scampering of children over seven,
A fenced-in pen for children under five,
A frail old woman more dead than alive
Uninterested, withdrawn from social dramas,
Patiently tended by two Chinese Amahs.

Flying fish from the bow waves skittering,
Mrs Frobisher's endless tittering

'I Travel Alone'

And at night the great stars glittering.

In Hong Kong, Mrs Ashpole
Had an alarming experience
Which, without reticence,
After the ship had sailed again
She recounted in the saloon.
It appeared that she had lunched
At the Peninsula Hotel
(Which she knew well)
In Kowloon
And that later,
Crossing the harbour in the ferry
An American in a tussore suit said a very
Unpleasant word.
At first she imagined that she hadn't heard
Correctly
And said politely, circumspectly
'I beg your pardon'
Whereupon he lewdly winked his eye
And, believe it or not,
Actually pinched her thigh!
Apparently she practically fainted
And if the ferry hadn't happened to reach the landing
At that very moment
She didn't know what she'd have done.
At all events she left him standing
And went off at a run
Feeling humiliated
And, you know, sort of tainted!
Fortunately she remembered
That she kept handy
In her bag
A tiny flask of brandy
From which she felt compelled to take a nip
In the rickshaw on the way back to the ship.

The ship arrived at dawn in Singapore
But in the city day had long begun
The wider streets were bland and empty still

But shops, beneath the flaking green arcades,
Blazed the shrill colours of their merchandise.
Dark rain clouds, harassed by the quickening light
Moved off across the flat metallic sea
And crouched upon the far horizon's edge
Like trained but savage circus animals
Awaiting sullenly their next performance.
Colonel Wintringham, in spotless drill,
Snuffing the air like an escaping prisoner,
Stepped firmly from the gangway to the dock
And strode, epitome of just authority,
Through raucous crowds of hotel porters, priests,
Beggars, vendors of bright, unlikely fruits
Sellers of silks and cottons, ornaments
Tortoise-shell and oriental beads
And, hailing a rickshaw boy in brisk Malay,
Settled himself at ease and bowled away.

> Superficially like the sailor
> With a wife in every port
> Colonel Wintringham could depend
> On finding an understanding friend
> From Cape Town to Venezuela
> Of a rather special sort.
> The ship didn't sail till seven
> And desire, like a rising stream,
> Flooded Colonel Wintringham's kind,
> Unregenerate, private mind.
> And Oh for the secret heaven!
> And Oh for the secret dream!

The siren hoots three times its final warning
The first one long, the second too much shorter,
Passengers at the deck rail waved to friends
New life begins before the old life ends.
The lights reflected in the harbour water
Like yellow serpents twist
And Colonel Wintringham stands
As spick and span as, in the far-off morning,
He'd set forth with his demons clambering

His body tense, his pulse is hammering,
To his peculiar tryst
Now, only the faintest tremor of his hands
Betray his recent, ardent sarabands.
Whistles are blown, the bugles shrilly bray again
The harbour sounds fade in the freshening breeze,
The crowded dock begins to slide away again.
Impassively the Colonel hears and sees
The last 'Good-byes', the coloured streamers fluttering
And two pale nuns interminably muttering.

Mrs Macomber in her steamer chair
Closed her tired eyes against the burning sky
And looked back over eighty-seven years
To when she was a child in Winchelsea.
The house was long and low, or so it seemed,
There was a sunken garden with small paths
Winding among bright flower beds, and beyond
The lichened red-brick wall, an old, old tree
Stretched out its branches to the distant sea.
An orchard lay behind the house and Spring
Scattered its shaded grass with primroses
Later the catkins and the bluebells came
And there was a wooden swing.
The memories of different years and different flowers
In different gardens flowed into her mind . . .

> Five planter's children playing Hide and Seek
> Ran shrieking back and forth along the deck
> White-coated stewards swooped between the chairs
> Delivering bowls of soup and sandwiches.

But Mrs Macomber stayed behind her eyes
Removed from all disturbance, quiet and still
Remembering other voyages long ago,
Remembering the walled city of Pekin
When first she went to live there as a bride;
The lacquered temples on the Western hills,
The early morning rides;
Watching the dawn
Staining with light the terracotta plains;

The Empress Dowager, sharp and malign,
Monstrously attired in Highland tartan
Receiving Ministers at four a.m.
And Mac, beloved Mac, in full court dress
Cursing Imperial capriciousness.
And then the children growing up and leaving
To cross these same warm seas to go to school;
The loving, dying, marrying and grieving,
The happy moments and the empty hours
Waiting for the news from England, waiting alone
In that blank echoing house in Wei Hai Wei.
Then suddenly, quite suddenly, when Mac was killed,
Becoming aware that youth and middle-age
Had slipped into the past and were no more
And that there was little to look forward to
Beyond the changing seasons and the cold,
Niggardly compensations of the old
Mrs Macomber in her steamer chair
Closing her eyes against the burning sky
Knew, without terror and without despair
That the time had come for her to die.

Mrs Macomber was laid to rest at four forty-five p.m.
The ship reduced its speed and slowly, slowly came to a halt.
The missionaries provided a suitable Requiem
And a little grey cat ran out of a hatch which wasn't anyone's fault.
The Captain read the service which was mercifully brief.
The coffin slid into the water from under its covering flag
And one of the Chinese Amahs, assaulted by sudden grief,
Fumbled to find a handkerchief in a little beaded bag.
Mrs Frobisher summed it all up that afternoon at tea
'There's nothing more impressive', she said, 'than a burial at sea.'

> The ship pursues its course, the days go by
> Romances bloom, tensions intensify.
> Mrs Macgrath and Mrs Drage have words
> Cawing and spluttering like angry birds
> Until Mrs Drage, with mottled, scarlet neck
> Utters a strangled cry and leaves the deck.
> That dreadful girl in the revealing jumper

'I Travel Alone'

Who had to be sent home from Kuala Lumpur
Is found, inside a lifeboat after dinner
Recumbent in the arms of Major Skinner.
Amusements are relentlessly devised
A Deck Quoits tournament is organised,
Competitors are bidden to confab in
The sacred precincts of the captain's cabin.
A dance is given, fancy dress 'de rigueur'
And Colonel Wintringham, his massive figure
Draped in a towel of enormous size
Coyly accepts the consolation prize.
The Deck Quoits tournament is fought and won
By Mr Frith and Mrs Cuthbertson.
The ship pursues its course, nights follow days,
The five-piece orchestra tirelessly plays
Selections from the classics, German *lieder*,
'Les Cloches de Corneville', 'Celeste Aida'
And, as a musical salute to Asia,
Extracts from *The Mikado* and *The Geisha*.

Colombo, viewed from the approaching ship
Looked, in the distance, like bright coloured stones
Flung on to emerald and cinnabar hills
Behind which, serried ranks of mountains stood
Some of them veiled in cloud and some quite clear
Sharply defined against the morning sky.
Mrs Frobisher, wearing shaded tones
Of pink and lavender, adorned with frills,
Emitting girlishly her usual trills
Of unprovoked amusement stepped ashore
Escorted by the victorious Mr Frith
Who'd given Mrs Cutherbertson the slip
 And, needing someone to go shopping with,
Had offered his services as cavalier.
Mrs Frobisher knew Colombo well
And, prior to lunch at the Galle Face Hotel
Led him immediately to a store
Where a be-turbaned, dark-eyed Bengalese
Welcomed them with soft, obsequious sighs
And emptied from little chamois leather sacks

A scintillating, miscellaneous flood
Of zircons, amethysts, aquamarines,
Star sapphires, rubies pale as watered blood,
Opals, agates, cat's eyes, tourmalines
And cultured pearls as big as garden peas.
Poor Mr Frith stared glumly at the stacks
Of gems, so few of which he could afford,
And wished to God that he'd remained on board.
However, after arguing awhile,
Appraising each small stone from every angle,
The Bengalese, to Mr Frith's surprise,
Smiled with a patient, understanding smile
And finally agreed to compromise.
A set of tourmalines for Mrs Frith
(Later to be set into a bangle)
Eight zircons, carefully matched, later to be
Fashioned with cunning ingenuity
Into some studs and links for evening dress,
Not flashy, mind you, but discreetly sober.
Then Mr Frith, dazed by his own largesse,
Gave Mrs Frobisher an opal pin
(Quite safe because her birth month was October).
The whole lot, plus a garnet crucifix
The Bengalese obligingly threw in,
Cost twenty-seven pounds, thirteen and six.

The Governor's Lady's steamer chair
Is set a little apart
And day after day she sits in it
And reads in it and knits in it
With a chiffon scarf to protect her hair
And loneliness in her heart.

She is sick of tropical greenery
And everything Asiatic
She is tired of lizards and parakeets,
Scarlet hibiscus and tom-tom beats
And her eyes are aching for scenery
That's a little less dramatic.

  She seems immune from despairs and joys

'I Travel Alone'

Her bones are brittle with breeding.
It isn't easy to reconcile
Her unexpected, disarming smile
With the hard façade of her social poise
Which is definitely misleading.

She answers politely when addressed
Her coat has a Redfern label.
Inwardly timorous and shy
She goes through life with her head held high
And, indestructibly self-possessed,
Dines at the Captain's table.

The voyage continues, still the bugles blow,
Meal follows meal, the temperature below
Rises to quite unprecedented heights
Curbing the most voracious appetites.

Mrs Drage, as though felled by a truncheon
Faints at the Purser's table during luncheon.
Outside, the Indian Ocean, stretched like glass,
Beneath a carapace of burnished brass,
Heaves with a gentle, oily under-swell
And Mrs Vining, feeling far from well
Suddenly gives a cry, clutches her head,
And runs precipitately to her bed.

But every evening, cold or hot,
Whether the sea is rough or not
Mrs Burden, Mr Knapp
(The one that wears the yachting cap),
Mr Haggerty from Rangoon,
Travelling with Mr Witherspoon,
Bobby Green and 'Nutty' Boyle
(Agents, both, from Standard Oil)
Mr Randall, Harry Mott,
And tiny Mr Appendrodt
Come rain, come shine, come joy, come doom,
Assemble in the smoking-room.

A word must be said for Mrs Rhys-Cunningham
Who embarked on the ship at Bombay

Accompanied by the Viscount Harringford,
The Honourable Evan and Mrs Blair
And a little bird-like man called Ossie Blenkinsop
Who was the life and soul of the party
And made comments on everybody and everything
In a high-pitched, rather affected voice.
They had all been staying with some Maharajah
And Mrs Rhys-Cunningham and Mrs Blair
Appeared each night at dinner in different saris
Gossamer light, magenta, yellow and blue,
Threaded with gold and silver. Even the men
Wore tokens of their host's munificence;
Ossie had links like golden lotuses,
Blair and Lord Harringford, square signet rings
Of intricately carved chalcedony.
In the saloon they graced a separate table
Around which stewards hovered, thick as bees,
Tensed to anticipate their slightest wishes
Eagerly plying them with special dishes.
Lord Harringford had lustreless, blond hair
Smoothed back from a benign but narrow forehead
And, though his complexion was a trifle florid,
He had a certain charm, also of course
One felt he looked much better on a horse.
Unlike the Honourable Evan Blair
Who seemed, by Nature, wrought for an arm-chair.
Mrs Blair was definitely jolly,
Thick-set and freckled with a raucous laugh,
One saw her tramping Dartmoor with a collie
Or, in some stately hall festooned with holly,
Handing out Christmas presents to the staff.

> Mrs Rhys-Cunningham's widowed state
> Made little appeal for pity
> Her taste in clothes was immaculate,
> Her income, more than adequate
> And her face extremely pretty.
>
> Of weariness she showed no trace
> In spite of her Indian Odysseys

Her figure was slim and moved with grace
Along the deck's restricted space
Like one of the minor goddesses.
She and her party remained aloof
Preoccupied and serene
From the *va-et-vient* and the warp and woof,
The daily recurring *Opéra Bouffe*
Of shipboard's defined routine.

So sure they were, so secure they were
So ineffably centrifugal
So set apart from the common weal,
Never in time for any meal
Disdainful of gong or bugle.

They failed to observe the look of hate
The lips so cynically curved,
Tantalisingly intimate
They giggled and talked and stayed up late
Enclosed in their private world.

Between Bombay and the Gulf of Aden
An unexpected storm pounced in the night
And, seizing the ship like a ratting terrier,
Shook it and savaged it. The tranquil sea
As though bored by its own monotony
Rose up and, whipped by the shrieking wind,
Changed into ambulant, grey mountain peaks
Advancing endlessly, and in between
Their walls of grim implacability
Fell sickening valleys streaked with veins of foam.
The ship, reducing speed, received the first
Violent assault with shuddering acquiescence,
Pitching and tossing, rolling drunkenly,
Battered and bruised, sodden with flying spray,
She stubbornly proceeded on her way.
The cabins creaked and groaned: vases of flowers
Flew through the air as though endowed with wings,
Avalanches of books and toilet things
Tumbled on to the sleepers in their bunks
While, in the baggage room, enormous trunks

Rumbled and crashed with each vibrating roll.
Mrs Macgrath, who left her porthole open,
Woke with a scream to see her lamé dress
Swirling about like some strange jellyfish
Together with her stockings, shoes and stays.

Poor Mr Frith sustained a nasty graze
When the large plate of fruit he always kept
Handy beside his bunk, suddenly leapt
And struck him on the temple while he slept.
Colonel Wintringham, in a sarong
Which gave due freedom to his massive legs
And left his body bare, awoke to find
A broken bottle of green brilliantine
Clotting the matted hair upon his chest
Where it malignantly had come to rest.
Mrs Frobisher arose and dressed
Uttering little moans and staggering,
The cabin stifled her, it lurched and heaved
Flinging her to and fro like a rag doll.
When finally her object was achieved
She sank disconsolate on her bunk
Armed with lifebelt and two winter coats,
And waited to be conducted to the boats.
Meanwhile the Governor's Lady, unafraid,
Asked the night stewardess to call her maid.
All the next day the hurricane continued,
Screamed through the rigging, tore at the plunging masts,
Hatches were battened down, the deck doors guarded
By weary stewards, empowered to prevent
Foolhardy passengers with iron stomachs
From venturing out to photograph the sea.
In the saloon 'fiddles' encased the tables,
Ropes were stretched taut across the creaking decks,
Stewards and stewardesses with covered basins
Swayed doggedly along the corridors
Moving unflurried through familiar hells
Of retchings, groaning and incessant bells.
In the deserted lounge, in time for tea,
The five-piece orchestra, reduced to three,

'I Travel Alone'

Valiantly and to its undying glory
Obliged with *Tosca* and *Il Trovatore*.
In the later afternoon, capriciously,
The storm clouds parted on the starboard beam
Revealing a strip of blue, unflurried sky.

An hour later, in a blaze of sun
The ship still wallowed, but the storm was done.
The sun beats down on Aden. The port officials drip,
The dusty buildings sizzle in the heat,
The grimy, black coal barges crowd obscenely round the ship
Like gaping coffins on a metal sheet.
The town has few attractions: no shaded avenues,
No fascinating vistas to explore.
The passengers have only two alternatives to choose,
To suffocate on board or go ashore.
Those who decide the latter is the less repellent plan
From the point of view of culture, draw a blank,
For they find the arid town has little more to offer than
Two so-called mermaids in a dingy tank.
These strange mis-shapen creatures, constricted and morose,
Hauled up long since in some bewildering net
Stare fishily, unseeingly, when visitors draw close,
Grateful at least, at least, for being wet.
Just before evening when the brazen sky begins to cool
The ship sails and the harbour fades from view
Astern, the wake, unwinding like white ribbon from a spool
Stretches and coils upon the deepening blue
And Aden, stumbling back against the night
Suddenly beautiful, sinks out of sight.

> From either bank of the Suez Canal
> The desert marches to the sky
> And, on the interminable sand
> Stretching away to the Promised Land
> Lean, meditative Arabs stand
> Watching the ships go by.
> So narrow is the waterway
> You feel that by stretching out an arm
> You could touch the hovels of mud and clay

Or pick a date from a dusty palm.
On the other side, beyond the day,
Beyond the night, the Sahara spills,
Beyond immediate prophecy
So far as to challenge Infinity
Until it at last, at last gives way
To lakes and beginnings of hills,
And then the tropics where coloured birds
Swift in flight as a falling star
Swooping over lumbering elephant herds
And the fevered jungles of Africa.

At Port Said, Mr Frith and Mrs Frobisher
Who'd been inseparable since Colombo
Strolled in the evening through crowded streets,
Mrs Frobisher dressed to the nines
Looking about her eagerly for signs
Indicative of strange exotic vices
For which the unattractive little town
Had, quite inaccurately, won renown.
They sat outside a café eating ices
Badgered by beggars and by fortune-tellers
By urchins bearing trays of vivid sweets
By servile Oriental carpet-sellers
Whose voices fluctuated with their prices.
The 'Gully-Gully' merchant's mumbo-jumbo
Left them depressed and dully mystified.
They watched, with lassitude, the agile tricks
Vanishing coins, recurrent baby chicks,
All the impressive, boring sleight of hand
Which nobody could ever understand.
Later they rose, jostled by 'lesser breeds'
Deafened by mendicant, subservient whining
And saw Mrs Macgrath and Mrs Vining
Bargaining for synthetic amber beads.
Presently Colonel Wintringham went by
Striding with back erect and shoulders high
And, trotting purposefully by his side,
A picturesque but dubious Arab guide.
Mrs Rhys-Cunningham wandered through the crowd

'I Travel Alone'

Accompanied by Ossie and the Blairs
Who, when Mrs Frobisher politely bowed
Acknowledged her with vaguely puzzled stares.
A seedy man drew Mr Frith apart
And swiftly flashed before his startled gaze
A snapshot of an ageing Syrian tart
Placidly naked, fastening her stays.
Later they tried to dissipate their gloom
With champagne cocktails in their smoking-room.

The Mediterranean welcomed the ship
And flattered her with promises
Of cleaner airs and fresher winds
And Europe drawing slowly closer.
Deck games were played with keener zest
And here and there fur coats appeared
And one dark night on the starboard side
Stromboli, spurting flame, defied
The gentle sea and the quiet sky.
Later the mountains of Sicily
Painted lavender shadows against
A blazing sunset of green and rose.
The Shuffleboard finals came and went
With Mrs Blake the ultimate winner.
The second prize went to Major Skinner
And the Captain gave a gala dinner.
After Marseilles the atmosphere on board
Altered perceptibly. In the saloon
Passengers, by mutual accord
Tacitly moved from their allotted places,
Closed up the ranks, filled in the gaps, ignored
The hitherto stern protocol, and soon
Banished from memory the familiar faces
Of those who had so treacherously planned
To leave the ship and go home overland.
Europe slid by upon the starboard side
To port, Africa hid below the sea
Gibraltar rose impressive, dignified
Knowing no rising sun could ever set
On such a symbol of Imperial pride

On such invulnerable majesty.
That night, the Rock, an ebon silhouette
Through Colonel Wintringham's binoculars
Vanished at last among the swaying stars.
The Bay of Biscay, true to form
Behaved in its usual way
Greeting the ship with rain and storm
And gunmetal seas and spray.
Once more the cabins creaked and groaned
Once more the wind through the rigging moaned
Like sinners on Judgment Day
The gale blew stronger and lashed the waves
Like an overseer with a whip
The rain blew level as music staves
From bow to stern of the ship.
Poor Mrs Vining, the sport of fate
Fell, embedding her upper plate
In the flesh of her lower lip.
But when the tempest had ceased to roar
And had muted its sullen arrogance
And the stubborn vessel at last forbore
To bow to the ocean's exigence
The clouds dispersed, the horizon cleared
Some pale, unconvincing stars appeared
And Mrs Cuthbertson swore she saw
A light on the coast of France.

Of course there was a ship's concert
There is always a ship's concert
Given ostensibly in aid of the Seaman's Fund
Given ostensibly to divert the passengers
But really given for several other reasons.
The Seaman's Fund, we know, accrued some benefit
The passengers, we know, are fairly diverted
But over and above and behind and below
These clear, unquestionable advantages
There are other issues, other implications.
The battle of straining egos for the light
For that sweet hour of temporary recognition,
There is also to be considered the Purser's pride

'I Travel Alone'

The raging hunger in him to be satisfied
Once, once at least in course of every voyage.
How can he carry on each day's routine
Pacify passengers, deal with small complaints
Keep a sharp, suave and understanding eye
On diverse temperaments, without some hope
Of one rich moment, when subservience ends
And he at least can dominate a while
Those, who by wealth and rank and circumstance
Are classified as his superiors?
At the ship's concert he can rise
Clad in benign authority and speak
A few well chosen introductory phrases.
Later, like other deities, rise again
And make a longer, more imposing speech,
Thanking the artists, thanking the orchestra
Thanking the Captain for his gracious presence
Thanking the audience for their kind reception
Thanking the universe, the moon and stars
For this clear, golden opportunity
To stand, upholder of a worthy cause
And hear the sound of personal applause.

The concert started with 'Veronique'
Played excessively loudly
And when it came to 'Swing High, Swing Low'
Mrs Blake in the second row,
Hummed the melody proudly.
Then a young man of strong physique
With the air of a swaggering rebel
Embarked to everyone's surprise
On 'Take a Pair of Sparkling Eyes'
In a voice that was almost treble.
Next came a girl from the Second Class
With spectacles and a fiddle
Who, unaware that she was tone deaf
Played Rubinstein's 'Melody in F'
And lost her place in the middle.
A table steward with lungs of brass
Bellowed a song of Devon

And Colonel Wintringham, drenched in sweat,
With Mrs Drage, sang an arch duet
Entitled 'The Keys of Heaven'.
A boy in a Javanese sarong
Made everyone rather restive
By executing a native dance
Which, whether on purpose or by chance,
Was definitely suggestive.
Turn followed turn, song followed song
Until all at last was ended
And the Purser's ears, crimson with praise,
Re-echoed the Governor's Lady's phrase
'It has all been simply splendid!'

England at last. At first only a smudge
A blue smudge on a windy blue-grey morning
High mackerel sky and spray, barely discernible
Splintering white against the sullen rocks,
The granite obstinacy of Land's End.
Seagulls appear, one perches in the rigging,
Its curved beak like a yellow scimitar.
Passengers crowd the rails, eager to catch
The first glimpse, after months and years away
Of their beloved and inalienable home.
This is a moment that must be remembered
Set in the heart and mind, branded upon
The retinas of tired English eyes,
Tired of violent colours, tired of glare
And heat and sand and jungles and bright birds.
Eyes that so often longingly have gazed
Through beaded curtains of torrential rain
To gentler rain falling on English woods,
Eyes that have stared nostalgically beyond
Flowers too vivid in the blazing light
To quieter flowers in herbaceous borders
Snapdragons, pinks, sweet-williams, lupins, phlox
And gawky, unexotic hollyhocks.
The ship draws near to the welcoming land
Houses are visible, cottages white and grey
Scramble down between low, forbidding cliffs

To crescent coves of shining golden sand
And twisted harbours filled with fishing boats.
The Lizard, crouching among its little waves
Inspires Mrs Vining to recall
That, when she was a girl of seventeen
Together with two cousins and a friend
She got caught by the tide at Kynance Cove
And had to spend several hours upon a ledge
Wet and bedraggled, frightened and woebegone
Until the coastguards came and rescued them.
The ship, most courteously, drew nearer still
And steams along less than a mile from shore.
Falmouth, Veryan, Porthpean, St Austell Bay,
Fowey, Looe, Polperro, all identified
By Mrs Vining's overwhelming pride
At being the only one on board who 'knew
Her Cornwall inside out and through and through'.

The Eddystone Lighthouse, slim and white
Like a pencil stuck in the blue,
Plymouth Hoe and Babbacombe Bay
Gaunt rocks changing from red to grey
Until the slow diminishing light
Banishes them from view.

No one on board can quite relax
Poor Mr Frith gets drunk
And Mrs Frobisher, bathed in tears,
Sits, surrounded by souvenirs
Each one of which she carefully packs
With her hopes, in her cabin trunk.

Colonel Wintringham cannot sleep
Barred are the gates of Slumberland
He cannot make up his mind between
His sister's cottage in Bushey Green
A trip to the continent on the cheap
Or a walking tour of Northumberland.

Inscrutable, disconsolate
Remote from understanding
Counting the dark hours as they pass

Wide awake in the Second Class
Mrs Macomber's Amahs wait
To be told where to go on landing.

How evil the mind's continued rage!
How cruel the heart that hardens!
Aware of this truth, with smiling face
And overflowing with Christian grace
Mrs Macgrath asks Mrs Drage
To tea in Ennismore Gardens.

Last-minute packing finished and done
The long and wearisome journey over
The Governor's Lady, standing apart,
With a sudden lifting of her heart
Sees, like a sentinel in the sun,
The arrogant cliffs of Dover.

Kent on the one side, Essex on the other
And the wide Thames Estuary lying in between.
Oilers, tankers, cargo-ships and tug-boats,
The churning yellow paddles of *The Margate Queen*.
Cockneys on a holiday, sound of concertinas
Vying with the seagulls squawking in the breeze,
Houses, wharves and factories, grey beside the river,
Behind them, marshes and a few tall trees.
Delicately, shrewdly, the black-funnelled liner
Dark hull whitened by the salt sea spray
Picks her way with dignity among her lesser sisters
And steams up to Tilbury through the warm June day.

> This then is the end. The end of longing,
> The realised anticipatory dream,
> The lovely moment, still unspoiled and tremulous
> Still lighter than a bubble, gay with hope,
> Still free from anti-climax, before Time
> Itself has had the time to tarnish it.
> The image of homecoming still unmarred
> By little disappointments, small delays
> And sudden, inexplicable dismays.

The siren hoots three times, three warning calls
The first one long, the second two much shorter.

And into the turgid, swirling river water
The anchor falls.

(1957)

Pleased as he was to see the anchor fall, a work of this complexity had undoubtedly taken a lot out of him. In January 1957 he had told his Diary: 'My epic verse is at last within sight of the end. Fifteen pages – it has been a long voyage and I am eager to get the god-damned ship and all who sail in her safely to Tilbury, because I have several other ideas rapping smartly on the door and I cannot let them in until this particular odyssey is completed.'

As the years went by and more and more of the 'wrong people' began to travel, Noël's view became noticeably less benign . . .

Pleasure Cruise

Was this the ship that launched a thousand faces
Upon the bosom of the seven seas?
Was this the ship that bore to far off places
The scum of culture-keen democracies?

Viewed from the shore her spirit seems unwilted
Calmly she swings at anchor in the tide
Her funnels tilting as they always tilted
As though remembering her early pride.

Remembering, as some gay painted lady
Remembers hopeful days when life was young
Before expedience imposed the shady
Transactions she must now exist among.

Was this the ship that slid into the river
With such panache, with so much proud disdain
Greeting her love with an exultant shiver
Her bows anointed with the best champagne.

Was this the craft that won that record ribbon
Snatched from the straining might of larger ships
Surely the whole *Decline and Fall* of Gibbon
Couldn't describe so dismal an eclipse.

Souvenir

In memory of a charming trip
On board a dull but noble ship
In memory of endless games
And scores of unrelated names
Including that of Doctor Wence
Who first discovered flatulence
Also the famous Elmer Hale
Who pitched a ball eight times for Yale
Without forgetting Witzenback
That hero of the Harvard Track
Nor Mrs Hiram J. Macfarr
Who wandered, nude, through Iowa.
Under these clarion trumpets' din
Sometimes a lesser name crept in
Such as Napoleon Bonaparte
Or even Plato or Mozart
But men of such obscure repute
Were seldom passed without dispute
So we returned with great relief
To Senator Augustus Spief
To Ada Chubb and Wendel Green
(The first to cauterise the spleen)
To Ethan Beck and General Bight
And Mabel Macnamara Wright
To Doctor Bowes, the insect man
Who perished in Afghanistan
Without a thought for Otto Kahn
Or Drian or Reynaldo Hahn.

Lines to a Fellow Passenger

Mr Samoa! Mr Samoa
Why are you such a unbearable boa?
Why do you turn first to one then the other
Crushing their spirits with 'Buddy' and 'Brother'?
Have you no vestige of equable poise?

Why do you make such a desperate noise?
Why do you bawl so that Heaven could hear
Every event in your private career?
Why, when a group is quite harmlessly drinking,
Must you hold forth and annihilate thinking?
Why, without knowledge or verification,
Must you impart so much false information?
Why do you pander to small Japanese
Knowing they're eagerly planning to seize
All the possessions America holds,
All that the flag of your country enfolds?
Why were you nice to them? Was it because
Some inner need for unworthy applause
Spurred you to please them, to joke and to try
To prove you were really a 'regular guy'
Mr Samoa! Mr Samoa!
Note what I gracefully hinted befoa
Will you, for God's sake, not be any moa
Such a pervasive and shattering boa?

The Little Men Who Travel Far

These little men who travel far
How infinitely dull they are
You find them in the ships that ply
Between Manila and Shanghai,
From Tripoli to Port Sudan,
Shimonosaki to Fusan
You find them everywhere they go
And always in a P and O.
These little men who travel far
Drinking forlornly at the bar
'This is my round' and then 'One more'
'Stop me if you've heard this before'
Each one endeavouring to cap
The story of the other chap.
From Trinidad to Panama,
From Brindisi to Zanzibar,

From Alexandria to Crete,
These lethal raconteurs compete.
The loudest laugh, the coarsest joke,
Each shouting down the last who spoke,
Each ego straining more and more,
Insensately to hold the floor.
The barman, with unsmiling eyes,
Smiles at such dismal vanities.
The smallest fish beneath the keel
With every fishy instinct feel
Each ancient pornographic quip
Stately descending through the ship
Until at last with one accord
They sink away, profoundly bored.
The little men who travel far
How sadly insecure they are.
The little men who travel far
How infinitely dull they are.

Of all the places he saw a few found themselves the subject of a Coward verse. And not always a complimentary one.

In the Mediterranean there was Malta, for instance . . . and the Royal Navy . . .

Malta

The Isle of Malta lies at ease
Secure in old tradition,
Lapped by translucent azure seas
And social competition.
That service spirit dominates
All shabby habitations,
Controlling fears and loves and hates
And marital relations.
The visitor who is unused
To dealing with officials
Will find his mother tongue reduced
To orgies of initials.
If Captain D is asked to T

To give himself more leisure
He signals WMP
Which means 'Without much pleasure'.

Go to Malta, Little Girl

If your neck craves the matrimonial halter
Go to Malta,
Little girl
For the Fleet provides the answer to the maiden's prayer.
Foolish virgins don't despair
Set your cap at them
Have a slap at them
If you're firm enough
You can make them do their stuff.
If you've missed copulation in Gibralta
Go to Malta,
Little girl.

Nor did Corsica linger fondly in memory . . .

Thoughts on Corsica

Descriptive

The Island of Corsica crouches at ease
Secure in its bloody tradition
Surrounded by changing, unamiable seas
And proudly immune from ambition.
The dogs and the chickens that scavenge the streets
The children that litter the ports
The goats, with their bulbous inelegant teats
And the insects of various sorts
The eagles that live on the furthermost peaks
And the natives that live in the vales
Appear to enjoy being battered for weeks

By the wild unaccountable gales.
When winds from the South, or the West, East or North
Smear the skies with an ominous black
The Corsican fishermen bravely go forth
But seldom, if ever, come back.

Hotel Napoleon Bonaparte, Ile Rousse

God bless the 'Messageries Maritimes'
For building this splendid hotel.
This modern, de luxe, and superb habitation
With passable food and sublime sanitation
This architect's vision in gay terracotta
This dream, which if only the weather were hotter
And also if only the sea could be calm
Could soothe our frayed nerves with its infinite charm
This haven of rest with the mountains behind it
Would surely hold peace if we only could find it.

Advice from a Lady Who Has Visited the Island Before

You really should see the Interior
It's honestly vastly superior
You won't leave the Island,
Please don't leave the Island,
Without having seen the Interior.
The coast is quite gay
In a kind of way
But you must leave your stupid old yacht for a day
And really explore the Interior,
Now what in the world could be drearier
Than *not* having seen the Interior?
Don't trouble to stay in Ajaccio
Or Calvi or San Bonifacio
But just take a car
From wherever you are
And drive like a streak
Round each crag and each peak

And see the *real* Corsica,
Genuine Corsica
(Hell-raising curves
But to Hell with your nerves!)
The coast is so dreadfully inferior
Compared with the *real* Interior.
You really *must* see the Interior.

Calvi

There is something very odd about fishermen
In this picturesque and vivid little port
Though the muscles roll like boulders
Up and down their brawny shoulders
And their sea legs are conveniently short
There is something very odd about fishermen
In this pretty and attractive little port.

What has miscarried here?
What has miscarried here?
Too many foreigners maybe have tarried here
Too many types from more decadent nations
Swaying their hips in San Tropez creations
Too many queer indeterminate creatures
Coaxing the sun to their nondescript features
What is occurring here?
What is occurring here?
Too many caps at provocative angles
Too much extravagant shrill phraseology
Too much exuberant psycho-pathology.

There is something very strange about fishermen
Though they're physically epitomes of grace
Though each child in the vicinity
Should prove their masculinity
And ardent procreation of the race
There is something *very* strange about the fishermen
In this charming and alluring little place.

The Bandit

A bandit inhabiting Corsica
Would never waste time on Divorsica
He'd kick the backside
Of his tedious bride
And gallop away on his horsica.

. . . though Venice inspired amused affection if not awe . . .

Venice

Last Wednesday on the Piazza
Near San Marco's *trecento* Duomo
I observed *una grassa ragazza*
With a thin, Middle Western *uomo*.

He was swatting a *piccola mosca*
She was eating a chocolate *gelato*
While an orchestra played (from *La Tosca*)
A flat violin *obbligato*.

They stared at a dusty *piccione*
They spoke not a single *parola*
She ordered some *Te con limone*
He ordered an iced Coca-Cola.

And while the *tramanto del sole*
Set fire to the Grand Canale
She scribbled haphazard *parole*
On glazed *cartoline postale*.

(1954)

Bali. The island that tourists came to know in the Dutch East Indies was very much the projection of outsiders such as American sociologist Margaret Mead and artists like Walter Spies (1895–1942). Between them they created a Western image of 'an enchanted land of aesthetes at peace with themselves and nature'.

Noël first visited Bali in May 1935, met and became friendly with Spies. When he left the Campuan guest house, he wrote this in the guest book:

Oh Walter Dear

Oh Walter dear, Oh Walter dear,
Please don't neglect your painting.
Neglect, dear Walter, if you must,
Your pleasure in the native's trust,
Neglect, if needs be, Social Grace
And Charity and Pride of Race.
Crush down, dear Walter, if you can,
Your passion for the Gamelan,
Neglect your love of birds and beasts,
Go to far fewer Temple Feasts,
Neglect your overwhelming wish
To gaze for hours at coloured fish.
You may delight in flowers and trees
And talking to the Balinese
But they, alas, tho' gay and sweet,
Are, notwithstanding, most effete
And not conducive to the state
You need, in order to create.
So, Walter dear, neglect to drink,
Neglect to eat and wash or think
Of opportunities to shirk
The stern necessity of work.
And when, at last, you madly rush
To squeeze your paint and grab your brush,
Do not neglect in memory
To give a kindly thought to me!

The island clearly lingered in memory and in the spring of 1936 he revisited it – and some of his themes – in verse . . .

Bali

As I mentioned this morning to Charlie,
There is far too much music in Bali.
And altho' as a place it's entrancing
There is also a *thought* too much dancing.
It appears that each Balinese native

From the womb to the tomb is creative,
From sunrise to long after sundown,
Without getting nervy or rundown,
They sculpt and they paint and they practise their songs,
They run through their dances and bang on their gongs,
Each writhe and each wriggle,
Each glamorous giggle,
Each sinuous action,
Is timed to a fraction.
And altho' the results are quite charming,
If sometimes a trifle alarming!
And altho' all the 'Lovelies' and 'Pretties'
Unblushingly brandish their titties,
The whole thing's a little *too clever*
And there's *too much artistic endeavour*!

Forgive the above mentioned Charlie,
I had to rhyme *something* with Bali.

(Spring 1936)

In the Far East – which he got to know well – the French Polynesian island of Bora Bora ('First Born'), which might easily have sparked a Coward *bon mot* by its name alone, did rather better than Bali:

Bora Bora

The wild lagoon in which the island lies
Changes its colours with the changing skies
And, lovely beyond belief,
The dazzling surf upon the outer reef
Murmurs its lonely, timeless lullaby
Warning the heart perhaps that life is brief
Measured against the sea's eternity.

In the lagoon beneath the surface grow
Wild fantasies of coral; to and fro
And, lovely beyond all praise,
The vivid fish interminably gaze;
Rubies and emeralds, yellows, blues and mauves

Endlessly nibbling at the coral sprays
Endlessly flitting through the coral groves.

The coco-palms paint shadows on the sand
Shadows that dance a languid saraband
And, lovely indeed to see,
Above the scented frangipani tree
The mountain's silhouette against the moon
Who, as she saunters through Infinity
Traces a silver path on the lagoon.

(March 1962)

In the West Indies Noël was not buying the publicity about Martinique. It was after all *French* . . .

Martinique

No Frenchman can forbear to speak
About the charms of Martinique
It seems it is a land of spice
And sugar, and of all things nice
A veritable Paradise
Un endroit fantastique.

The Compagnie Transatlantique
Sends lots of ships to Martinique
Because, they say, it's nicer far
Than many other places are
More glamorous than Zanzibar
Cleaner than Mozambique.

They also say it has more 'chic'
Than Tunis in the Nord d'Afrique
Possessing 'Plages' with finer 'sable'
A climate 'Toujours admirable'
In fact, they say, it's 'Formidable'
This God-damned Martinique.

In praising this celestial Freak
They, one and all, omit to speak

About its flat cathedral bells
Its indescribable hotels
The noisesome and disgusting smells
That make the Island reek.

In fact, there *were* times when all of those overestimated destinations could go to hell . . .

Oh Dear

Oh dear, oh dear
What am I doing here
It's all so very queer
Oh dear, oh dear, oh dear!

Batavia's a bugger
A bastard and a sod
So I'm back on board the lugger
With a hey ho and a bollocks ahoy
I'm back on board the lugger
Thank the Sweet Lord God.

These verses may appear to some
A teeny bit obscene
I'm only writing them to test
This fartarsing machine.
I've put a brand new ribbon in
And oiled each bloody screw
I've cleaned each letter with a pin
Each fucking letter with a pin
And now I really *must* begin
Some dreary work to do
With a hey whack knackers aho
Some dreary work to do.
If lots of sticks and stones and bits of larva
Abruptly come cascading through the air
And bollocksed up the sunny isle of Java
I don't believe that I should really care.
If pestilence, by order of the Saviour

> Exclusively descended on the Dutch
> Killing those podgy bastards in Batavia
> I don't think I should mind so *very* much.

Well, all except one, perhaps. He gave the Quinta Bates and its American-born owner, Mrs Anna Bates, 5 Coward Stars.

The hotel was located in Arequipa, the second city in Peru. Mrs Bates ran it with a benevolently iron hand and was known by the locals as 'Tia' (aunt). When she died at eighty-five, one of them said, 'She was like *charpa*, the land turtle – hard outside, tender inside.'

Noël wrote:

> Her name is plainly Mrs Bates
> A strange capricious whim of Fate's
> To crown with such banality
> So great a personality.

He was to use the Quinta Bates (suitably modified) as the imaginary setting for *Point Valaine* (1935).

The Quinta Bates (Aunt Bates)

> No wand'ring Nomad hesitates
> To patronise 'The Quinta Bates',
> He finds it comfortable inside
> And innocent of social pride.
> He finds, on entering the gate
> An atmospheric opiate.
> The spirit of the place conserves
> An anodyne for jangled nerves.
> The water's hot, the beds are soft,
> The meals are many a time and oft.
> The flowers are sweet, the grass is green,
> The toilet is austerely clean.
> Which, in this ancient continent,
> Occasions vast astonishment.
> The food is more than 'luxe' enough,

The cook not only cooks enough
But builds each afternoon for tea
A model of gastronomy.
The furniture is nicely placed
And signifies a catholic taste.
The periods are slightly mixed,
Some are between and some betwixt.
All 'tourists' who grumble fail
To comprehend this jumble sale.
The visitors are jumbled too
Here sit the Gentile and the Jew,
The Mining Engineer, the Don,
The Governess from Kensington,
The debutante from Sulphur Springs,
The Archaeologist who sings,
The Matron from the Middle West,
The Minister from Bucharest,
The brittle lady Novelist,
The arid Christian Scientist
Conversing with fraternal grace
In this remote maternal place.
And now I feel it would be nice
In praising this small Paradise,
To mention with an awe profound
The one who makes the wheels go round.
Her name is plainly Mrs Bates,
A strange capricious whim of Fate's
To crown with such banality
So great a personality.
Her friends, who love the Quinta's frame,
Disdain this unromantic name,
And much prefer to call this dear,
Kind and enchanting person, 'Tia'
For 'Tia' is a word that trips
With more allurement from the lips
And can be used endearingly
With apposite felicity.
Tho' Tia is completely kind,
She has a keen and lively mind,

And when things seem too hard to bear,
She'll soundly and robustly swear
She's learned her life in Nature's School
And isn't anybody's fool.
Of every place I've been to yet
This I shall leave with most regret.
The Quinta is to blame for this
Peculiar metamorphosis.
I think the 'Carlton' and the 'Ritz',
Those Palaces at St Moritz,
The 'Crillon' and the drab 'Meurice',
The 'Grandes Auberges' of Cannes and Nice
The 'Continental' in Belgrade,
And in Berlin 'The Esplanade',
And every hotel in the States
Should emulate the 'Quinta Bates'.
                    (Arequipa, February 1932)

One of the main troubles with travel were one's fellow travellers . . .

From One Chap to Another: A Complaint

I told the Desboroughs about my wife
And they couldn't have minded less,
I also told them about my life
In the heart of the FMS.*

I also told them she had red hair
But the snooty Desboroughs didn't care;
I mentioned once that we had a child
And the beastly Desboroughs merely smiled.
I chanced to mention the Sultan's Aunt
Who had given my wife a rubber plant,
I also mentioned, in passing, twice
That the Chinese merchants were awfully nice
And so adored me, the simple souls
That they gave me presents of several scrolls

*FMS: Federated Malay States

With my name at the top in a Chinese hand
Which none but the Chinese understand.
I also showed them a queen Sarong
A gift from the Sultan of Lang Kwi Kiong
And a slightly rusty Malayan knife
Which was forced on me by the Sultan's wife.
When I tried to describe a Malay dawn
The odious Desboroughs suppressed a yawn.
When I showed them the Rajah's private sword
The haughty Desboroughs were frankly bored
So discerning between us no clear bond
I dine each night with a *cendré* blonde
From whom it is easy to invoke
A winsome laugh at the oldest joke
And she sits quite still in a low cut dress
And is frightfully thrilled with the FMS.

I told the Desboroughs about my wife
And they couldn't have looked more dead,
I also told them about my life
And they giggled and went to bed.

Jeunesse Dorée

Ian Macnamara Wrexham-Smith
Always desired a friend to travel with
So it befell, one day on the Riviera
He ran across Guido di Falconiera.
In fact the whole delightful thing began
Outside the Martinez Hotel in Cannes.

A mutually reminiscent chat,
A joke or two about some passing hat.
A swift, sure recognition of the truth
Concerning this or that sun-gilded youth
A few Bacardi cocktails and the pact
Of friendship was a gay, accomplished fact.

The early spring of nineteen thirty-one
Found them together basking in the sun

'I Travel Alone'

Wearing, in charming complement to each
Silk dressing-gowns, one yellow and one peach
Which, thanks to Lanvin's ingenuity,
Could be reversed and changed entirely.

The whole of July, nineteen thirty-two
They spent, in sailor trousers, in Corfu.
A little later in the self-same year
They both of them elected to appear,
At that strange party given by Hans Rosen,
In gaily coloured scarves and 'Lederhosen'.

The month of August, nineteen thirty-three
Saw them in pale blue shorts in Sicily.
In nineteen thirty-four and thirty-five
They took a long, and most enchanting drive
From Buda Pesth, via Florence, to Bavaria
In linen shirts the shade of old wistaria.

In nineteen thirty-six the whole Aegean
Was ravished by the spectacle of Ian
And Guido, wearing Schiaparelli drawers
Closely akin to *crêpe-de-chine* plus fours.
This, tho' a quite innocuous caprice,
Hardly enhanced the glory that was Greece.

In nineteen thirty-seven all the Lido
Gazed with a certain vague dismay at Guido
And Ian as they minced along the *plage*
Wearing gold lockets which were far too large,
Closely knitted rompers, children's size,
With 'diamanté' anchors on their thighs.

Late in September, nineteen thirty-eight,
Something that neither could anticipate
Sundered their gentle lives after the most
Delightful month on the Dalmatian coast
During which time they both of them had been
Wearing, alas, an acid shade of green.

When they set out by steamer for Trieste
Guido (for once conventionally dressed)

Struck up a conversation with a Croat
Wearing a rather bizarre Gipsy's coat
And when they finally arrived in Fiume,
Ian retired, in silence, to his room.

Later, a rather violent dispute
Spattered with tear-stains Guido's Tussore suit
Very much later still a further scena
Ended in sobs outside the Bar Marina
With the result that on the morning boat
Guido departed firmly, with the Croat.

So we must hope that Ian Wrexham-Smith
Finds someone more sincere to travel with.

'I love to go and I love to have been, but best of all I love the intervals between arrivals and departures.'

Present Indicative (1937)

9.

'IF LOVE WERE ALL'

'Heigh-ho, if love were all.'
Bitter Sweet (1929)

'How idiotic people are when they're in love. What an age-old devastating disease.'

Like everyone else, Noël found Love was a problem he could never solve to his satisfaction. He refers to it time and time again in his song lyrics.

In *Bitter Sweet* the heroine Sari asks 'What is Love?'. Then there is the disconcerting new sensation that must be Love, 'Something Very Strange (Is Happening to Me'); the anticipation of Love waiting to be found, 'I'll Follow My Secret Heart (Till I Find Love'), 'Someday I'll Find You'; the hope of recapturing Love Lost ('I'll See You Again'); the realisation of the impossibility of holding on to Love ('The Dream Is Over'); the determination not to repeat the painful pattern ('Time and Again', 'Never Again').

Then, finally, the acceptance that, even when one experiences love, it can't really be the answer to everything ('If Love Were All').

Which led him to the conclusion that:

> I believe that since my life began
> The most I've had is just
> A talent to amuse.

Taken as a statement about his own life, it was meant to be rejected by those who knew him and, of course, it was. He had so many talents, people said, it was absurd to claim just one and such a light one.

Nonetheless, it took attention away from one aspect of life in which he felt he'd failed to acquit himself . . . Perhaps he needed to redefine it: 'Passionate love has been like a tight shoe rubbing blisters on my Achilles heel . . . How idiotic people are when they're in love. What an age-old devastating disease.'

By the end of his life, Noël had decided that being 'in love' was out. Love was what lasted.

In a late interview Noël was asked to sum up his life in one word. He paused uncharacteristically, then said, 'Now comes the terrible decision as to whether to be corny or not. The answer is one word. LOVE . . .'

In his verse over the years he would explore it in all its forms.

There was Love Reflective . . .

This Is to Let You Know

> This is to let you know
> That there was no moon last night
> And that the tide was high

And that on the broken horizon glimmered the lights of ships
Twenty at least, like a sedate procession passing by.

This is to let you know
That when I'd turned out the lamp
And in the dark I lay
Then suddenly piercing loneliness, like a knife,
Twisted my heart, for you were such a long long way away.

This is to let you know
That there are no English words
That ever could explain
How, quite without warning, lovingly you were here
Holding me close, smoothing away the idiotic pain.

This is to let you know
That all that I feel for you
Can never wholly go
I love you and miss you, even two hours away,
With all my heart. This is to let you know.

White Cliffs, St Margaret's Bay, Kent, c. 1945–46

There was Love Lost – But Fondly Recalled . . .

I Knew You without Enchantment

I knew you without enchantment
And for some years
We went our usual ways
Meeting occasionally
Finding no heights nor depths among our days
Shedding no tears
Every so often when we felt inclined
Lying like lovers in each other's arms
Feeling no qualms
In our light intimacy
So resolute we were in heart and mind
So steeled against illusion, deaf and blind

'If Love Were All'

To all presentiment, to all enchantment
(I knew you without enchantment).

It is so strange
Remembering that phase
Those unexacting, uneventful days
Before the change
Before we knew this serio-comic, tragic
Most unexpected, overwhelming magic.
I knew you without enchantment.

And to-day I cannot think of you without my heart
Suddenly stopping
Or, in those long grey hours we spent apart
Dropping, dropping
Down into desolation like a stone.
To be alone
No longer means to me clear time and space
In which to stretch my mind.

I see your face
Between me and the space I used to find
Between me and the other worlds I seek
There stands your sleek
And most beloved silhouette
And yet
I can remember not so long ago
We neither of us cared
Nor dared
To know
How swiftly we were nearing the abyss
(This foolish, quite ungovernable bliss)
Let's not regret
The empty life before. It was great fun
And hurt no one
There was no harm in it
At certain moments there was even charm in it.

But oh my dearest love, there was no spell
No singing heaven and no wailing hell.
I knew you without enchantment.

But, all in all – Noël concluded – sensitively as he might write about it, Love was not one of the many skills of which he was The Master . . .

I Am No Good at Love

I am no good at love
My heart should be wise and free
I kill the unfortunate golden goose
Whoever it may be
With over-articulate tenderness
And too much intensity.

I am no good at love
I batter it out of shape
Suspicion tears at my sleepless mind
And, gibbering like an ape,
I lie alone in the endless dark
Knowing there's no escape.

I am no good at love
When my easy heart I yield
Wild words come tumbling from my mouth
Which should have stayed concealed;
And my jealousy turns a bed of bliss
Into a battlefield.

I am no good at love
I betray it with little sins
For I feel the misery of the end
In the moment that it begins
And the bitterness of the last good-bye
Is the bitterness that wins.

10.

'THE PARTY'S OVER NOW'

'I would prefer Fate to allow me to go to sleep when it's my proper bedtime. I never have been one for staying up too late.'

Diaries (1967)

In those last years he began to dwell – at least in private – on what came next.

Cole Lesley recalled a mordant exchange with Noël: 'Ah, well,' said Cole, 'we live and learn.' 'Yes,' replied Noël, 'and then we die and forget it all.'

As early as 1937 he had written, 'The finality of death is bewildering on first acquaintance and the words "never again" too sad to believe entirely.'

And in a fragment of *Beyond These Voices*, an unpublished novel, he has the leading character say:

> One of the pleasures of growing older is the realisation that to be alone does not necessarily imply loneliness. For many years it has been my habit wherever I may be, to take an evening off, to relax my nerves, to gaze objectively at the world about me and the world within me; to know, for a few brief hours, that no contribution is required of me, neither wit, wisdom, sparkling repartee nor sage advice. On these quiet occasions I am always stimulated by the feeling that adventure may be just around the corner; not adventure in the sexual or dramatic sense, but adventure of the mind; something to distract, an idea, a sudden flick of memory, an observed incident, trivial in itself perhaps, but sharp and clear enough to quicken my creative impulse and fire my imagination.

He began to live increasingly in memory and this contemplative verse seems to have been the last he wrote.

When I Have Fears

When I have fears, as Keats had fears,
Of the moment I'll cease to be
I console myself with vanished years
Remembered laughter, remembered tears,
And the peace of the changing sea.

When I feel sad, as Keats felt sad,
That my life is so nearly done
It gives me comfort to dwell upon
Remembered friends who are dead and gone
And the jokes we had and the fun.

How happy they are I cannot know
But happy am I who loved them so.

There was to be one more literary return to the islands. Noël left behind a draft manuscript for *Beyond These Voices*, though there is no indication as to when it was written. It is set in Samolo in the late 1950s and reads more elegiacally than *Pomp and Circumstances* – almost as though both the writer and the narrator, Kerry Stirling, were taking their leave. It begins:

> I have come home again, this time, I suspect, for good. The years that are left to me I intend to pass here on the island where the winds are soft and the climate temperate and where, except for a few weeks twice a year in the rainy season, there is always sunshine.
>
> This thought fills me with gentle pleasure for I am tired. Not physically tired, for I am in the best of health and look and feel a great deal younger than I am, but spiritually a little under the weather. This is not a disagreeable sensation; on the contrary it is rather pleasant, for there is space around me and time ahead of me, time enough at least to enable me to give myself up to my quiet *malaise* and wait, without agitation, until the unhurried days smooth it away.

By the time he arrived in Jamaica that last time, there were, as it turned out, only days left. Noël Coward died peacefully in the early morning of 26 March 1973.

And, indeed, the winds that day were soft . . .

I'm Here for a Short Visit Only

> I'm here for a short visit only
> And I'd rather be loved than hated
> Eternity may be lonely
> When my body's disintegrated
> And that which is loosely termed my soul
> Goes whizzing off through the infinite
> By means of some vague, remote control
> I'd like to think I was missed a bit.

He needn't have worried.

'I want to get right back to nature and relax': Noël in his beloved Jamaica

Index of Titles

Verse titles only; entries in quotation marks denote the first lines of verses which were not assigned a title by the author.

1901 44
Advice from a Lady Who Has Visited the Island Before 330
After a Surfeit of Sir Philip Sidney 295
'Agamemnon and Sappho' 60
Any Part of Piggy 14
'Apple Blossoms' 61
Bali 333
Ballad of Graham Greene, The 298
Bandit, The 332
Battle of Britain Dinner, New York, 1963, The 201
'Baybay's gone . . .' 123
'Because of the vast political intrigues' 153
Beyond 18
Bill 157
Birth of Hope, The 141
Birthday Ode 129
Blackness of Her Hair . . . , The 18
Boots 294
Bora Bora 334
Boy Actor, The 265
Bread and Butter Letter to Jean and Bill Fleming 193
Bread and Butter Letter to Lord and Lady Killearn 191
Bread and Butter Letter to Mr and Mrs R. G. Casey 195
'Bride Cake, The' 62
Calvi 331
Canary, The 13

Candelabra 77
Canton Island 183
Caprice de Noël 87
Casa Medina 192
Chelsea Buns 73
Child Prodigy, The 270
Children's Tales 77
Christmas Cheer 87
Church of England 94
Columbine and Harlequin 22
Concert Types 269
Condolence 255
Contemporary Thought 83
Contours 73
Contralto, The 269
Convalescence 179
Conversion of a Cynic, The 19
'A Country Fair' 67
Curve In Curve Out 93
Daddy and Boo 54
'Dancing Class, The' 63
'Darling Alfred, dainty Lynn' 280
Darling Kay and Little Lad 128
Dawn 106
'Dear Admiral . . .' 190
'Dear Mr Graham Greene, I yearn' 299
'Dearest Binkie, dearest Bink' 277
'Dearest Mrs Lorn Loraine' 151
'Dearest sympathetic lovely Lorn' 155
Death 250
'Deirdre' 100
Descriptive 329

Do I Believe? 251
Don'ts for Dab 124
Don'ts for My Darlings 137
Early Peruvian Love Song 52
Elizabeth May 31
Emperor's Daughter, The 95
Epitaph for an Elderly Actress 285
Every Day 96
Exultance 52
The Great Awakening 15
A Fallen Postscript 150
Family Circle 75
Father and Son 256
Fécamp 165
First Love 101
'Flamenco' 99
Freundschaft 102
From One Chap to Another: A Complaint 339
Garden of Allah, The 291
Garibaldi 74
Go to Malta, Little Girl 329
'Go, Joycie, with your upper parts uncovered' 119
Gob 54
Goblins 17
Goldeneye Calypso 134
Goldeneye Opus No. 2 135
'Greasy Garbage' 65
Guava Jelly 74
Happy New Year 186
Harlem 91
Harlot's Song 97
Heigho for Hockey 55
'Here I lie sweetly in bed' 115
Hic Haec Hoc 85
Honeymoon 1905 46
Hotel Napoleon Bonaparte, Ile Rousse 330

House Guest 133
How Does Your Garden Grow 89
Humorist, The 270
Hungry Land 90
I Am No Good at Love 348
'I could really not be keener . . .' 140
'I had a little onion' 12
I Knew You without Enchantment 346
I Resent Your Attitude to Mary 281
I Will Protect My Sister 85
I'm Here for a Short Visit Only 352
I've Got to Go Out and Be Social 233
I've Just Come Out from England 187
If I Should Ever Wantonly Destroy 254
If Through a Mist 242
If Wishes Were Horses 20
Ignatius Hole 260
In Masculine Homage 236
'In the deep hush before the dawn' 117
Irene Vanbrugh Memorial Matinée: The Epilogue 274
Island of Bosh, The 24
Jamaica 131
James and Belinda 28
Jeunesse Dorée 340
Lady at the Party, The 234
Legend 103
Let the People Go 203
Letter from the Seaside 1880 41
Letter to Beatrice Eden 244
Lie in the Dark and Listen 169
Lines to a Fellow Passenger 326
Lines to a Film Censor (1940) 289
Lines to a Little God 261
Lines to a Remote Garrison 167
Lines to an American Officer 180
Lines to God 250

Index of Titles

Little Men Who Travel Far, The 327
'Lock your cabin door my darling' 129
'Lornie Darling, how I loved your news' 117
Lornie Is a Silly-Billy 114
'Lornie, dear Lornie . . .' 154
'Lornie, whose undying love' 147
Love Ditty to a Turnip 11
Lower Classes, The 53
Ma People 92
Major Leathes 160
Malta 328
Martinique 335
'Master's back and all alone' 154
'A May Morning' 65
Meditation on Death 251
Midst the Hustle and the Bustle . . . 241
A Miniature 250
Misericordia 82
Morning Glory 235
'Morning Glory' 136
Moss 93
Mrs Gibbon's Decline and Fall 81
Mrs Mallory 229
'My Bedroom' 59
Necromancy 90
Neurotic Thoughts on the Renaissance 71
News Ballad 162
Not Yet the Dodo 206
Note on Our New National Heroine 171
Notes on an Admiral's Hangover 168
Notes on Liaison 161
Notes on the Correct Entertainment of Royalty 125
Nothing Is Lost 255
Nous n'avons plus de chichi 72

Novel by Baroness Orczy 290
Nursemaid, The 105
Ode to Italia Conti 267
Ode to Joyce 119
Oh Dear 336
'Oh Lady Clementi!' 199
Oh Walter Dear 333
'Oh, Beatrice dear, what a superb weekend' 244
Old Things Are Far the Best 104
Oleograph 85
Olwen, Olwen 164
On Leaving England for the First Time 303
Onward Christian Soldiers 260
Open Letter to a Mayor 237
Opera Notes 296
P&O 1930 305
Passion 52
'Pastoral' 101
Paul 159
Personal Note 14
Personal Reminiscence 26
Peter 158
Pianist, The 269
Picnic Near Toledo 98
'Pied-à-Terre' 64
Pierrot and Pierrette 21
Pleasure Cruise 325
Political Hostess 173
'Poor Shakespeare' 62
Postscript 185
A Prayer: Most Merciful God 253
'Pretty, Pretty, Pretty Lorn' 147
A Question of Values 295
Quiet Old Timers 239
Quinta Bates, The (Aunt Bates) 337
Raratonga 19
Reflections 198

Reflections by Master on Awakening 115
Reply-Reply 162
'Reply-Reply!' 149
Reunion 200
Reversion to the Formal 89
Rhapsody 24
Richmond Boating Song 104
'Romance' 66
Routine for a Critic (Dirge) 287
Rubaiyat of a Man About Town 34
A Sad, Sad Story 38
Sampan 94
Saturday, January the Sixth (1940) 120
Scoundrel, The (verse from) 240
Send Me My Hat 83
Sicilian Study 103
Silly Boy 76
Sing of the Shepherd's Night 175
'Sir Campbell is coming' 163
Social Grace 231
'Sonata for Harpsichord' 60
Sonnet to a Hermit Crab 14
Soprano, The 270
Souvenir 326
Souvenir of Infancy 40
Spotted Lilies 80
Sunburn 106
Sunday Morning at Wiesbaden 81
Suppositions and Expectations 33
'Swiss Family Whittlebot, The' (Sketch – 1923) 51
Tarantella 293
Telegram to My Mother on Her Eightieth Birthday 112
Tenor, The 269
Theatre Party 97
Theme for Oboe in E Flat 84

'There was an old Marquis of Puno' 25
These Are Brave Men 166
This Is the Moment 254
This Is to Let You Know 345
Thoughts on Beatrice Lillie 278
Till I Return 39
Tintagel 178
To a Maidenhair Fern 72
To Admiral Sir James Somerville 191
To Admiral the Lord Louis Mountbatten 197
To an Octogenarian 112
'To an Old Woman in Huddersfield' 64
To Badrulbador Frampton 82
To His Excellency Field Marshal Viscount Wavell 196
To Lorn 114
To Mary MacArthur 273
To Meg Titheradge 272
To Mr James Agate 288
'To My Favourite Hostess' 59
To My Literary Parasites 82
'To Noël Coward' 62
'To pretty winsome Joyce' 118
To Rudyard Kipling 106
Toast to Sir Hugh and Lady Foot and Blanche Blackwell 139
Tooting Bec 37
Torero 99
Tribute to Ivor Novello 275
A Tribute to Lorn from Master 115
Tribute to Marlene Dietrich 283
Venice 332
Victorian Rhapsody for Lesser Minds 80
Voice in the Bamboo Shoot, The 95
'We came to the Ivy . . .' 124

Index of Titles

We Must Have a Speech from a Minister 176
What a Saucy Girl 241
When Babsie Got the Bird 271
When I Have Fears 351
'When I visit Venice, Italy' 116
'Where are the bright silk plaids . . .' 177
'Whisht Paple, The' 100
Whoops! Ella Wheeler Wilcox 243
'Why did you fall, Winnie?' 148
With All Best Wishes for a Merry Christmas 1939 156
Written from a Mansard Window in a Velvet Dress 79
'Yellow Nocturne' 65
'Youth' 102

ALSO BY BARRY DAY

THIS WOODEN 'O': SHAKESPEARE'S GLOBE REBORN

MY LIFE WITH NOËL COWARD
(with Graham Payn)

NOËL COWARD: THE COMPLETE LYRICS

NOËL COWARD: IN HIS OWN WORDS

NOËL COWARD: COMPLETE SKETCHES AND PARODIES

THEATRICAL COMPANION TO COWARD
(with Sheridan Morley)

THE UNKNOWN NOËL
new writing from the Coward archives

COWARD ON FILM: THE CINEMA OF NOËL COWARD

THE LETTERS OF NOËL COWARD

THE ESSENTIAL NOËL COWARD COMPENDIUM

THE NOËL COWARD READER

OSCAR WILDE: A LIFE IN QUOTES

P. G. WODEHOUSE: IN HIS OWN WORDS

P. G. WODEHOUSE: THE COMPLETE LYRICS

JOHNNY MERCER: THE COMPLETE LYRICS
(with Robert Kimball)

DOROTHY PARKER: IN HER OWN WORDS

SHERLOCK HOLMES
in his own words and the words of those who knew him

SHERLOCK HOLMES AND THE SHAKESPEARE GLOBE MURDERS

SHERLOCK HOLMES AND THE ALICE IN WONDERLAND MURDERS

SHERLOCK HOLMES AND THE COPYCAT MURDERS

SHERLOCK HOLMES AND THE APOCALYPSE MURDERS

SHERLOCK HOLMES AND THE SEVEN DEADLY SINS MURDERS

MURDER, MY DEAR WATSON
(*contributor*)